B+T

D0569736

MAY 3 0 2008

The POLITICS of FREEDOM

DAVID BOAZ

The POLITICS of FREEDOM

TAKING ON THE LEFT, THE RIGHT, AND THREATS TO OUR LIBERTIES

CATO INSTITUTE

WASHINGTON, D.C.

Copyright © 2008 by Cato Institute.
All rights reserved.

Library of Congress Cataloging-in-Publication Data

Boaz, David, 1953–
    The politics of freedom : taking on the left, the right, and threats
to our liberties / David Boaz.
        p. cm.
    Includes index.
    ISBN 978-1-933995-14-4 (alk. paper)
        1. United States—Politics and government—2001–
    2. Liberalism—United States. 3. Conservatism—United States.
    I. Title.

    JK275.B63 2007
    320.60973—dc22
                                                            2007051296

Cover design by Jon Meyers.

Printed in the United States of America.

CATO INSTITUTE
1000 Massachusetts Ave., N.W.
Washington, D.C. 20001
www.cato.org

DAVID BOAZ

The POLITICS *of* FREEDOM

TAKING ON THE LEFT, THE RIGHT, AND
THREATS TO OUR LIBERTIES

CATO
INSTITUTE
WASHINGTON, D.C.

Copyright © 2008 by Cato Institute.
All rights reserved.

Library of Congress Cataloging-in-Publication Data

Boaz, David, 1953–
    The politics of freedom : taking on the left, the right, and threats
to our liberties / David Boaz.
        p. cm.
    Includes index.
    ISBN 978-1-933995-14-4 (alk. paper)
    1. United States—Politics and government—2001–
    2. Liberalism—United States. 3. Conservatism—United States.
    I. Title.

    JK275.B63 2007
    320.60973—dc22

                                                                    2007051296

Cover design by Jon Meyers.

Printed in the United States of America.

CATO INSTITUTE
1000 Massachusetts Ave., N.W.
Washington, D.C. 20001
www.cato.org

Contents

Introduction

Thomas Paine said that freedom had been hunted and harassed around the world and that only America offered it a home. Today, it seems to many Americans that freedom is on the run here, too. War and taxes, the nanny state and the Patriot Act, unsustainable entitlements all threaten the liberty Americans enjoy.

But our situation is not as bleak as that might sound. In the essays collected here I write most often about threats to freedom. But just as I chide the mainstream media for ignoring the good news about prosperity, technology, health, and life expectancy, I sometimes need to remind myself of the good news about freedom—which of course is what makes possible all that other good news.

It's true that our recent political history does provide ample cause for depression. Forty years of Democratic control of Congress gave us what the Republicans in 1994 called "government that is too big, too intrusive, and too easy with the public's money." Dissatisfaction with that record and with the Clinton administration's efforts to make government yet bigger and more intrusive led to a historic Republican victory.

It didn't take long for the Republicans to get just as comfortable in power as the Democrats had become, especially after the election of George W. Bush gave the GOP control of the presidency and both houses of Congress. For decades the Republicans had promised voters that they would reduce the size and power of government if only they controlled the White House . . . if only they controlled the Senate . . . if only they controlled the entire government. Beginning in 2001, they did.

And what did complete Republican control of the federal government deliver? Federal spending up one trillion dollars in six years. An explosion of pork-barrel projects. The centralization of education. The biggest expansion of entitlements since Lyndon Johnson. A proposed constitutional amendment to take marriage law out of the hands of the states. Federal intrusion into private family matters. Spying, wiretapping, "sneak and peek" searches. A surge in executive power. And a seemingly endless war.

No wonder the voters quickly tired of that and returned Congress to the Democrats. As Dr. Phil would say, How's that working out for ya?

Within two months of the Democratic takeover, the *Washington Post* reported that Democrats were charging lobbyists big bucks to meet Nancy Pelosi and the chairmen of the congressional committees that write tax laws, regulations, and spending bills—including, they noted, some of the favorite clients of now-imprisoned GOP power broker Jack Abramoff. After six months, they'd held hearings and press conferences and all-night slumber parties.

But the war goes on. The spending goes on. We're up to 32,000 earmarks in the latest spending bills. Congress has not limited the president's claim of sweeping powers of detention and surveillance. Democrats are proposing huge increases in federal spending—on top of Bush's trillion-dollar increase—and the tax hikes to pay for them.

Which is presumably why a poll in late 2007 showed that 68 percent of Americans said the country was on the wrong track. Only 25 percent approved of Congress's performance, with independents slightly more negative than either Democrats or Republicans.

The politics of big government continues to flounder. Maybe it's time for the politics of freedom.

The State We're In

Assaults on freedom come from all sides these days. The right and the left, the military-industrial complex and the teachers unions, the environmentalists and the family-values crowd, they all have an agenda to impose on us through government. Political scientists offer a number of labels for the vast and powerful state that threatens our constitutional freedoms:

The Nanny State

On both left and right we're bombarded by people who just want the government to take care of us, as if we were children. This takes many forms. Bill Clinton was famous for "I feel your pain"—with programs to match. George W. Bush responded with "compassionate conservatism" and "We have a responsibility that when somebody hurts, government has got to move." Both conceptions offer a sweeping mandate for the federal government, one never envisioned by the Founders nor even by FDR. They combine Progressivism with Prozac.

Once in a while politicians reveal the patronizing attitude toward the voters that underlies these promises. Vice President Al Gore told an audience, "The federal government should never be the baby sitter, the parents," but should be "more like grandparents in the sense that grandparents perform a nurturing role and are aware of what parenting was like but no longer exercise that kind of authority."

Bush's chief of staff Andy Card disagreed: The government should be the parents, he said; "this president sees America as we think about a 10-year-old child," in need of firm parental protection.

And so we get sexual harassment laws from the Democrats and niggling regulations on workplaces, and smoking bans, and fat taxes, and gun bans, and programs to tuck us in at night.

And from the Republicans we get federal money for churches; and congressional investigations into textbook pricing, the college football bowl system, the firing of NFL star Terrell Owens, video games, the television rating system, you name it; and huge new fines for indecency on television; and crackdowns on medical marijuana and steroids and ephedra; and federal subsidies to encourage heterosexuals to marry; and bans to prevent homosexuals from doing so.

And on both sides the politicians and the intellectuals tell us they're just trying to encourage "socially desirable behavior"—not a role that Thomas Jefferson and James Madison envisioned the government playing.

The Entitlements Crisis

Everyone in Washington knows that the burden of "entitlement" programs like Social Security, Medicare, and Medicaid is growing to an unsustainable level. But not only does no politician want to talk about the problem, they continue to pile on more benefits that make the situation worse.

Entitlements already cost taxpayers more than $1 trillion a year, about 40 percent of the federal budget. That's a heavy enough burden. But the first members of the huge baby-boom generation are retiring this year. In barely 20 years, economists predict, entitlements will almost double as a share of national income. Today's young workers will find themselves staggering under the burden of supporting tens of millions of retired boomers.

After years of discussion of this looming fiscal crisis, what have the politicians done? They all declare themselves "fiscal conservatives" and then keep on spending. They reject reform proposals and promise more benefits. "Nobody shoots at Santa Claus," Al Smith used to say of Franklin Roosevelt's New Deal hand-outs, and politicians have found that a useful reminder ever since. Instead of fiscal responsibility, in 2003 Democrats and Republicans combined to pass a prescription drug entitlement for Medicare recipients. Critics said it might cost a trillion dollars over the next decade.

But even that figure drastically underestimates the problem. Jagadeesh Gokhale, an economist at the Cato Institute, calculated the real costs of our current entitlement programs. The numbers are simply incomprehensible: The total cost of the drug benefit alone will eventually be more than $16 trillion, on top of the $45 trillion that Medicare was already going to cost taxpayers. That's how much *more* money we'll eventually have to raise in taxes if we're going to pay off these debts.

Terror, War, and Surveillance

Radical Islamism is a real threat to freedom in the Muslim world, where people often face a desperate choice between secular dictators and religious totalitarians. Americans need not worry about living under an Islamic theocracy, but terror is certainly a threat to our life, liberty, and pursuit of happiness. Thus we need a strong national defense, better intelligence, and international cooperation to track and prevent terrorism.

But ever since the September 11 attacks, we have let fear and panic drive us to put up with infringements on freedom that change the nature of our society without any real increase in safety. It was understandable after September 11 that we would grant the federal government new powers to investigate threats of terrorism. But laws like the Patriot Act were passed without careful scrutiny, and without providing for the normal checks and balances of constitutional government. The more power government has in such areas, the more important it is to constrain that power within the law, with congressional oversight and judicial review.

In this new world the Bush administration is pushing secret subpoenas, secret searches, secret arrests, and secret trials. American citizens have been held without access to a lawyer, and without access to an impartial, civilian judge. The Great Writ of habeas corpus is denied. The administration's "torture memos" have been most notorious for their carefully oblique definitions of what constitutes torture and for the fact that they were kept secret for years. What has been too often overlooked in discussions of the memos is their assertion that the president cannot be restrained by laws passed by Congress. They claim executive powers that far exceed what our constitutional tradition allows. As Gene Healy and Timothy Lynch write in their study "Power Surge," "The Constitution's text will not support anything like the doctrine of presidential absolutism the administration flirts with in the torture memos."

One problem with the new powers that we have granted to government to fight terrorism is that they aren't used just to investigate and prosecute terrorists. There's a bait-and-switch game going on. Citing the threat of another 9/11, administration officials demand and get greatly expanded powers to deal with terrorism. But then it turns out that the new powers aren't restricted to terrorism cases. And indeed the Bush administration has been using the powers granted in the Patriot Act with increasing frequency in criminal investigations that have little or no connection to terrorism. Those cases range from drugs and pornography to money laundering, theft of trade secrets, and simple fraud. No doubt we could prevent or punish more crimes if we allowed the federal government to put a surveillance camera in every conference room and every living room. But we don't want to live in that kind of society. We're moving in that direction, though, by granting government new powers to deal with terrorism and not restricting the scope of those powers.

And of course the fight against terrorism isn't the only source of expanded powers for police and prosecutors. Long before 9/11 legal

scholars were bemoaning the "drug exception to the Fourth Amendment." The Supreme Court ruled that government investigators do not need warrants to conduct aerial surveillance of areas that any pilot could legally fly over, including both the fenced yards of private homes—where they might be looking for marijuana—and highly secure chemical factories, where the Environmental Protection Agency was looking for evidence of air pollution violations.

Every new war, real or metaphorical—war on terror, war on drugs, war on obesity—is an excuse for expanding the size, scope, and power of government. A good reason to organize antiwar movements.

The Politics of Statism

For any friend of freedom, one of the most frustrating aspects of our current political system is the absence of political leaders challenging any of these expansions of state power. It's hard to find politicians, Republican or Democratic, who don't support one or another aspect of the nanny state. Practically every member of Congress turns away when the problem of our unsustainable welfare state is mentioned. "It won't go bankrupt before the next election, so it's not my problem," seems to be their attitude. As for the wars on both terrorism and drugs, most politicians just want to avoid being labeled as "weak." The Patriot Act passed the Senate with only one dissenting vote, even though few if any members of Congress had actually read the bill. Most Democrats, including most major presidential candidates, joined virtually all Republicans in voting for the authorization for war with Iraq. And virtually no elected officials will protest the insanity of the war on drugs, or even vote against its continued escalation.

It's not that politicians couldn't show a little courage once in a while. After all, gerrymandering and campaign finance regulations have given House members a reelection rate of over 98 percent. With so little to fear from the voters, they ought to be able to vote their consciences. But there aren't many citizen-politicians these days; they all want to be part of a permanent ruling class, in office forever until they collect their congressional pensions, so they try to play it safe. All the talk about increased polarization between Democrats and Republicans just obscures the increasing agreement on most aspects of the welfare-warfare state, a sprawling federal government that promises to meet our every need, as long as we give it ever-increasing amounts of money, and keeps us embroiled in conflicts around the globe.

It's no wonder that ever-larger numbers of Americans express disgust with the current political establishment, even though the election laws make it very difficult to organize and fund a new party, an independent campaign, or even an insurgency within the major parties.

The Good News about Freedom

After a litany of problems like that, it's easy to get discouraged, to believe that we're losing our freedom, year after year. Libertarians often quote Thomas Jefferson: "The natural progress of things is for liberty to yield and government to gain ground."

But let's take a moment to think about some of the laws we *don't* have anymore: Slavery and established churches. Segregation and sodomy laws. Sunday-closing laws, 90 percent income tax rates, wage and price controls. In many ways Americans are freer today than ever before.

Politicians shouldn't get much of the credit for that. They tend to react, not to lead. Social change and a mass movement challenged segregation before Congress responded. Popular resentment over rising taxes led to Proposition 13 and then the election of Ronald Reagan. A court challenge struck down the last few sodomy laws, which had fallen into disuse anyway. Economists produced enough evidence on the costs of transportation, communications, and financial regulation that Congress finally had to recognize it.

It's certainly not time to rest on our laurels. But we should take pride in the freedom that we have wrested from government and remain optimistic about the future of freedom.

The Libertarian Vision

When I argue for a society that fully recognizes each person's right to life, liberty, and the pursuit of happiness, I'm often asked: Where's an example of a successful "libertarian society"? The answer to that question is easy: The United States of America.

As I noted above, the United States has never been a perfectly free society. But our Constitution and our national sense of life have guaranteed more freedom to more people than in any other society in history, and we have continued to extend the promises of the Declaration of Independence to more people.

More than any other country in the world, ours was formed by people who had left the despots of the Old World to find freedom in the new, and who then made a libertarian revolution. Americans tend to think of themselves as individuals, with equal rights and equal freedom. Our fundamental ideology is, in the words of the political scientist Seymour Martin Lipset, "antistatism, laissez-faire, individualism, populism, and egalitarianism." Some people don't like that fact. Professors Cass Sunstein and Stephen Holmes complain that libertarian ideas are "astonishingly widespread in American culture."

And indeed they are. My recent work with David Kirby found that in several different public opinion surveys, 15 to 20 percent of Americans give libertarian answers to a range of questions—answers that in combination distinguish them from both liberals and conservatives. But that figure seriously underestimates the prevalence of libertarian ideas. Many American conservatives are fundamentally committed to small government and free enterprise. Many American liberals believe firmly in free speech, freedom of religion, and the dignity of every individual. Both liberals and conservatives may be coming to better appreciate the value of the Constitution in restraining the powers of the federal government. The sharpening of the red-blue divide in the past decade causes liberals and conservatives to deepen their opposition to "the other team." But it may obscure the number of Americans on both sides of the divide who are fundamentally libertarian in their attitudes.

As one measure of that, after the 2006 election the Cato Institute commissioned Zogby International to ask poll respondents if they would describe themselves as "fiscally conservative and socially liberal." Fully 59 percent of the respondents said "yes." That is, by 59 to 27 percent, poll respondents said they would describe themselves as "fiscally conservative and socially liberal." When we asked the same question but noted that such a combination of views is "known as libertarian," a robust 44 percent of respondents still answered "yes."

The Message of This Book

Part of the challenge for libertarians is to help those Americans understand that their fundamental political value is freedom. Instead of being frightened and distracted by politicians, they should recognize that the main issue in politics—in 2008 and beyond—is the freedom of the individual and the power of government. That challenge has been a key theme of my writings, as this book shows. I've tried to collect here a wide range of essays, op-eds, and shorter items written over the past couple of decades, both before and after the 1997 publication of *Libertarianism: A Primer* and *The Libertarian Reader*. Most are presented in exactly the form they were originally published. I've made a few cuts to avoid repetition and changed a few titles. Some of the older articles may seem dated; on the other hand, sometimes they show that bad ideas just keep turning up again in new contexts. People may have forgotten, for example, that Americans were weirdly paranoid about the Japanese in the 1980s. Or that the price of 64K microchips was once potentially a cause for major government intervention. Or that the Democrats of the 1990s had many ridiculously ambitious and thoroughly collectivist schemes that we are clearly better off without.

In some ways the idea of freedom is very simple. Recall the bestseller, *All I Really Need to Know I Learned in Kindergarten*. You could say that you learn the essence of libertarianism—which is also the essence of civilization—in kindergarten:

> Don't hit other people,
> Don't take their stuff, and
> Keep your promises.

Most people understand that idea in their personal lives. Now if only we could get people to apply it to "public policy" as well: Don't use force to make other people live the way you think they should. Don't use the power of taxation, regulation, or eminent domain to take their stuff. Don't interfere with contracts—the promises other people make—and don't make promises the taxpayers can't keep. A politician who ran on such a platform would find a large and receptive audience.

There's never been a golden age of liberty, and there never will be. There will always be people who want to live their lives in peace, and there will always be people who want to exploit them or impose their own ideas on others. There will always be a conflict between Liberty and Power.

In the long run, freedom works, and people figure that out. I have no doubt that at the dawn of the fourth millennium more of the human beings in the universe will live in freer societies than do today. In the shorter run the outcome is less predictable, and it will depend on our own efforts to capitalize on our strengths and learn to counter the trends that work against free and peaceful societies.

PART 1

The Libertarian Idea

Pro-Choice

The long struggle against communism kept libertarians and traditionalist conservatives allied despite their often significant philosophical differences. Since the demise of the Soviet Union, many commentators have speculated on the likelihood of growing strains in the libertarian-conservative relationship. Usually the speculation has centered on splits between libertarians and the religious right over such moral or "social" issues as abortion, gay rights, school prayer, and the drug war. Lately, however, a lot of mainstream conservatives have decided to challenge libertarians on the basic issue of, well, liberty. As Walter Olson pointed out in the July issue of *Reason*, the *Weekly Standard* has become a veritable Anti-Libertarian Central, bristling with articles like "Up from Libertarianism" and "The Libertarian Temptation."

The more intellectual conservatives have focused their fire on "the right to choose"—not just, or not even, the right to choose abortion, but the general right to choose one's course in life. William Kristol, editor of the *Standard*, writes in *Commentary*, "Conservatism's more fundamental mandate is to take on the sacred cow of liberalism—choice." Adam Wolfson, executive editor of *The Public Interest*, despairs in a different issue of *Commentary* that "the 'right to choose' is something which not only upper-middle-class liberals but all Americans take for granted." He worries that people have come to expect that they have a right to choose not just abortion but premarital sex, pornography, and even drugs.

Note that Kristol and Wolfson are criticizing not just particular choices but the right to choose itself. It is, of course, entirely reasonable for public-spirited citizens to urge others to make better choices—to practice temperance or even abstinence with regard to drugs and sex, to avoid divorce, to spend more time with their children, to treat employees with respect, to give more to charity. But the distinction between a free and an unfree society is that such advice remains just that, and the adult individual remains free to accept or reject it without legal sanction.

Conservatives wrap themselves in the mantle of American tradition, but on this key point they have trouble making it fit. The Declaration of Independence not only claims for all people the rights of life, liberty, and the pursuit of happiness but declares that governments derive their powers "from the consent of the governed." Thomas Jefferson and the other signers apparently believed that choice was involved in the very foundation of the American republic. That's what "consent" means: that we have a choice, and we have chosen to delegate some of our rights to a government under the Constitution, though we retain the right "to alter or abolish it" if it becomes destructive of our rights.

Kristol and Wolfson are struggling, not just against the principles on which America was founded, but against the modern world. It is capitalism that has given us moderns so many choices. Capitalism is the economic system of free people; it is what happens when you let people alone. The virtues that capitalism rewards—prudence, discipline, initiative, self-reliance, new ideas—and the affluence it creates tend to push people in the direction of confidence in their own abilities, skepticism about organized authority, and a desire to manage their own affairs in all realms of life. That's why capitalism is not in the long run compatible with political repression or governmental restrictions on freedom.

Freedom is also necessary for the development of strong moral character. Surely Kristol and Wolfson don't want to undermine the bourgeois virtues, but the effect of restricting choice is to eliminate the incentive and the opportunity for people to make good choices and develop good habits. People do not develop prudence, self-reliance, thrift, and temperance when their choices are imposed by force. Welfare-state liberals undermine moral character when they subsidize indulgence in destructive choices. Big-government conservatives undermine character when they deny people the right to shape their own characters through their choices.

Conservatives seem to have a surprising amount of difficulty distinguishing between coercive, government-imposed restrictions on choice and the kinds of voluntary social institutions that, after we consent to participate in them, limit our choices. The distinguished historian Gertrude Himmelfarb told a gathering recently that civil society is not rooted in liberty; it includes such freedom-limiting institutions as marriage, churches, and universities. There's a confusion here about the meaning of freedom. We sometimes use "free" to mean "able to do what I want to do without constraint." The refrain of a 1950s country song by Hank Snow goes, "You've got a house and a wife and a job, Bob, but I'm still free." Yes, a house and a wife and a job limit one's freedom in the sense that one has voluntarily agreed to pay the mortgage every month, to be faithful, and to show up for work every day. The various contracts we enter involve various degrees of commitment: under traditional "employment at will" doctrine, I can quit my job—or be fired—at any time; a mortgage is more difficult to escape; and it is quite reasonable that a marriage, especially when children are involved, is even more difficult to leave. But in accepting such limitations on our freedom of action we do not give up liberty—we exercise it.

Of course, in the assault on choice, welfare-state liberals and big-government conservatives find themselves coming together. The leftist writer

Robert Kuttner deplores Americans' "excess amount of choice" in his latest anti-market jeremiad, *Everything for Sale*. No doubt Kuttner is surprised to find himself on the same side of such a basic issue as Kristol and Wolfson, but that may be a harbinger of the politics of the future.

Cato Policy Report, July/August 1997

Pro-Life

Back in 1997 I wrote an editorial, titled "Pro-Choice," about conservatives and liberals who want to deny people choice in all sorts of areas. So I thought it was time I wrote a "pro-life" editorial. This time I want to focus on one of the most important choices: the choice of life over death. (And once again, I'm not writing about abortion.) Not much controversy here, right? Everyone prefers life to death. Everyone wants to live as long as possible. You'd think so. But no, it turns out that lots of people are not so sure that life is a good thing.

The most obvious are Osama bin Laden and his network of terrorists. Islamic martyrs "love death as you love life," bin Laden tells an interviewer. "The Americans are fighting so they can live and enjoy the material things in this life," a Taliban spokesman says, "but we are fighting so we can die in the cause of Allah." In a video for his followers, bin Laden intones, "The love of this world is wrong."

And there he reaches the crux of the issue. He is wrong. This world is well worth loving. It is right and good for human beings to try to make the most of life on this earth. The Americans are indeed "fighting so they can live and enjoy the material things of this life." Not just material things, of course—we fight for such values as love, sex, family, friendship, community, integrity, and courage. But at the root of all these is the love of life in all its wonder and happiness.

One of the biggest complaints modern Americans have about life is how stressed they feel, how they are pulled in so many directions. Why are we stressed? Not because we have to work longer hours than we used to. Whatever the statisticians may tell us about the hours we work, we know that our grandparents and their grandparents worked harder than we do to achieve a much lower standard of living. How many hours a week would I have to work at their jobs, and in their economy, to afford a small house without air conditioning, radio, television, or a refrigerator? No, the problem today is that capitalism has given us so many options; but who would want to give up all that abundance?

Or all the *interestingness*? Whatever your interests, the modern world is filled with enough to keep you busy for a lifetime. Every day there's more news about science, politics, international affairs, sports, entertainment, and so on—not to mention new books, new movies, new music, new religions, even new family and friends. I for one don't want to die because I want to find out what happens next—in everything from sports to politics to TV soaps to the newest scientific discoveries.

Sadly, the Islamic terrorists are not the only people who see life as a limited blessing. The debates over genetic engineering have brought out our native-born anti-lifers in droves. One of the most-quoted bioethicists of our time, Daniel Callahan of the Hastings Center, says: "The worst possible way to resolve [the question of life extension] is to leave it up to individual choice. There is no known social good coming from the conquest of death."

Callahan is a liberal, in the modern welfarist sense. Conservatives such as philosopher Leon Kass, named to head President Bush's Council on Bioethics, and scholar Francis Fukuyama, a member of the council, sound remarkably similar. In a debate at the Cato Institute, Fukuyama said, "The whole effort to defeat death, it seems to me, is a kind of striving that speaks of a kind of serious lack of a certain kind of moral perspective." A certain kind, perhaps.

Kass writes, "The finitude of human life is a blessing for every human individual." In a speech in Jerusalem two years ago, he complained that Jewish scholars "nearly always come down strongly in favor of medical progress and on the side of life—more life, stronger life, new life." He objects to their making "victory over mortality" the goal of medical science. This Jewish attitude has also been noticed in the Middle East, where Hamas leader Ismail Haniya says that Jews "love life more than any other people, and they prefer not to die."

And then there are the environmental extremists, who think there's just too much human life on earth. Jacques Cousteau told the UNESCO *Courier* in 1991, "In order to stabilize world populations, we must eliminate 350,000 people per day." Earth First! founder Dave Foreman writes, "We humans have become a disease, the humanpox." Celebrated young novelist William T. Vollman says, "I would say there are too many people in the world and maybe something like AIDS or something like war may be a good thing on that level."

There are many ways to divide people according to their political beliefs—communist and anti-communist, liberal and conservative, libertarian and statist, reactionary and modernist, and so on. But the issue of whether you celebrate life on this earth and want to extend it or think that "the conquest of death" lacks any value seems a good place to draw a line. With enemies of life in abundance, maybe we need what Hayek called a party of life, a "party that favors free growth and spontaneous evolution," a party that appreciates and encourages the enjoyment of life on this earth. And since choice is an essential part of human life, the pro-life party must be pro-choice as well. The Declaration of Independence, which not only declares that governments derive their powers "from the consent of the governed" but also claims for all people the rights of life, liberty, and the pursuit of happiness, can serve as the party manifesto.

Cato Policy Report, July/August 2002

Rights, Responsibilities, and Community

> We hold these truths to be self-evident, that all men are created equal, that they are endowed by their creator with certain unalienable rights, that among these are life, liberty, and the pursuit of happiness. That to secure these rights, governments are instituted among men, deriving their just powers from the consent of the governed.
>
> United States Declaration of Independence

A journalist asked me recently what I thought of a communitarian proposal to "suspend for a while the minting of new rights." How many ways, I thought, does that get it wrong? Communitarians seem to see rights as little boxes; when you have too many, the room gets full. In my view, we have only one right—or an infinite number. The one fundamental human right is the right to live your life as you choose, as long as you do not infringe on the equal rights of others. But that one right has infinite implications. As James Wilson, a signer of the Constitution, said in response to a proposal that a Bill of Rights be added to the Constitution, "Enumerate all the rights of man! I am sure, sirs, that no gentleman in the late Convention would have attempted such a thing."[1] After all, a person has a right to wear a hat, or not; to marry, or not; to grow beans, or apples, or to open a haberdashery. Indeed, though that right is not recognized in current federal law, a person has a right to buy an orange from a willing seller even though the orange is only 2⅜ inches in diameter.

It is impossible to enumerate a priori all the rights we have; we usually go to the trouble of identifying them only when someone proposes to limit one or another. Treating rights as tangible claims that must be limited in number gets the whole concept wrong.

Rights and Responsibilities

It is certainly true that every right carries with it a correlative responsibility. My right to speak freely implies your responsibility not to interfere with my exercise of that right. Your right to private property implies my responsibility not to steal it, or to force you to use it in the way I demand. In short, the protection of my rights entails my responsibility to respect the rights of others. So why do I feel uncomfortable when I hear communitarians talk about "rights and responsibilities"? The problem is that there are three senses of the term "responsibility" that are frequently confused.

First, there are the responsibilities noted above, the obligations that correlate with other people's rights. Second, there are the responsibilities that some would insist we assume in order to exercise our rights. This sense, frequently found in communitarian writings, echoes the *ancien régime* approach, the notion of rights as privileges that we retain only so long as we use them responsibly. That idea degrades the American tradition of individualism. It implies that we have our rights only as long as someone—the government, in practice—approves of the way we use them. In fact, as the Declaration of Independence tells us, humans have rights before they enter into governments, which are created for the very purpose of *protecting* those rights.

People rarely try to take away our rights when they think we are using them responsibly. No one tries to censor popular, mainstream speech; rather, it is obscene or radical speech that is frequently threatened. We must defend even the irresponsible use of rights *because* they are rights and not privileges. To paraphrase the moving words of Martin Niemoller in a modern American context: "They came first for the pornographers, and I didn't speak up because I wasn't a pornographer. Then they came for the drug dealers, and I didn't speak up because I wasn't a drug dealer. Then they came for the insider traders, and I didn't speak up because I wasn't an insider trader. Then they came for the Branch Davidians, and I didn't speak up because I was a mainstream Protestant. Then they came for me, and by that time no one was left to speak up."[2] Governments will never begin by taking away the rights of average citizens and taxpayers. But by establishing legal precedents in attacks on the rights of despised groups, governments lay the groundwork for the narrowing of everyone's rights.

Third, there are the moral responsibilities that we have outside the realm of rights. The Communitarian Platform claims that "the language of rights is morally incomplete."[3] Of course, that is true; rights pertain only to a certain domain of morality, a narrow domain in fact, not to all of morality. Rights establish certain minimal standards for how we must treat each other: We must not kill, rape, rob, or otherwise initiate force against each other. That leaves a great many options to be dealt with by other theories of morality. But that fact does not mean that the idea of rights is invalid or incomplete *in the domain where it applies*; it just means that most of the decisions we make every day involve choices that are only broadly circumscribed by the obligation to respect each other's rights.

Libertarians are often charged with ignoring or even rejecting these moral responsibilities. There may be some truth to the first charge. Libertarians obviously spend most of their time defending liberty and thus criticizing government. They leave it to others to explore moral obligations and exhort people to assume them. I see two reasons for this. First, there is the question of specialization. We do not demand of the AIDS researcher, "Why aren't you searching for a cure for cancer as well?" With government as big as it is, libertarians find the task of limiting its size thoroughly time consuming. Second, libertarians have noticed that too many non-libertarians want to enforce, legally, every moral virtue. As my colleague William Niskanen puts it, welfare-state liberals fail to distinguish between a virtue and a requirement, while contemporary conservatives fail to distinguish between a sin and a crime. (The unique contribution of communitarians to current debate often seems to be that they make both of these grievous errors.) Libertarians thus fear, with reason, that if we declare drug abuse a vice, someone will want to outlaw it; if we declare charity a moral obligation, someone will want to make it a federal program; if we extol the virtues of community participation, someone will institute compulsory national service.

When libertarians ignore these moral values in their social analysis, however, they are failing to heed the lessons taught by all their intellectual heroes. Adam Smith wrote *The Theory of Moral Sentiments*.[4] F. A. Hayek stressed the importance of morals and tradition.[5] Ayn Rand set out a fairly strict code of personal ethics.[6] Thomas Szasz's work—often caricatured by critics—challenges the reductionists and behaviorists with a commitment to the old ideas of good and bad, right and wrong, and responsibility for one's choices.[7] Charles Murray emphasizes the value and, indeed, necessity of community and responsibility.[8] Libertarians should do more to make clear the role of moral responsibility in their philosophy. However, they will no doubt continue to emphasize that government can undermine the values necessary for a free society—honesty, self-reliance, reason, thrift, education, tolerance, discipline, property, contract, and family—but it cannot instill them.

Libertarians and communitarians alike should decry the flight from individual responsibility that has characterized the past several decades in the United States. Intellectuals, usually governmentally funded, have concocted a whole array of explanations why nothing that happens to us is our own fault. These intellectuals tell us that the poor are not responsible for their poverty, the fat are not responsible for their overeating, and the alcoholics are not responsible for their drinking.

Many Americans have responded enthusiastically to these justifications for irresponsibility. Just consider a few contemporary examples: Smokers sue cigarette companies, seeking to blame their lung cancer on someone else—even though someone who smoked two packs of cigarettes a day for 25 years was exposed to a warning about the dangers of smoking 365,000 times, not counting the endless discussions of smoking and cancer in the media. A Los Angeles jury was lenient with Reginald Denny's attackers because they could not really be blamed for getting caught up in a mob reaction. Government offers subsidized insurance for people who build homes in the paths of hurricanes, floods, and fires, then offers special assistance to cover whatever the cheap insurance did not cover after an entirely predictable disaster. Everyone from politicians to reckless drivers uses alcohol as an excuse, a mitigating factor, rather than accepting responsibility for their decisions to use alcohol.

Libertarians believe that people should be free to live their lives as they choose. But freedom requires that people assume the consequences of their actions. Use drugs if you choose, but understand that you are going to jail if you drive recklessly or commit a crime under the influence of drugs. Engage in unsafe sex if you choose, but do not expect other people to pay your medical bills after you ignore medical warnings *and* fail to buy health insurance. Put your life savings into a home on the Atlantic coast, but do not expect the rest of us to give you free or subsidized hurricane insurance.

Misnamed Rights

The communitarian complaint about "the proliferation of rights" is not all wrong. There is indeed a problem in modern America with the proliferation of phony rights. When "rights" become merely claims of legal entitlement attached to interests and preferences, the stage is set for political and social conflict. There is no conflict of genuine human rights in a free society. There are many conflicts between the holders of so-called "welfare rights"—rights that require someone else to provide us with things we want, whether education, health care, social security, welfare, farm subsidies, or unobstructed views across someone else's land. This is the fundamental problem of interest-group democracy and the interventionist state. In a liberal society, people assume risks and obligations through contract; an interventionist state imposes obligations on people through the political process.

A socialist system—or an interventionist state, which is just partial socialism—requires uniform solutions to problems rather than the myriad variety of solutions available through the market process. If education is publicly provided, we can expect that it will be one-size-fits-all education in the "One Best System" of the Progressives, and children with different learning styles or values will just have to learn to cope. If the state sets up a retirement system, it will be designed for middle-class, white, working father/nonworking mother families; blacks, single people, and working and childless women will receive inferior benefits, and the system will stay the way it was designed decades after society changes.

The notion of rights as entitlements combined with public property and public money leads to all sorts of political and social conflicts and to an absence of order and civility. Many of the complaints of communitarians concern how public property should be used. Should smoking be allowed in public buildings? Should smelly homeless people be allowed in public libraries? Should panhandlers, prostitutes, and drug dealers be allowed on public streets? Should either Bibles or condoms be distributed in public schools? There are no good answers to these questions within the context of public property. No matter what we choose, some citizens will be forbidden to use the public property in the way they prefer.

That is why it would be best to privatize as much property as possible, to depoliticize the decision-making process about the use of property. Take smoking as a paradigmatic case. In a government building, either some taxpayers will be denied the right to smoke or others will be denied the right to breathe clean air. (The same dilemma applies if the government makes rules that apply to private property.) But if we leave most property private, and allow owners to make rules about smoking—as we should, if we properly understand property rights—then many different kinds of rules will arise, and more people can be satisfied. Owners of restaurants will try to accommodate their customers—whether that means banning smoking, establishing no smoking areas, or allowing smoking throughout the establishment. Customers can patronize restaurants that offer the combination of services—food quality, service, location, price, smoking rules—that suits them best. The language of rights tells us to leave the decision about smoking rules out of the realm of coercion; it tells us nothing about what rules to make in each privately owned home, office, airplane, or retail establishment.

On a more important point, one that may seem more difficult to leave to the private, voluntary sector of society, we are all worried about the rising level of crime in our society. We are torn between the desire to crack down on crime and our respect for civil liberties. It seems impossible to bring order to our streets without restricting civil liberties. But again, much of the problem is rooted in the public nature of the streets. I recently had dinner in a restaurant after an evening of shopping, so it was quite late when I left the restaurant. As I walked down deserted commercial streets, past shuttered shops, it occurred to me that I was not afraid. Why? Because I was in a shopping mall, a private community with private streets. By exercising very minimal control over access to the community and reserving the right to expel suspicious characters, the owners of the mall can provide a safe and comfortable community for their customers. One way to reduce the number of potential criminals in a society is to exclude them from access to the community; but the Constitution forbids us to expel suspicious people from public areas. If more areas were private, potential criminals would realize sooner the costs in isolation and exclusion of threatening behavior, and there would be more safety in our society.

Civil Society

There is widespread concern in our society, which communitarians have effectively tapped, about the decline of community, civility, and order. This problem manifests itself in everything from the disorder on our streets to a general sense that people just do not care about their neighbors as much as they once did. I suggest that those who worry about this decline of community have failed to recognize the important distinction between civil society and the state.

According to Reinhard Bendix, "Civil society refers to all institutions in which individuals can pursue common interests without detailed direction or interference from the government:"[9] That would include families, businesses, schools, churches, clubs, community and neighborhood groups, fraternal associations, and so on. Civil society grew up rapidly in the young America. Alexis de Tocqueville pointed out, "Americans of all ages, all stations in life, and all types of dispositions are forever forming associations. . . . What political power could ever carry on the vast multitude of lesser undertakings which associations daily enable American citizens to control?"[10]

Communities are not created by the state. Society is composed of individuals who belong to many different communities. The liberal view says that society is an association of individuals governed by legal rules, or perhaps an association of associations—but not one large community, or one family, in Mario Cuomo's and Pat Buchanan's utterly misguided conception. The rules of the family or small group are not, and cannot be, the rules of the extended society.

And yet, from the Progressive Era on, the state has increasingly disrupted natural communities and mediating institutions in America. Public schools replaced private community schools, and large, distant, unmanageable school districts replaced smaller districts. In 1920, 18 million Americans got health care through fraternal societies, but the rise of the welfare state caused those voluntary associations to atrophy. Social Security not only took away the need to save for one's own retirement, but weakened family bonds by reducing parents' reliance on their children. Zoning laws reduced the availability of affordable housing, limited opportunities for extended families to live together, and removed retail stores from residential neighborhoods, reducing community interaction. Daycare regulations limited home day care. In all these ways, civil society was crowded out by the state.

Today, the federal government spends over $1.5 trillion a year, and says we as citizens should sacrifice more.

Democratic governments today presume to regulate more aspects of our lives more closely than even the autocratic governments of the *ancien régime* ever did. Governments in the United States assign our children to schools and select the books they will learn from, require us to report our most intimate economic transactions, demand eighty permit applications if we want to start a business in Los Angeles, restrict whom we may love and what we may read, prescribe the number and gender ratio of toilets in buildings open to the public, tell us whom we must hire and whom we may fire, bar our most efficient businesses from high-tech markets, deny terminally ill patients access to pain-relieving and life-saving drugs, strangle our financial institutions with archaic rules, prosecute investors for crimes that have never been defined, and devote 19,824 words to a directive on the federal peanut program. And, though it rarely comes to this in civilized modern societies, it should be remembered that behind every ridiculous regulation stands the government's willingness to enforce it, with violence if necessary.

Lately, it seems, our response to every problem—from the expense of childcare to the fear of carjacking—is to demand a new federal law, and politicians are more than happy to comply. So what happens to communities as the state expands? The welfare state takes over the responsibilities of individuals and communities and in the process takes away much of what brings satisfaction to life: If government is supposed to feed the poor, then local charities are not needed. If a central bureaucracy downtown manages the schools, then parents' organizations are less important. If government agencies manage the community center, teach children about sex, and care for the elderly, then families and neighborhood associations feel less needed. Civil rights laws, adopted with the best of intentions, are used to challenge many voluntarily formed communities; from black colleges, to a private school in Hawaii that hires only Protestant teachers, to landlords whose effort to discriminate in favor of responsible tenants may be charged with a racially disparate impact.

What is the cost to our society of having government take over more and more roles that individuals and communities used to serve? Alexis de Tocqueville warned us of what might happen:

> After having thus successively taken each member of the community in its powerful grasp and fashioned him at will, the government then extends its arm over the whole community. It covers the surface of society with a network of small, complicated rules, minute and uniform, through which the most original minds and the most energetic characters cannot penetrate, to rise above the crowd. The will of man is not shattered, but softened, bent, and

guided; men are seldom forced by it to act, but they are constantly restrained from acting. Such a power does not destroy, but it prevents existence: it does not tyrannize, but it compresses, enervates, extinguishes, and stupefies a people, till each nation is reduced to nothing better than a flock of timid and industrious animals, of which the government is the shepherd.[11]

As Charles Murray puts it, "When the government takes away a core function [of communities], it depletes not only the source of vitality pertaining to that particular function, but also the vitality of a much larger family of responses."[12] The attitude of "let the government take care of it" becomes a habit. Communitarians should look to big government for an explanation of why the tendrils of community have shriveled. They do acknowledge this problem: "Free individuals require a community, which backs them up against encroachment by the state and sustains morality by drawing on the gentle prodding of kin, friends, neighbors, and other community members rather than building on government controls," writes Amitai Etzioni in *The Spirit of Community*.[13] And again, "Much of what Communitarians favor has little to do with laws and regulations, which ultimately draw on the coercive powers of the state." Yet they call for more and more new laws. They should take their libertarian rhetoric more seriously.

Conclusion

The twentieth century has seen a steady growth of the state. We have weakened mediating institutions, leaving just lone individuals and an ever-more-powerful state. We have lost the civility we expect from civil society. Our task now should be to restore real, voluntarily chosen communities. But that means limiting, devolving, and decentralizing government—and it means allowing communities to make mistakes and to operate in ways that we do not like. We can empower communities only by giving them the power to run their own affairs. As long as they are private, voluntary communities—including schools, churches, clubs, associations, and condominium-style housing developments—the policy of the government should be hands-off.

We will strengthen civil society and community by limiting the power of the state. When we recognize people's rights and treat them as responsible adults, I believe they will respond by assuming responsibility; not just for themselves, but for their communities. Oliver Wendell Holmes said, in a Supreme Court decision, "Taxes are what we pay for civilized society."[15] He had it exactly backwards. Taxes are, in fact, a reflection of our failure to achieve a fully civilized society. Civilized people get what they want by voluntary means, through persuasion or exchange. The use of force to acquire property is uncivilized, and the history of civilization is the history of limitations on the use of force. As we enter the twenty-first century, let us move toward a more civilized society by giving full legal recognition to the rights that were proclaimed in the Declaration of Independence.

Notes

1. Jonathan Elliot, ed., 2 *Debates in the Several State Conventions on the Adoption of the Federal Constitution* (1836, 2d. edition; reprint, Philadelphia: J. B. Lippincott, 1941), 454.

2. Martin Niemoller, (1892–1984), attributed.

3. Amitai Etzioni, *The Spirit of Community* (New York: Crown, 1993), 277.

4. Adam Smith, *The Theory of Moral Sentiments* (Indianapolis: Chicago Press, 1988).

5. F. A. Hayek, *The Fatal Conceit* (Chicago: University of Chicago Press, 1988).

6. Ayn Rand, "How Does One Live a Rational Life in an Irrational Society?" and "The Objectivist Ethics," in *The Virtue of Selfishness* (New York: Signet, New American Library, 1964).

7. Thomas Szasz, *Insanity, the Idea and Its Consequences* (New York: John Wiley & Sons, 1987), chap. 8.

8. Charles Murray, *In Pursuit: Of Happiness and Good Government* (New York: Simon & Schuster, 1988).

9. Reinhard Bendix, *Kings or People* (Berkeley and Los Angeles: University of California Press, 1978), 523.

10. Alexis de Tocqueville, *Democracy in America* (New Rochelle, N.Y.: Arlington House, 1965), 2:114–16.

11. Ibid., 338.

12. Murray, *In Pursuit: Of Happiness and Good Government*, 274.

13. Etzioni, *The Spirit of Community*, 23.

14. Ibid., 47.

15. *Compania de Tabacos v. Collector*, 275 U.S. 87, 100 (1904).

International Rights and Responsibilities for the Future, ed. Kenneth W. Hunter and Timothy C. Mack (Praeger, 1996)

Competition and Cooperation

Defenders of the market process often stress the benefits of competition. The competitive process allows for constant testing, experimenting, and adapting in response to changing situations. It keeps businesses constantly on their toes to serve consumers. Both analytically and empirically, we can see that competitive systems produce better results than centralized or monopoly systems. That's why, in books, newspaper articles, and television appearances, advocates of free markets stress the importance of the competitive marketplace and oppose restrictions on competition.

But too many people listen to the praise for *competition* and hear words like *hostile*, *cutthroat*, or *dog-eat-dog*. They wonder whether cooperation wouldn't be better than such an antagonistic posture toward the world.

Billionaire investor George Soros, for instance, writes in the *Atlantic Monthly*, "Too much competition and too little cooperation can cause intolerable inequities and instability." He goes on to say that his "main point . . . is that cooperation is as much a part of the system as competition, and the slogan 'survival of the fittest' distorts this fact."

Now it should be noted that the phrase "survival of the fittest" is rarely used by advocates of freedom and free markets. It was coined to describe the process of biological evolution and to refer to the survival of the traits that were best suited to the environment; it may well be applicable to the competition of enterprises in the market, but it certainly is never intended to imply the survival of only the fittest individuals in a capitalist system. It is not the friends but the enemies of the market process who use the term "survival of the fittest" to describe economic competition.

What needs to be made clear is that those who say that human beings "are made for cooperation, not competition" fail to recognize that the market *is* cooperation. Indeed, as discussed below, it is people competing to cooperate.

Individualism and Community

Similarly, opponents of classical liberalism have been quick to accuse liberals of favoring "atomistic" individualism, in which each person is an island unto himself, out only for his own profit with no regard for the needs or wants of others. E. J. Dionne Jr. of the *Washington Post* has written that modern libertarians believe that "individuals come into the world as fully formed adults who should be held responsible for their actions from the moment of their birth." Columnist Charles Krauthammer wrote in a review of Charles Murray's *What It Means to Be a Libertarian* that until Murray came along the libertarian vision was "a race of rugged individualists each living in a mountaintop cabin with a barbed wire fence and a 'No Trespassing' sign outside." How he neglected to include "each armed to the teeth" I can't imagine.

Of course, nobody actually believes in the sort of "atomistic individualism" that professors and pundits like to deride. We do live together and work in groups. How one could be an atomistic individual in our complex modern society is not clear: would that mean eating only what you grow, wearing what you make, living in a house you build for yourself, restricting yourself to natural medicines you extract from plants? Some critics of capitalism or advocates of "back to nature"—like the Unabomber, or Al Gore if he really meant what he wrote in *Earth in the Balance*—might endorse such a plan. But few libertarians would want to move to a desert island and renounce the benefits of what Adam Smith called the Great Society, the complex and productive society made possible by social interaction. One would think, therefore, that sensible journalists would stop, look at the words they typed, and think to themselves, "I must have misrepresented this position. I should go back and read the libertarian writers again."

In our time this canard—about isolation and atomism—has been very damaging to advocates of the market process. We ought to make it clear that we agree with George Soros that "cooperation is as much a part of the system as competition." In fact, we consider cooperation so essential to human flourishing that we don't just want to talk about it; we want to create social institutions that make it possible. That is what property rights, limited government, and the rule of law are all about.

In a free society individuals enjoy natural, imprescriptible rights and must live up to their general obligation to respect the rights of other individuals. Our other obligations are those we choose to assume by contract. It is not just coincidental that a society based on the rights of life, liberty, and property also produces social peace and material well-being. As John Locke, David Hume, and other classical-liberal philosophers demonstrate, we need a system of rights to produce social cooperation, without which people can achieve very little. Hume wrote in his *Treatise of Human Nature* that the circumstances confronting humans are (1) our self-interestedness, (2) our necessarily limited generosity toward others, and (3) the scarcity of resources available to fulfill our needs. Because of those circumstances, it is necessary for us to cooperate with others and to have rules of justice—especially regarding property and exchange—to define how we can do so. Those rules establish who has the right to decide how to use a particular piece of property. In the absence of well-defined property rights, we would face constant conflict over that issue. It is our agreement on property rights that allows us to undertake the complex social tasks of cooperation and coordination by which we achieve our purposes.

It would be nice if love could accomplish that task, without all the emphasis on self-interest and individual rights, and many opponents of liberalism have offered an appealing vision of society based on universal benevolence. But as Adam Smith pointed out, "in civilized society [man] stands at all times in need of the cooperation and assistance of great multitudes," yet in his whole life he could never befriend a small fraction of the number of people whose cooperation he needs. If we depended entirely on benevolence to produce cooperation, we simply couldn't undertake complex tasks. Reliance on other people's self-interest, in a system of well-defined property rights and free exchange, is the only way to organize a society more complicated than a small village.

Civil Society

We want to associate with others to achieve instrumental ends—producing more food, exchanging goods, developing new technology—but also because we feel a deep human need for connectedness, for love and friendship and community. The associations we form with others make up what we call civil society. Those associations can take an amazing variety of forms—families, churches, schools, clubs, fraternal societies, condominium associations, neighborhood groups, and the myriad forms of commercial society, such as partnerships, corporations, labor unions, and trade associations. All of these associations serve human needs in different ways. Civil society may be broadly defined as all the natural and voluntary associations in society.

Some analysts distinguish between commercial and nonprofit organizations, arguing that businesses are part of the market, not of civil society; but I follow the tradition that the real distinction is between associations that are coercive—the state—and those that are natural or voluntary—everything else. Whether a particular association is established to make a profit or to achieve some other purpose, the key characteristic is that our participation in it is voluntarily chosen.

With all the contemporary confusion about civil society and "national purpose," we should remember F. A. Hayek's point that the associations within civil society are created to achieve a particular purpose, but civil society as a whole has no single purpose; it is the undesigned, spontaneously emerging result of all those purposive associations.

The Market as Cooperation

The market is an essential element of civil society. The market arises from two facts: that human beings can accomplish more in cooperation with others than individually and that we can recognize this. If we were a species for whom cooperation was not more productive than isolated work, or if we were unable to discern the benefits of cooperation, then we would remain isolated and atomistic. But worse than that, as Ludwig von Mises explained, "Each man would have been forced to view all other men as his enemies; his craving for the satisfaction of his own appetites would have brought him into an implacable conflict with all his neighbors." Without the possibility of mutual benefit from cooperation and the division of labor, neither feelings of sympathy and friendship nor the market order itself could arise.

Throughout the market system individuals and firms compete to cooperate better. General Motors and Toyota compete to cooperate with me in achieving my goal of transportation. AT&T and MCI compete to cooperate with me in achieving my goal of communication with others. Indeed, they compete so aggressively for my business that I have cooperated with yet another communications firm that provides me with peace of mind via an answering machine.

Critics of markets often complain that capitalism encourages and rewards self-interest. In fact, people are self-interested under any political system. Markets channel their self-interest in socially beneficent directions. In a free market, people achieve their own purposes by finding out what others want and trying to offer it. That may mean several people working together to build a fishing net or a road. In a more complex economy, it means seeking one's own profit by offering goods or services that satisfy the needs or desires of others. Workers and entrepreneurs who best satisfy those needs will be rewarded; those who don't will soon find out and be encouraged to copy their more successful competitors or try a new approach.

All the different economic organizations we see in a market are experiments to find better ways of cooperating to achieve mutual purposes. A system of property rights, the rule of law, and minimal government allows maximum scope for people to experiment with new forms of cooperation. The development of the corporation allowed larger economic tasks to be undertaken than individuals or partnerships could achieve. Organizations such as condominium associations, mutual funds, insurance companies, banks, worker-owned cooperatives, and more are attempts to solve particular economic problems by new forms of association. Some of these forms are discovered to be inefficient; many of the corporate conglomerates in the 1960s, for instance, proved to be unmanageable, and shareholders lost money. The rapid feedback of the market process provides incentives for successful forms of organization to be copied and unsuccessful forms to be discouraged.

Cooperation *is* as much a part of capitalism as competition. Both are essential elements of the simple system of natural liberty, and most of us spend far more of our time cooperating with partners, coworkers, suppliers, and customers than we do competing.

Life would indeed be nasty, brutish, and short if it were solitary. Fortunately for all of us, in capitalist society it isn't.

The Freeman: Ideas on Liberty, September 1997

Liberalism and Change

The United States is a society based on change. We have no cultural memory of generations or centuries when life remained much the same. The one constant to which Americans have become accustomed is change.

Many explanations can be adduced for this phenomenon—our society's relative youth, constant new frontiers, continual immigration. But the fundamental explanation is that the United States is the world's most liberal society in the classical sense of the term. It was founded by liberals, on explicit liberal principles, and it has remained largely true—despite many deviations—to those principles.

The benefits of change are obvious. We can point to new developments from the cotton gin to the automobile to the computer chip that have made our lives better. The clearest way to understand the benefits of change is to recognize that our society supports more than 200 million people at the highest standard of living in the history of the world, in a land area that once provided mere subsistence to only a few million.

But change has costs. As consumer preferences shift or new competitors arise, some people lose their businesses or their jobs. Their skills become outmoded. When an industry or even a firm shuts down, a whole way of life may disappear. Millions of Americans have had to give up farm life. Millions more are faced with the loss of their lifetime jobs as smokestack industries decline. Some people find this change too much to bear.

Many of us today may think of the 1920s—when Mises wrote *Liberalism*—as the good old days, even a golden age, and certainly a time well before the harrowing pace of modern life. Yet even then people were complaining about the need to adjust to change. They argued, said Mises, that "the material advances of recent generations . . . have, of course, been really very agreeable and beneficial. Now, however, it is time to call a halt. The frantic hustle and bustle of modern capitalism must make way for tranquil contemplation." (p. 189 in the 1985 edition from the Foundation for Economic Education)

Few people today are so explicit in their hostility to change. They don't want to stop all change, just the particular changes that infringe on their patterns of life. Modern "liberals" and leftists find a receptive audience among displaced workers and others beset by economic change for their programs of stagnation: Rent control, farm parity, plant closing restrictions, limits on automation. Similarly, New Right conservatives appeal to middle Americans fearful about today's lifestyle changes with their programs to "restore traditional moral values."

There are, it would appear, few things that Ludwig von Mises and George Will would agree on, but one of them is this point, as phrased by Will: "The essential aim of liberalism, and the central liberal value, is the maximization of individual choice." Mises wrote about the maximization of choice primarily as a means to achieve greater wealth for everyone in society. But he did not limit his liberal principles to what George Will would call the "merely economic" sphere of life. Here is Mises on liberal policy toward what we might today call lifestyle issues: "If the majority of citizens is, in principle, conceded the right to impose its way of life upon a minority, it is impossible to stop at prohibitions against indulgence in alcohol, morphine, cocaine, and similar poisons. Why should not what is valid for these poisons be valid also for nicotine, caffeine, and the like? Why should not the state generally proscribe which foods may be indulged in and which must be avoided because they are injurious? . . . We see that as soon as we surrender the principle that the state should not interfere in any questions touching on the individual's mode of life, we end by regulating and restricting the latter down to the smallest detail." (pp. 53–54)

The problem for conservatives like Will is that capitalism means individual choice. And, as Mises noted, when people are allowed to be free, some of them will choose courses of action that others disapprove. When that happens, some want the government to step in. Whether it is to control rents, prevent disinvestment in farming, or keep women in the home, they are willing to use the state to keep society from changing.

This is a fundamentally reactionary view of the world, a lingering impulse from pre-capitalist times. Before capitalism, and in a few parts of the world still largely untouched by capitalist society, life did stay much the same for generations. Men and women knew that they would grow up, live, and die just as their fathers and mothers did. This was not a pastoral ideal; it was a life that was nasty, brutish, and short, and the subsistence society could support only a few people compared to today's population.

Into this stagnant world came liberalism. By freeing people from ancient bonds, it showed them that progress was possible. They could change their lives, they could have more material comforts, their powers of creation and achievement were liberated. And with the coming of liberalism came an end to settled society. Change became the only constant.

Liberalism gave people the freedom to make choices. Economic freedom created prosperity, which gave more people the wherewithal to take advantage of the new choices available to them. This process of choice and change is the distinguishing characteristic of capitalism.

Liberals must recapture the progressive spirit that characterized liberalism in its early days. We must make it clear that liberalism, and only liberalism, is the political philosophy of progress, and that those who seek to resist change stand in the way of what Mises called "an ever progressing improvement in the satisfaction of human wants." (p. 192)

The Freeman: Ideas on Liberty, November 1985

The Gun behind the Law

A newspaper photo depicts a bank nationalization in Peru: dozens of helmeted police officers pouring through a door. When we Americans hear the words "bank nationalization," we are apt to imagine a piece of paper being signed by a bank president and a deputy assistant treasury secretary. We can thank our friends in Peru for making the meaning of the term a little clearer. What really occurred there is that some people forced other people to give up their property at the point of a gun.

The gun is evident in the picture, but it is no less real when an American is forced to give up his property by a law or regulation. Such commonly used terms as "national economic policy," "social regulation," "revenue enhancement," "profamily legislation," and "minimum-wage law" all obscure the simple fact that some people are forcing others to do as they're told.

But Peru is not the United States, it will be said; our government would never send riot troops to take over a bank. That is largely because it wouldn't have to—Americans don't resist the demands of government. What would happen if they did?

During World War II Sewell L. Avery, who was chairman of Montgomery Ward, refused to comply with orders from the War Labor Board. President Franklin D. Roosevelt angrily ordered his cabinet to bring Avery into compliance. When Avery continued to ignore federal demands, Attorney General Francis Biddle flew to Montgomery Ward's headquarters in Chicago and ordered soldiers to carry the chairman out of his office. A picture of that unprecedented exercise of federal power made every newspaper in the country. Avery continued to run the business by telephone, however, and eventually President Roosevelt sent the army in to take over Montgomery Ward's books, change the combinations on its safes, and discharge managers who refused to cooperate. What is unusual about that episode is Avery's defiance. The government's willingness to go to such lengths to enforce its demands stands behind every law, every executive order, every regulation.

Imagine, say, that an orange grower insists on selling all the fruit he grows—in violation of federal marketing orders. Bureaucrats shuffle a few papers and send out an injunction assessing a fine. The grower says he has no intention of paying a fine for the crime of selling nutritious fruit to willing customers and continues to sell his oranges. More bureaucrats enter the picture and order his customers not to buy from him. They ignore the government's orders. Next bureaucrats descend on the farm with cease-and-desist orders, which the grower chooses to ignore.

What happens then? Either the government backs down and allows the grower to continue selling all his oranges, in which case there isn't much point to having marketing orders on the books, or the bureaucrats return to his farm with armed force. They lock the gates, discharge the employees, and keep the grower off his land. If the grower says, "This is my property, and like my ancestors at Lexington and Concord, I'm prepared to defend it," the bureaucrats must be willing to use their weapons to "implement national agricultural policy."

It rarely comes to that, of course, but neither is the threat of violence idle. In 1979, 10 policemen went to John Singer's house in Utah to demand that he stop educating his children at home and send them to a government-sanctioned school. Singer refused and brandished a gun to keep the police off his property. They shot him in the back. In December 1987 the Customs Service asked for permission to shoot down aircraft suspected of smuggling drugs, a policy it described as "us[ing] appropriate force" to "ensure compliance."

If more Americans decided to ignore absurd, special-interest, and counterproductive laws, it would soon be apparent that physical force lies behind the Federal Register. Does anyone believe that Americans would pay a large percentage of their income to the federal government if not for the ultimate threat of imprisonment and violence?

As the bankers of Peru have learned, every law is enforced at the point of a gun—a fact we should carefully consider when we are tempted to conclude that some perceived problem should be solved by enacting a law.

Cato Policy Report, January/February 1988

Are Libertarians Anti-Government?

For the past several years, especially since the Oklahoma City bombing, the national media have focused a lot of attention on "anti-government" extremists. Libertarians, who are critical of a great deal that government does, have unfortunately but perhaps understandably been tossed into the "anti-government" camp by many journalists.

There are two problems with this identification. The first and most obvious is that many of the so-called anti-government groups are racist or violent or both, and being identified with them verges on libel.

The second and ultimately more important problem is that libertarians are not, in any serious sense, "anti-government." It's understandable that journalists might refer to people who often criticize both incumbent office-holders and government programs as "anti-government," but the term is misleading.

A government is a set of institutions through which we adjudicate our disputes, defend our rights, and provide for certain common needs. It derives its authority, at some level and in some way, from the consent of the governed.

Libertarians want people to be able to live peacefully together in civil society. Cooperation is better than coercion. Peaceful coexistence and voluntary cooperation require an institution to protect us from outside threats, deter or punish criminals, and settle the disputes that will inevitably arise among neighbors—a government, in short. Thus, to criticize a wide range of the activities undertaken by federal and state governments—from Social Security to drug prohibition to out-of-control taxation—is not to be "anti-government." It is simply to insist that what we want is a limited government that attends to its necessary and proper functions.

But if libertarians are not "anti-government," then how do we describe the kind of government that libertarians support? One formulation found in the media is that "libertarians support weak government." That has a certain appeal. But consider a prominent case of "weak government." Numerous reports have told us recently about the weakness of the Russian government. Not only does it have trouble raising taxes and paying its still numerous employees, it has trouble deterring or punishing criminals. It is in fact too weak to carry out its legitimate functions. The Russian government is a failure on two counts: it is massive, clumsy, overextended, and virtually unconstrained in scope, yet too weak to perform its essential job. (Residents of many American cities may find that description a bit too close for comfort.)

Not "weak government," then. How about "small government"? Lots of people, including many libertarians, like that phrase to describe libertarian views. And it has a certain plausibility. We rail against "big government," so we must prefer small government, or "less government." Of course, we wouldn't want a government too small to deter military threats or apprehend criminals. And *Washington Post* columnist E. J. Dionne, Jr., offers us this comparison: "a dictatorship in which the government provides no social security, health, welfare or pension programs of any kind" and "levies relatively low taxes that go almost entirely toward the support of large military and secret police forces that regularly kill or jail people for their political or religious views" or "a democracy with open elections and full freedom of speech and religion [which] levies higher taxes than the dictatorship to support an extensive welfare state."

"The first country might technically have a 'smaller government,'" Dionne writes, "but it undoubtedly is not a free society. The second country would have a 'bigger government,' but it is indeed a free society."

Now there are several problems with this comparison, not least Dionne's apparent view that high taxes don't limit the freedom of those forced to pay them. But our concern here is the term "smaller government." Measured as a percentage of GDP or by the number of employees, the second government may well be larger than the first. Measured by its power and control over individuals and society, however, the first government is doubtless larger. Thus, as long as the term is properly understood, it's reasonable for libertarians to endorse "smaller government." But Dionne's criticism should remind us that the term may not be well understood.

So if we're not anti-government, and not really for weak or small government, how should we describe the libertarian position? To answer that question, we need to go back to the Declaration of Independence and the Constitution. Libertarians generally support a government formed by the consent of the governed and designed to achieve certain limited purposes. Both the form of government and the limits on its powers should be specified in a constitution, and the challenge in any society is to keep government constrained and limited so that individuals can prosper and solve problems in a free and civil society.

Thus libertarians are not "anti-government." Libertarians support limited, constitutional government—limited not just in size but, of far greater importance, in the scope of its powers.

Cato Policy Report, July/August 1998

The Ownership Society

President Bush says he wants America to be an "ownership society." What does that mean?

People have known for a long time that individuals take better care of things they own. Aristotle wrote, "What belongs in common to the most people is accorded the least care: they take thought for their own things above all, and less about things common, or only so much as falls to each individual." And we all observe that homeowners take better care of their houses than renters do. That's not because renters are bad people; it's just that you're more attentive to details when you stand to profit from your house's rising value or to suffer if it deteriorates.

Just as homeownership creates responsible homeowners, widespread ownership of other assets creates responsible citizens. People who are owners feel more dignity, more pride, and more confidence. They have a stronger stake, not just in their own property, but in their community and their society. Geoff Mulgan, a top aide to British prime minister Tony Blair, explains, "The left always tended to underestimate the importance of ownership, and how hard it is for a democracy that does not have widespread ownership of assets to be truly democratic. . . . To escape from poverty you need assets—assets which you can put to work. There is a good deal of historical evidence . . . as well as abundant contemporary evidence, that ownership tends to encourage self-esteem and healthy habits of behaviour, such as acting more for the long term, or taking education more seriously."

Former prime minister Margaret Thatcher had that goal in mind when she set out to privatize Great Britain's public housing. Her administration sold 1.5 million housing units to their occupants, transforming 1.5 million British families from tenants in public housing to proud homeowners. She thought the housing would be better maintained, but more importantly she thought that homeowners would become more responsible citizens and see themselves as having a real stake in the future and in the quality of life in their communities. And yes, she thought that homeowners would be more likely to vote for lower taxes and less regulation—policies that would tend to improve the country's economic performance—and thus for the Conservative Party, or for Labour Party candidates only when they renounced their traditional socialism.

Margaret Thatcher saw that private ownership allows people to profit from improving their property by building on it or otherwise making it more valuable. People can also profit by improving themselves, of course, through education and the development of good habits, as long as they are allowed to reap the profits that come from such improvement. There's not much point in improving your skills, for instance, if regulations will keep you from entering your chosen occupation or high taxes will take most of your higher income.

The United States today has the most widespread property ownership in history. This year an all-time high of 68.6 percent of American households own their own homes. Even more significantly, increasing numbers of Americans are becoming capitalists—people who own a share of productive businesses through stocks or mutual funds. About half of American households qualify as stockholding in some form. That's up from 32 percent in 1989 and only 19 percent in 1983, a remarkable change in just 20 years. That means almost half of Americans directly benefited from the enormous market appreciation between 1982 and 2000 and are prepared to see their wealth increase again when the current stock market slump ends.

But it also means that about half of Americans are not benefiting as owners from the growth of the American economy (though of course they still benefit as wage-earners and consumers). In general, those are the Americans below the average income. The best thing we could do to create an ownership society in America is to give more Americans an opportunity to invest in stocks, bonds, and mutual funds so that they too can become capitalists. And the way to do that is obvious.

Right now, every working American is required to send the government 12.4 percent of his or her income (up to about $88,000) via payroll taxes. That's $4,960 on a salary of $40,000 a year. But that money is not invested in real assets, and it doesn't belong to the wage-earner who paid it. It goes into the Social Security system, where it's used to pay benefits to current retirees. If we want to make every working American an investor—an owner of real assets, with control of his own retirement funds and a stake in the growth of the American economy—then we should let workers put their Social Security taxes into private retirement accounts, like IRAs or 401(k)s. Then, instead of hoping someday to receive a meager retirement income from a Social Security system that is headed for bankruptcy, American workers would own their own assets in accounts that couldn't be reduced by Congress.

President Bush has talked about such a reform since his first campaign, and his President's Commission to Strengthen Social Security proposed three ways to achieve this goal. If he chooses to make Social Security reform part of his reelection campaign, then we may see congressional action in 2005. Sen. John F. Kerry has pledged never to "privatize Social Security." He should be asked why he thinks working-class Americans should not be allowed to invest their savings in stocks and bonds, as his family has done so successfully.

Other reforms that could enhance the ownership society include school choice—which would give parents the power to choose the schools their children attend—and wider use of Health Savings Accounts, which transfer control over health care decisions from employers, insurance companies, and HMO gatekeepers to individual patients.

Advancing an ownership society can also improve environmental quality. People take care of things they own, and they're more likely to waste or damage things that are owned by no one in particular. That's why timber companies don't cut all the trees on their land and instead plant new trees to replace the ones they do cut down. They may be moved by a concern for the environment, but the future income from the property is also a powerful incentive. In the socialist countries of Eastern Europe, where the government controlled all property, there was no real owner to worry about the future value of property; consequently, pollution and environmental destruction were far worse than in the West. Vacláv Klaus, prime minister of the Czech Republic, said in 1995, "The worst environmental damage occurs in countries without private property, markets, or prices."

Another benefit of private property ownership, not so clearly economic, is that it diffuses power. When the government owns all property, individuals have little protection from the whims of politicians. The institution of private property gives many individuals a place to call their own, a place where they are safe from depredation by others and by the state. This aspect of private property is captured in the axiom, "A man's home is his castle." Private property is essential for privacy and for freedom of the press. Try to imagine "freedom of the press" in a country where the government owns all the presses and all the paper.

The many benefits of an ownership society are not always intuitively obvious. The famous Harvard economist John Kenneth Galbraith wrote a bestselling book in 1958 called *The Affluent Society*, in which he discussed the phenomenon of "private opulence and public squalor"—that is, a society in which privately owned resources were generally clean, efficient, well-maintained, and improving in quality while public spaces were dirty, overcrowded, and unsafe—and concluded, oddly enough, that we ought to move more resources into the public sector. Thousands of college students were assigned to read *The Affluent Society*, and Galbraith's ideas played a major role in the vast expansion of government during the 1960s and 1970s.

But Galbraith and American politicians missed the real point of his observation. The more logical answer is that if privately owned resources are better maintained, then we should seek to expand private ownership.

Widespread ownership of capital assets has many benefits for society: It means that property is better maintained and long-term values are higher, including environmental quality. It means that people have a greater stake in their community and thus become better citizens. It protects people from the arbitrary power of government and gives them more freedom and more confidence as citizens. It produces prosperity because markets can't work without private property. Private retirement accounts and reduced taxes on investment would encourage more ownership for all Americans.

Cato.org, 2004

The Importance of History

Why so much interest in history at the Cato Institute? The lead article in this publication examines whether Franklin Roosevelt's New Deal got America out of the Great Depression. A few issues back, Michael Chapman looked at FDR's cousin Theodore and declared him "no friend of the Constitution." Recently Cato has hosted authors Anne Applebaum to talk about the Gulag and Thomas Fleming to discuss Woodrow Wilson and World War I.

Why all this history? Why not just stick to current policy issues? There are three reasons.

First, we study topics such as the Gulag for the same reason that there's a Holocaust Memorial Museum on the Mall in Washington: to remind ourselves, Never again. Never again must such things happen. (Though Applebaum writes, sadly, "This book was not written 'so that it will not happen again,' as the cliche would have it. This book was written because it almost certainly will happen again.")

Second, as the American Founders understood, the study of history is our best guide to the present and the future. In his great "liberty or death" speech, Patrick Henry proclaimed, "I have but one lamp by which my feet are guided, and that is the lamp of experience. I know of no way of judging the future but by the past." The authors of the Federalist Papers wrote of history as "the oracle of truth" and "the least fallible guide of human opinions." The American revolutionaries were close students of the ancient republics and the history of England. They traced their own demands to the "ancient and undoubted rights of Englishmen" and beyond that to the common law, Magna Carta, and the popular assemblies of the early English peoples. The first publication of the Declaration of Independence in book form in 1776 combined the document with lengthy excerpts from the influential *Historical Essay on the English Constitution*. As historian H. Trevor Colbourn wrote, "The history made by the American Revolutionaries was in part the product of the history they read."

The Founders understood that freedom is best defended when a philosophical claim is supported by a historical claim. From their study of history they learned of the ancient rights of Englishmen, the importance of individual virtue in preserving freedom, and the dangers of power and thus the necessity of constraining and dividing it. Consider Hamilton's warning in Federalist 75 about the powers of the president in foreign affairs, a warning of particular relevance today: "The history of human conduct does not warrant that exalted opinion of human virtue which would make it wise in a nation to commit interests of so delicate and momentous a kind, as those which concern its intercourse with the rest of the world, to the sole disposal of a magistrate created and circumstanced as would be a President of the United States." (I copied that text from www.speaker.house.gov, where it is accompanied by a picture of Speaker Dennis Hastert; I hope he has read the essay.)

History helps us to understand the development of our civilization, including the ideas that shape it. Often the ideas that we now regard as universal principles arose in response to particular circumstances. Magna Carta and similar medieval charters reflect the struggle to constrain the power of kings. From such guarantees of specific liberties, eventually liberty developed. The rights guaranteed in the Bill of Rights reflected particular historical experiences: with religious wars, censorship, confiscation of property, the Star Chamber, and the constant tendency of government to seek more power.

Third, people get much of their understanding of government and policy from history. The way we view the Constitution, the industrial revolution, the robber barons, the New Deal, and other historical events shapes our view of the present. Far too often these days our public institutions such as schools and universities fail to give students a proper appreciation for the great achievement of the Founders in creating a society in which government is constrained by law. Instead, we get revisionist accounts of Washington and Jefferson and hagiographic treatment of the Roosevelts, all of it accompanied by calls for more power to be entrusted to Washington.

American students need to learn about the greatness of America. But that requires an understanding of what makes a nation great. Is America great because we put a man on the moon or defeated Saddam Hussein? Or is America great because it's the country that has offered more freedom to more people to pursue their own happiness than any other nation on earth?

Some think that a great nation must be governed by great men wielding great power. History suggests otherwise. Right after he wrote, "Power tends to corrupt and absolute power corrupts absolutely," the historian Lord Acton went on to say, "Great men are almost always bad men." And great men with great powers are no substitute for our Constitution. The truly great men are the ones who have fought for liberty, who have walked away from power, who have helped to bring power under the rule of law. Limited government is a great achievement, a recent achievement in the sweep of history, and history teaches us that it can be lost. Appreciating where it came from and how rare and fragile it is will help us to preserve it.

Cato Policy Report, July/August 2003

PART 2

A Necessary Evil

The Hubris of Politics

Sen. Richard Lugar (R-Ind.), reflecting on his presidential campaign, writes in the *Washington Post*, "I argued for a ban on assault weapons, for which I see no legitimate social purpose."

Leave aside the substance of the specific issue and consider the sweeping audacity of "for which I see no legitimate social purpose." One might well ask, Who appointed Senator Lugar the arbiter of what can be sold in the United States? And how many of the millions of products for sale could be determined to have a "legitimate social purpose"? Cigarettes? Electric toothbrushes? Jolt Cola? Copies of *It Takes a Village*? Most products have a private, not a social, purpose. The food and clothes that I buy serve *my* needs, not society's.

Senator Lugar's statement is a perfect example of the mentality people develop after too many years in public office. They seem to think that every opinion of theirs should be made law and enforced by the police.

Lugar is hardly unique. The day after his article ran in the *Post*, the Senate Banking Committee held hearings on a bill, sponsored by Chairman Alfonse D'Amato (R-N.Y.) along with Sens. John Kerry (D-Mass.), Barbara Boxer (D-Calif.), and others, that would prohibit banks from charging fees to noncustomers who use their automatic teller machines. Senator D'Amato says, "Congress should not *condone* ATM surcharging" (his emphasis). He seems to believe that Congress must roam across America, looking for immoral activities that cannot be condoned—like providing people a useful service for a price—because Congress has some sort of moral responsibility for every activity in our society.

Again, consider the presumptuousness of such a bill and the relative contributions of banks and senators to our lives. Civil society, hampered at every turn by petty political rules, takes thousands of years to develop the technology, the complex market mechanisms, and the levels of trust necessary for individuals to be able to get cash, at midnight, in an airport or a 7-Eleven thousands of miles from home, from a bank that they do no other business with—and members of Congress decide that the bank shouldn't be able to charge a dollar for that service. Imagine what kind of banking services we'd have if we had to wait for Congress to develop the necessary institutions, and then imagine what we might have if Congress got entirely out of the business of controlling, hamstringing, and bullying banks.

Too many people in Washington think nothing happens—or should happen—in America except at their behest. In their own minds, political society has entirely replaced civil society. Sen. Edward M. Kennedy (D-Mass.) said in 1992, "The ballot box is the place where all change begins in America"—conveniently forgetting the market process that has brought us such changes as the train, the skyscraper, the automobile, the personal computer, and charitable or self-help endeavors from settlement houses to Alcoholics Anonymous to Comic Relief.

This disease has infected too many people in our society. The "Mini Page," a Sunday supplement for children distributed in many newspapers, urged children recently, "Look through your paper for problems the country is facing. Which Cabinet members do you think might help solve them?" It might have done better to ask, "Which Cabinet members do you think caused the problems?" But the real mistake here is thinking that all problems have a political solution. In fact, most of the social problems that people have faced throughout history have been ameliorated or solved through the voluntary workings of civil society and the market process. We didn't relieve ourselves of the burden of backbreaking labor, or bring the world closer together through a series of transportation revolutions, by passing laws; we worked, saved, invested, and created economic progress. Even if a particular goal was achieved by people on a government payroll, it was only the wealth produced by private individuals that allowed government to undertake the project—and we should always consider what that money might have accomplished had it been spent voluntarily by those who produced it.

Critics of the welfare state are often charged with wanting "to tear down government programs and put nothing in their place." But what kind of political philosophy is it that looks at the vibrancy of America and sees "nothing" except what the government does?

Hillary Clinton's philosophy, apparently. The First Lady said recently, "This is an ominous time for those of us who care for the arts in America. A misguided, misinformed effort to eliminate public support for the arts not only threatens irrevocable damage to our cultural institutions but also to our sense of ourselves and what we stand for as a people." A similar argument was made in the conservative *Weekly Standard* in a cover article by Joseph Epstein titled "Why, Despite Everything, Republicans Should Not Abandon the Arts." But whatever Mrs. Clinton and Mr. Epstein may think, no one is proposing to "abandon" the arts. Some Republicans are proposing that of the $37 billion spent on the arts in the United States (according to the American Arts Alliance), the $167 million that is coercively extracted from taxpayers should be eliminated. Who could view such a cut as "threatening irrevocable damage"—except someone who looks at the bounty of civil society and sees a barren wasteland enlightened only by the activities of the federal government?

Every morning's newspaper—at least if your morning newspaper is the *Washington Post*—is filled with the pronouncements of politicians and policy wonks on what people should be forced to do to make this a better world. The denizens of political society should develop a little humility and a little appreciation of what people achieve through voluntary cooperation, if only politicians will let them.

Cato Policy Report, July/August 1996

Government without Principles

> Atlanta, Jan. 1—Gov. Zell Miller proposed Tuesday that the state provide the parents of every Georgia newborn with a classical music cassette or compact disc in order to boost the infant's intelligence later in life.

We could make fun of poor Governor Miller. We could congratulate him on offering parents a choice of a cassette or CD, and wonder why he won't also offer them a choice of musical styles. Or we could note that at least one expert quoted in the *New York Times* indicates that the research on music and intelligence is far from conclusive. We could question the wisdom of a governor who goes straight from reading an article in *Time* magazine to establishing a state program.

But the real issue here is what we might call government without a compass, government that careens wildly from scheme to scheme because it has no guiding principles. If Governor Miller thinks it is the role of government to provide musical recordings to the parents of newborns, is there any task he considers inappropriate for government? And in that regard is he any different from any other governor, member of Congress, or president?

We used to have rules for government. Unique among nations, the United States was founded on a clear conception of the role of government. The Declaration of Independence, our founding document, declared that "all men . . . are endowed by their Creator with certain unalienable rights . . . life, liberty, and the pursuit of happiness" and that "to secure these rights, governments are instituted among men."

The Constitution established a government of delegated, enumerated, and thus limited powers. That is, Americans understood that they had their rights prior to and independent of government. In the Constitution, they delegated some of their rights to a federal government. In so doing, they enumerated the specific powers that they were placing with the government, and that enumeration limited the new government's power. The Declaration set out a clear principle for the role of government, and the Constitution set up a government according to that principle.

For many years Americans expected the federal government, at least, to operate largely according to the rules of the Constitution. With a few exceptions, it did not interfere in matters best left to states, localities, or civil society, and most Americans encountered the federal government only in the form of the postman. But after a century or so, the national government began to hand out subsidies and dabble in economic regulation. Just a little bit at first, then a little more and a little more. By the 1930s Charles Warren could write a book called *Government as Santa Claus*.

Each new subsidy and regulation weakened the original conception of limited government. After all, people reasoned, if government can help the farmers of Ohio, why not Illinois? And if the farmers, why not the veterans? And if the veterans, why not the elderly? And eventually there ensued what James Buchanan has called the collapse of the constitutional consensus, when everyone made a mad dash for the piñata of federal largesse.

By the 1970s the federal government was being called on to bail out individual failing companies such as Penn Central and Chrysler. Today, every day's newspaper reveals that there is no subject so petty, so local, or so absurd that some politician won't propose to have government tax, regulate, mandate, forbid or subsidize it. And alas, there are all too few Americans left who don't ask the government to subsidize their businesses and their hobbies and ban all of their neighbors' annoying habits.

The Consumer Product Safety Commission issues mandatory rules for bunk beds. Twentysomethings in Howard County, Maryland, the offspring of prosperous lawyers and lobbyists, complain that the county government doesn't provide any hobbies or social activities for them. Rep. Bill Paxon (R-N.Y.) proposes that the federal government subsidize the hiring of 100,000 new teachers, a local function if there ever was one. The futile war on drugs leads to 13-year-olds being suspended from school because they have Advil in their purses. Half the stories in every newspaper should be headlined "Stop me before I legislate again." In such a climate government has become Big Brother, Santa Claus, and Mary Poppins all rolled into one. The vice presidency of the United States, a position once held by John Adams and Thomas Jefferson, is now held by a man who declares that the federal government should be like a grandparent to the American people.

In the modern world, Zell Miller is the ideal governor, a man who thinks his every idea, his every newspaper clipping, his every impulse should be coercively enforced—with the bill sent to the productive people of Georgia.

Government not guided by firm principles is government adrift, government run amok, like a gargantuan two-year-old with an Uzi. It's time to tell the politicians, When all else fails, read the original instructions.

Cato Policy Report, January/February 1998

The Lobbyist Scandals

When you spread food out on a picnic table, you can expect ants. When you put $3 trillion on the table, you can expect special interests, lobbyists and pork-barrel politicians.

That's the real lesson of the Abramoff scandal.

Jack Abramoff may have been the sleaziest of the Washington lobbyists but he's not unique. As the federal government accumulates more money and more power, it draws more lobbyists like honey draws flies.

People invest money to make money. In a free economy they invest in building homes and factories, inventing new products, finding oil, and other economic activities. That kind of investment benefits us all—it's a positive-sum game, as economists say. People get rich by producing what other people want.

But you can also invest in Washington. You can organize an interest group, or hire a lobbyist, and try to get some taxpayers' money routed to you. That's what the farm lobbies, AARP, industry associations, and teachers unions do. And that kind of investment is zero-sum—money is taken from some people and given to others, but no new wealth is created.

If you want to drill an oil well, you hire petroleum engineers. If you want to drill for money in Washington, you hire a lobbyist. And more people have been doing that.

The number of companies with registered lobbyists is up 58 percent in six years. The amount of money lobbyists report spending has risen from $1.5 billion to $2.1 billion in that time, according to the PoliticalMoneyLine website, which compiles data from public reports.

And why not? After all, federal spending is up 39 percent in the same period. That means another $640 billion a year for interest groups to get their hands on.

With federal spending approaching $3 trillion a year—and even more money moved around by regulations and the details of tax law—getting a piece of that money can be worth a great deal of effort and expense. That's why they call the hallway outside the Senate Finance Committee "Gucci gulch," because that's where the lobbyists in their expensive shoes hang out waiting to buttonhole members of Congress and their staffs.

Nobel laureate F.A. Hayek explained the process 60 years ago in his prophetic book *The Road to Serfdom:* "As the coercive power of the state will alone decide who is to have what, the only power worth having will be a share in the exercise of this directing power."

The United States is not Russia or Nigeria, states where government power really is the only thing worth having. But when the government has more money and power, then more of society's resources will tend to be directed toward influencing government.

A study in the *Journal of Law and Economics* found that 87 percent of the increase in campaign spending over an 18-year period was attributable to the rise in federal spending during that period.

Abramoff specialized in manipulating regulations, especially the licensing of casinos. If gambling wasn't so tightly licensed and regulated, then it wouldn't produce extraordinary profits and lavish lobbying. He excelled at crassness and cynicism. But his efforts were small potatoes compared with the hugely expensive and complex programs of the federal government and the lobbying generated by all that spending and regulation.

During the 1970s, when Congress created massive new government regulations, businesses had to invest more heavily in lobbying. Some of it was defensive—to try to minimize the cost and burden of regulation.

But of course some of the lobbying was more cynical, to ensure that costs fell more heavily on competitors. One study in 1980 showed that 65 percent of the CEOs of Fortune 500 companies came to Washington at least every two weeks. That was up sharply from 1971, when only 15 percent of CEOs visited Washington even once a month.

In 2003 Congress passed a trillion-dollar prescription drug benefit for Medicare recipients. Not surprisingly, there was more lobbying on health care than on any other issue that year, some $300 million by PoliticalMoneyLine's calculation. AARP was the biggest single spender. But unions and pharmaceutical companies accounted for most of the total.

In most states education is the biggest budget item, and the teachers unions are the biggest lobbyists. As states start to spend more on Medicaid than on schools, health care lobbyists may become more numerous and effective than the education establishment.

Meanwhile, the taxpayers have little voice in the halls of Congress. The National Taxpayers Union spent less than $175,000 on lobbying in 2004. And the NTU is one of the very few organizations whose lobbying is aimed at decreasing the size and overall reach of government.

As long as the federal government has so much money and power to hand out, we'll never get rid of the Abramoffs. Restrictions on lobbying deal with symptoms, not causes.

Pittsburgh Tribune Review, January 15, 2006

Root of the Evil

Review of Elizabeth Drew, *Politics and Money*. New York: Macmillan, 1983.

The thesis of *Politics and Money* is simple: The raising and spending of campaign money is corrupting the democratic process. Drew has pulled together some disturbing examples:

The number of political action committees (PACs) increased 500 percent between 1974 and 1982. Lobbyists boast openly of the influence they command because of their PAC dollars, while Democratic Congressional Campaign Committee Chairman Tony Coelho assures us, "We [i.e., congressmen] don't sell legislation; we sell the opportunity to be heard." Raymond Donovan raised $600,000 for the Reagan campaign and was rewarded with a Cabinet post. Dan Rostenkowski, chairman of the House Ways and Means Committee, hasn't faced a serious challenger in 24 years, yet he had $495,000 in campaign funds at the end of 1982.

Perhaps the most unsettling aspect of the book is Drew's disregard for free speech. She cites Archibald Cox's statement that "it is at least a fifty-fifty possibility that all the framers of the Constitution had in mind when they wrote the First Amendment was a prohibition on prior censorship," thus dismissing 200 years of free-speech struggles. Her search for rationales for censorship leads her down several paths: Maybe it isn't free speech "when an organization raises money from all over the country and then spends it to broadcast"; after all, such money is used for "much speech but few ideas." Finally, she suggests that "we redefine what we mean by 'freedom of speech,' and uncouple the idea of 'the marketplace of ideas' from the idea of 'the free market.'"

This is a very revealing phrase. Many civil libertarians wish to make a dichotomy between the market for goods and the market for ideas so that they can support free speech but not economic freedom; Drew more perceptively recognizes that dividing the two is a good way to jettison freedom of speech. For what do we mean by "free speech," after all? Even in a totalitarian country, one cannot censor thoughts nor can one totally censor speech, which is fleeting. What the First Amendment really protects is *products* through which ideas are expressed: books, newspapers, meeting halls, television broadcasts, etc. Speech, to have any effect, must be transmitted through physical products, so if those products are subject to manipulation by the state, freedom of expression loses its meaning. The market for goods and the market for ideas are inextricably linked.

In any case, Drew doesn't want to eliminate all free speech. A cynic might say she wants to preserve it for people like herself. With her annoying "some say, others reply" habit, she writes of her bete noire, the right-wing political action committees: "Others reply that what [they] are doing, and the scale on which they are doing it, goes beyond political expression—that they manipulate people's desire for political expression. . . . These committees are highly skilled, directed organizations that use people's feelings about certain issues to gain influence." Well, just what are they doing except organizing people to give their views an influence in politics they wouldn't otherwise have?

Elsewhere, Drew quotes politicos of both right and left to make the point that conservatives do better with direct mail fundraising because their contributors are "suburban and rural, and they tend to be very frustrated. They don't have any [other] outlet for their political feelings." Liberals, on the other hand, tend to be educated, upper middle class, and able to influence politics more directly. Following this line of thought, she suggests that the kind of independent expenditure that ought to be legal is "a group of professors taking an ad in a newspaper." (An example provided by Professor Cox.)

Elections, she muses, ought to be like town meetings where "everyone gets an equal allocation of time and a fair chance to express his point of view." And just how would the average person have an "equal allocation" compared to, say, John Chancellor or Katharine Graham—or Elizabeth Drew? One way businessmen and people in Opelika can equalize the imbalance between themselves and Elizabeth Drew is by giving money to candidates and committees. A measure that eliminated the use of money in politics wouldn't give everyone an equal chance—it would simply give the advantage to speakers, writers, the well-educated, and others with an above-average ability to influence the political system. It would also weight elections toward incumbents, a result Drew would probably not approve of.

But one of the points that Drew never seems to grasp is that no measure will really eliminate money from politics. She recognizes the failure of current laws. Limits on individual contributions caused the enormous growth in PACs after 1974, and limits on contributions to federal races led to large donations to state parties for "local" expenditures. However, she fails to recognize that the new laws she recommends will invariably come to naught as well. The problem is that in a relatively open society people will always find a way around laws that attempt to prevent them from swaying the government.

Why? That brings up the fundamental failing of *Politics and Money*. With all her getting of information, Drew has not got understanding. In fact, she states the problem just backwards in her opening chapter: "Until the problem of money is dealt with, it is unrealistic to expect the political process to improve in any other respect." On the contrary, as long as we have an exceedingly large and powerful government, handing out some $800 billion a year, interest groups are going to try to get their hands on that money and power.

People and businesses know that you have to invest to make money. Usually, people invest in oil wells, factories, their own education and skills, and the like. But they can also invest in the political process, and as long as that seems more profitable than alternative uses of their money, they will do so. Money isn't corrupting politics, politics is corrupting money—money that would otherwise be spent to produce goods for consumers.

Republicans, pragmatic businessmen that so many of them are, have no trouble adapting the lingo of the marketplace to the political market. Former Republican National Chairman Bill Brock, of the Brock Candy Company, reminded business PACs that "the business of business is to take risks," and urged them to support Republican congressional challengers rather than sharing their funds with Democratic incumbents. And Republican lobbyist Robert K. Gray, who raised some $16 million for the Reagan inauguration from individuals and companies who just might want to be favorably regarded by the new president, said, "This is free enterprise at its best."

It isn't free enterprise, of course, but many of the same rules do apply. As government increasingly comes to dominate social and economic life, power over government becomes the most important power in society. It is naive to think that special interests won't work night and day to gain a piece of that pie. Since most government programs are designed to reward one group handsomely and spread the costs over millions of taxpayers, there are always lobbyists urging the passage of a particular bill, while taxpayers rarely find it in their interest to protest. Is it any wonder that more and more programs are passed?

Our modern corporate welfare state is perhaps reaching its maturity; the interest groups are settled in comfortably. Drew reports that, in the House Energy and Commerce Committee, "prospective members were talked of in terms of the interests they appeared to represent": coal, oil, environmentalists. She refers favorably to Representative Jim Leach (R-Iowa), who calls the proposal to limit PAC contributions "a kind of domestic SALT agreement between big business and big labor." And where do the rest of us come in?

Elizabeth Drew has put together some useful research on how much interest groups will spend to gain access to the greatest accumulation of wealth in the history of the world. As long as that cornucopia of benefits exists, however, efforts to limit influence over its distribution are dealing with symptoms, not causes.

Inquiry, November 1983

How the Republicans and Democrats Maintained Their Market Share

In this era of vigorous economic competition, oligopolies like the Big Three automakers and the three major television networks have seen their market shares slip. In a free market, the same fate might befall the two-party duopoly. But the politicians have a plan to prevent that.

Back in the mid-1970s, the two parties and the three big networks were riding high. ABC, CBS, and NBC commanded 91 percent of the primetime viewing audience in 1976. The Democrats and Republicans did even better: they received 98.3 percent of the vote in the 1976 elections for the House of Representatives.

But those towering market-share figures concealed a lot of dissatisfaction. Popular unrest over Vietnam, Watergate, and a stagnant economy had driven both parties' approval ratings down, and many people were calling for the creation of a new party.

Simultaneously, increasing affluence and the cultural revolutions of the 1960s fractured the television audience. Many people wondered why Americans were largely restricted to three networks, all seeking the lowest common denominator of viewing interest.

Both the parties and the networks worried that their comfortable oligopolies might soon be eroded by such popular discontent. Of course, the politicians had better tools available to deal with the challenge than did the network honchos.

The politicians declared that what people were upset about was the fundraising excesses of the 1972 Nixon campaign, so they passed strict new regulations on campaign finance. The 1974 amendments to the Federal Election Campaign Act limited contributions to any candidate for federal office to $1,000 per person per election (primary and general elections counted as separate elections). They also limited political action committees—which pool the donations of many individuals—to $5,000 per candidate. Many members of Congress were clear about their aim: to strengthen the two-party system in the face of popular outrage.

Several other provisions were later struck down by the Supreme Court: a limit of $25,000 in personal spending by a candidate, a limit on what independent committees could spend, and a ceiling of $70,000 in spending by House candidates.

But the contribution limits served their purpose. Despite all the dissatisfaction with the two major parties, no viable independent or third-party challenge emerged. The two-party share of the House vote remained at virtually 100 percent—rising a bit to 98.8 percent in 1988, dropping to a nail-biting 97.4 percent in 1996. Deprived of the chance to raise seed money from wealthy and strongly committed individuals, no new party could get off the ground.

Even within the two parties, no presidential nominee as independent of the party establishment as Barry Goldwater or George McGovern has been nominated since 1974. Both Goldwater and McGovern, like unsuccessful challenger Eugene McCarthy, depended on seed money from wealthy supporters to launch their campaigns.

Compare the success of the political strategists with their network counterparts. The networks couldn't pass a law limiting their competitors' access to money. Try as they might to develop attractive programming, they saw their market share decline steadily: from 91 percent in 1976 to 83 percent in 1980, to 61 percent in 1988, to 46 percent in 1996.

Just imagine how things might have been different if the networks had been allowed to control the rules for the television industry, the way Congress can make the rules for congressional elections. Imagine that the networks had passed a law in 1974 saying that anyone could start a new network, but that no company could spend more than $1,000 to advertise on it. With revenues restricted like that, would we be watching Fox, CNN, ESPN, AMC, USA, Lifetime or other new networks today? No, in that case ABC, CBS and NBC might still have 91 percent of their market.

Government regulations often backfire; they often create unintended consequences. But not always. In the case of campaign spending controls, the consequences were clearly intended. The establishment politicians set out in 1974 to protect their market share, and they succeeded beautifully.

But today, the politicians are worried again. Congressional reelection rates ranging from 98 percent in 1990 to a low of 90 percent in 1994 (with 95 percent in 1996) just aren't good enough. After all, that means some members of Congress aren't reelected—and what incumbent can be happy with that situation?

So there's discussion of still stricter limits on campaign finance. One favorite "reform" is to limit overall spending on congressional campaigns. The much-touted McCain-Feingold bill would limit total spending to $500,000 in House races and a cap in Senate races based on population. How did they come up with those particular limits? Well, in 1996 every House incumbent who spent less than $500,000 won reelection, while only 3 percent of challengers who spent that little were successful. And every senator who spent less than the McCain-Feingold limits in both 1994 and 1996 won, while every challenger who spent less than the limit lost. What a coincidence.

Contribution and spending limits mean less competition for incumbents. The market-share leaders in every industry would like to have such restrictions on potential competitors. So we have an easy choice to make: do we want our political campaigns to be as competitive as, say, our television choices, or as uncompetitive as, well, our current political choices?

The Washington Times, August 7, 1998

No Consensus

Again and again, individuals insist on making their own decisions—much to the frustration of governments and planners.

A weekend article in the *FT* comes with this teaser: "A generation ago, Shin Dong-jin was trying to stop South Korean women from having babies. Now his planned parenthood foundation has the opposite problem—there aren't enough babies being born. He must persuade the country to go forth and multiply."

Apparently Shin Dong-jin is just the only person in South Korea who knows, at any given time, how many children people should have. But people make their own decisions.

The *FT* piece reminded me of some other recent articles about how stubborn people just won't do what the planners want. A front-page headline in the *Washington Post* read: "Despite planners' visions, outer suburbs lead in new hiring." I was particularly struck by the lead:

> As a consensus builds that the Washington region needs to concentrate job growth, there are signs that the exact opposite is happening.

> Over the past five years, the number of new jobs in the region's outer suburbs exceeded those created in the District and inner suburbs such as Fairfax and Montgomery counties . . . contradicting planners' "smart growth" visions of communities where people live, work and play without having to drive long distances.

Maybe if tens—hundreds—of thousands of people aren't abiding by the "consensus," there is no consensus: there is just a bunch of government-funded planners attending conferences and deciding where people ought to live. It's like, "Our community doesn't want Wal-Mart." Hey, if the community really doesn't want Wal-Mart, then a Wal-Mart store will fail. What that sentence means is: "Some organized interests in our community don't want Wal-Mart here because we know our neighbors will shop there (and so will we)."

Similarly, another *Post* story reported that the Ford motor company has dropped a pledge to build 250,000 gas-electric hybrid cars per year by the end of the decade. Environmentalists accused the company of backpedaling: it seems not many people want to buy hybrid cars—even though the planners want them to.

Again and again, individuals insist on making their own decisions rather than conforming to planners' visions and purported consensuses. In authoritarian and totalitarian countries, they may be forced to comply. But in relatively free countries, they seek to buy the cars they want, live where they want and have the number of children they want. Markets respond to consumer desires while governments try to impose visions.

Take a rapidly growing part of a county or a school district—the newspapers will be full of stories about how difficult it's going to be to build enough schools there, and how it takes five years to plan a new school, and how the county should limit growth and encourage people to live in areas that already have schools. But you don't see any stories about how difficult it will be to create grocery stores or video stores: businesses just go build them.

Governments would do better to set a few rules of the game and let market enterprises respond to what people really rather than try to push people into conforming to planners' visions and phony consensuses.

Comment Is Free, July 11, 2006

War, Collectivism, and Conscription

National service is back, this time under the auspices of the Democratic Leadership Council, headed by Sen. Sam Nunn (D-Ga.). The DLC proposes that young people enlist in either military service or social programs for a term of one or two years, after which each participant would receive a voucher that could be used for college expenses, job training, or a down payment on a home. The current federal student aid programs would supposedly be phased out; student aid would then be available only to national service enlistees, making it "politically unassailable."

The DLC believes that the proposal would entail "sacrifice" and "self-denial" and that it would revive "the American tradition of civic obligation." Its booklet on the proposal does not mention the American tradition of individual rights. The proposal is also intended to "broaden the political base of support for new public initiatives that otherwise would not be possible in the current era of budgetary restraint." In other words, it would be a way for government to hand out benefits by enlisting cheap labor—and just offstage, one can hear the murmur "conscript labor." But not this year.

The last chapter of the booklet, inevitably, is titled "The Moral Equivalent of War," a phrase harking back to the famous 1910 essay in which William James proposed that young Americans be conscripted into "an army enlisted against Nature" that would cause them to "get the childishness knocked out of them, and to come back into society with healthier sympathies and soberer ideas."

The fascination of collectivists with war and its "moral equivalent" is undying. In our time President Carter revived the Jamesian phrase to describe his energy policy, with its emphasis on government direction and reduced living standards. It was to be his peacetime substitute for the sacrifice and despotism of war.

In 1982 British Labour party leader Michael Foot was asked to cite an instance of socialism in practice that could "serve as a model of the Britain you envision," and he replied, "The best example that I've seen of democratic socialism operating in this country was during the second world war. Then we ran Britain highly efficiently, got everybody a job. . . . The conscription of labor was only a very small element of it. It was a democratic society with a common aim."

More recently the American socialist Michael Harrington wrote, "World War I showed that, despite the claims of free-enterprise ideologues, government could organize the economy effectively." He hailed World War II as having "justified a truly massive mobilization of otherwise wasted human and material resources" and complained that the War Production Board was "a success the United States was determined to forget as quickly as possible." He went on, "During World War II, there was probably more of an increase in social justice than at any [other] time in American history. Wage and price controls were used to try to cut the differentials between the social classes. . . . There was also a powerful moral incentive to spur workers on: patriotism."

Collectivists such as Foot and Harrington don't relish the killing involved in war, but they love war's domestic effects: centralization and the growth of government power. They know, as did the libertarian writer Randolph Bourne, that "war is the health of the state"—hence the endless search for a moral equivalent of war.

As Don Lavoie demonstrated in his book *National Economic Planning: What Is Left?*, modern concepts of economic planning—including "industrial policy" and other euphemisms—stem from the experiences of Germany, Great Britain, and the United States in planning their economies during World War I. The power of the central governments grew dramatically during that war and during World War II, and collectivists have

pined for the glory days of the War Industries Board and the War Production Board ever since.

Walter Lippmann was an early critic of the collectivists' fascination with war planning. He wrote, "A close analysis of its theory and direct observation of its practice will disclose that all collectivism . . . is military in method, in purpose, in spirit, and can be nothing else." Lippman went on to explain why war—or a moral equivalent—is so congenial to collectivism:

> Under the system of centralized control without constitutional checks and balances, the war spirit identifies dissent with treason, the pursuit of private happiness with slackerism and sabotage, and, on the other side, obedience with discipline, conformity with patriotism. Thus at one stroke war extinguishes the difficulties of planning, cutting out from under the individual any moral ground as well as any lawful ground on which he might resist the execution of the official plan.

National service, national industrial policy, national energy policy— all have the same essence, collectivism, and the same model, war. War, though sometimes necessary, involves mass murder. Why would anyone want its moral equivalent?

Cato Policy Report, July/August 1988

The Fatal Conceit in the Bush-Clinton Years

We stand at the midpoint of the Bush-Clinton years—years that history will record were marked by higher taxes, higher spending, more regulation, and a general failure to recognize the lessons of history and to join the market-liberal revolution that is sweeping the rest of the world. From Moscow to Buenos Aires, from Wellington to Lombardy, from Stockholm to Soweto, people are throwing off repressive government and moving toward human rights and free markets.

Yet here in the United States, after four years during which the federal government grew dramatically without any ideological argument's being advanced for big government, a new administration elected by 22 percent of the American electorate is promising bigger and more expansive government in every imaginable area. Just consider the proposals of Bill and Hillary's first 100 days: a massive tax increase, a high-tech subsidy program, a government industry partnership to build better automobiles, a national commission to ensure a strong competitive airline industry, national youth service, a 20-year plan for defense industry conversion, managed trade with Japan, a new computer chip to allow the government access to all forms of electronic communication, and the pièce de résistance, 500 bureaucrats organized into 15 committees and 34 working groups to re-create in 100 days one-seventh of the American economy. Or at least that *seemed* to be the pièce de résistance, until Hillary Clinton announced in May that her next project would be "redefining who we are as human beings in the post-modern age." That should make recreating an $800-billion industry seem like a piece of cake.

We try to avoid using the F-word at Cato, so I'll just call this program "corporate statism." But it is the most sweeping example of what F. A. Hayek called the Fatal Conceit—the idea that smart people can plan an economic system that would serve human needs better than the unplanned market—that America has ever seen. In all their years of college, Bill and Hillary Clinton and their Rhodes Scholar friends apparently never encountered the wonderful words of Dr. Johnson:

> How small, of all that human hearts endure,
> That part which laws or kings can cause or cure!

I frequently hear our friends say that we've won the intellectual battle and that only the mopping up remains. I can't agree. We have achieved something tremendous in the past 15 years. We have intellectually—and for the most part practically—defeated the most coherent, most comprehensive alternative to the free society that the world has seen. Robert Heilbroner, one of America's most interesting socialist intellectuals, writes in the *New Yorker*, the cynosure of the American establishment, that "less than 75 years after it officially began, the contest between capitalism and socialism is over: capitalism has won." And again, "It turns out, of course,"—I love that "of course"—"that Mises was right" about the impossibility of socialism.

But we are now faced with a new challenge: Socialism is dead, but corporatism, paternalism, industrial policy, and the welfare state are still very much alive. Most academics and most journalists still believe in some form of active government intervention in society. Even though confidence in government is at an all-time low—lower than during the last years of Nixon, lower than during the last years of Carter—82 percent of Americans want to impose price controls on medical care. Market liberals still have a big intellectual battle to fight.

Market liberalism offers the vision of a free, prosperous, and pluralistic society for all people, in the United States and around the world. As Hayek wrote, "we must make the building of a free society once more an intellectual adventure. [We need] a truly liberal radicalism which does not spare the susceptibilities of the mighty [and] does not confine itself to what appears today as politically possible."

Our Magical President

"Mr. President, Please Make Us Proud." That was the cover story in the January 28 issue of *Parade*, the nation's most widely circulated magazine with 37 million copies distributed inside Sunday newspapers. The magazine had asked "teens across America" what they would "ask our new President to do for them [and] their families, schools and communities."

And boy, did the teens have ideas. "Help save our planet," they implored. "Everybody, no matter how much money they have, should be able to go to college. . . . The government could help us all." "Please care about homeless people." "How come our burnt-up houses and our school can't get remodeled?" No task is too small for the president—"Can you make a national hotline where teens can get advice when they're sad or angry?"—or too large—"Will you help to mend my broken heart?"

A few weeks earlier *Washington Post* columnist Courtland Milloy reported on letters written by District of Columbia elementary school students in an essay contest sponsored by Xerox Corp. What did the youngsters have to say to the president-elect? You should give everyone health care, Mr. President. You should give us new school materials, computers, and so on. You should end homelessness and provide homes and medical treatment for drug addicts. None of the children, of course, addressed who would pay for all those goodies, or what one might give up to get those programs, or whether the programs themselves would work. After all—homes, schoolbooks, health care—who could be against that?

The last letter Milloy highlighted demonstrated an even more expansive view of the president's powers: "Hopefully, now that you are President, you can stop all of this madness, this violence, and ignorance. I am depending on you." Fourth-graders believe the president can do anything, and only a *bad* president would fail to do good.

Many of us grow up. We come to realize that homes and computers have to be produced, that wishes and results are not the same things. And we learn that the president doesn't have magical powers; he can't cure cancer, or hate, or poverty, or economic fluctuations.

Unfortunately, a lot of people don't grow up. They retain a magical view of the power of the president, or of government generally. In magical societies people believe that speaking words gives power over things and persons. Many of our policymakers believe that to write and vote for a bill called the Social Security Act is to give people "social security." To name a bill the Bipartisan Campaign Reform Act of 2001 will actually reform campaigns. But of course adults know from bitter experience that legislative actions often fail, or backfire, or have unintended consequences, or disappear into bureaucratic sinkholes.

Still, we are told, if we just pass more laws about health care, education, homelessness, equality, and so on, we will at the very least affirm our own goodness—if one magical spell doesn't work, you need another.

Liberals are not the only people who have this magical view of government, of course. Many conservatives believe that a law banning the use and abuse of drugs will actually eliminate the use and abuse of drugs. Some even believe that a White House Office of Marriage Initiatives will cause more Americans to get and stay married.

Throughout history humans have attributed supernatural powers to their leaders. King Canute had to go down to the sea and command the tide to stop in order to show his advisers that his powers were limited. Most rulers, however, preferred to enjoy the presumption of magical powers. We have largely discarded our belief in the divine right of kings, and we have come to understand that no man is God, that even a powerful man is just a man, without supernatural powers. Now we are so advanced that we attribute magical powers only to men who are chosen in elections.

One of the tasks of believers in liberty and limited government is to persuade the public that governments—hereditary or elective—do not have magical powers. Benefits from government must be paid for. Government can no more "stop all this madness, this violence, and ignorance" than it can guarantee bounteous supplies of electricity at controlled prices. When voters come to understand those realities, politics and public policy will make more sense.

In the end, we should take note of one teen who actually has some sense of the tradeoffs in the real world and some understanding of what a president can do, perhaps because he has some experience in the real world. "I worked every day last summer," he told *Parade*, "repairing and setting up cattle fences, from 8 a.m. to 5 p.m. in very hot weather. I got a good tan, but other than that it wasn't worth it—just to have the government take a third of my money and have it go to someone I don't even know who didn't earn it in the first place. Do something about taxes." Now there's something a president could actually do. America has at least one adult: Lucas Harris, 16, of Spanish Fork, Utah.

Cato Policy Report, July/August 2001

PART 3

The Political Economy of Market and State

Chrysler, Microsoft, and Industrial Policy

What kind of government would subsidize Chrysler and penalize Microsoft and Wal-Mart? Not one that should be trusted with an industrial policy, that much is sure.

In 1979 the Chrysler Corporation was going under, for a number of complex economic and marketing reasons that could be summarized as "no one wanted to buy their cars." The Big Three automobile companies had grown fat and happy, facing little competition in the world's richest market. Then American tastes began to change. Baby-boomers liked the looks and the reverse snob appeal of small foreign cars, and the energy crisis of the 1970s created widespread interest in more fuel-efficient cars.

The Big Three ignored the signs of discontent for too long. By 1979 Chrysler was on the verge of bankruptcy. The taxpayers came to the rescue, offering the company $1.5 billion in loan guarantees (of which it ultimately claimed $1.2 billion) to keep it in business. When the loan guarantees weren't quite enough, the U.S. government also imposed "voluntary" quotas on Japanese automobile imports.

Together, the federal money and the restrictions on competition let Chrysler survive, of course, but only at the price of a less efficient economy. Every American car-buyer had to pay more because of the quotas. That was money he couldn't use to buy something else, maybe something produced by an efficient American company. And the credit that was channeled to Chrysler was thus diverted from more creditworthy borrowers. We'll never know who those borrowers would have been, but somewhere in America there are people who would have used that $1.2 billion in loans to build houses, start businesses, expand factories, hire more workers. Despite the government help, Chrysler's payroll fell from 160,000 to 74,000 in just four years. In fact, Chrysler went bankrupt in all but name.

The chief characteristic of a capitalist economy is change. While Chrysler and other giants were struggling, small companies were being born. Most of those new companies failed; they didn't serve customers as well as their competitors, and they didn't have the political clout to get loan guarantees and import quotas. But some of the start-ups succeeded.

Two of the biggest success stories of the 1980s were Wal-Mart Stores Inc. and Microsoft Corp. Their founders, Sam Walton and Bill Gates, became billionaires. They got rich the only way you can in a free market: by producing something other people wanted.

Through the 1980s, giant companies were laying off employees in huge chunks, making front-page headlines; employment in the Fortune 500 fell by three and a half million. But Wal-Mart and Microsoft were quietly hiring. High-tech companies stay small. Even though the software industry is now the country's sixth-largest industry, its biggest success, Microsoft, grew only from 1,000 to 5,600 employees between 1986 and 1992, which was still a lot better than IBM's 200,000 layoffs. And about 2,000 of those Microsoft employees became millionaires through their stock ownership.

Wal-Mart, however, became one of the country's largest employers. It grew from 62,000 employees in 1986 to 328,000 in 1992. Most of us never noticed; it's front-page news when Sears lays off 20,000 people at once, but it's never a big story when Wal-Mart hires 177 people every business day for six years.

So how did the U.S. government react to these tremendous success stories, to the story of a college dropout and a middle-aged man in Arkansas becoming the richest people in America? No doubt with awards, honors, presidential receptions, you say?

No such luck. In fact, the U.S. government's response to the success of Microsoft was to launch a Federal Trade Commission investigation, later compounded by a Justice Department investigation, of whether Microsoft "has monopolized or has attempted to monopolize" markets for personal computer software and peripherals. Eventually Microsoft gave in and agreed to restrictions on its contracting and pricing policies in order to avoid long and costly litigation.

And in Arkansas, a judge ordered Wal-Mart to raise its prices to avoid damaging its competitors. Thanks a lot, Judge. Wal-Mart built its phenomenal success on having a wide selection of products at the lowest possible prices. The genius of Sam Walton's system was not a new product, nor a single big idea. No, Walton's system involved saving a penny here, a penny there, to create a distribution system that allowed his stores to sell for less than anybody else. Why should a man spend his life designing such a system if the government is going to come along and order him to raise his prices?

Antitrust advocates claim that big companies such as Microsoft and Wal-Mart (which were small companies just a few years ago) will cut prices to consumers, drive their competitors out of business, and then raise prices through the roof. There are a couple of problems with this scenario, notably the fact that it's pretty hard to imagine eliminating all the other drugstores or software companies and the fact that no company has ever been able to implement this strategy.

And in these cases the facts indicate no such risk. When the FTC opened its investigation of Microsoft, for instance, the alleged monopolist controlled only about 10 percent of the MS-DOS applications business, which in any case is not the only operating system on the market. Its highly touted Windows program was installed on just 5 million PCs, or about 7 percent of the total. Microsoft did not have a single industry leader in the word processing, spreadsheet, and database markets. Some monopolist.

Meanwhile, in Conway, Arkansas, where a judge ruled that Wal-Mart was seeking to drive other pharmacies out of business, in 1987 there were 12 pharmacies. Today all 12 are still in business, and two more have opened. The profits of the plaintiffs in the lawsuit increased from 1986 to 1990.

Wal-Mart and Microsoft earned their billions the old-fashioned way—they gave customers what they wanted. Punishing them—and subsidizing market failures like Chrysler—is absolutely the reverse of the free enterprise system.

But those little forays into the marketplace are not enough for the Clinton administration. The very smart people in the White House think that they know how much pharmaceutical drugs should cost, what kind of cars Detroit should build, how information should be transmitted to our homes, how much Japanese consumers should buy from each of our industries, and how to "match the skills of the workforce against the things we have to produce in the next 20 years." They're spending $200 million this year—and planning to spend $744 million in 1997—on the Advanced Technology Program to subsidize high-tech, high-risk business ventures that the private sector won't touch.

You can bet on it: If Clinton's industrial policy gurus had been in charge for the last 20 years, we wouldn't have Microsoft or Wal-Mart. We would have computers as big as a room, slide rules at every engineer's desk, higher-priced and less-efficient stores, and less economic growth. People who reward Chrysler and punish Wal-Mart and Microsoft shouldn't be given more power.

Washington Times, July 26, 1994

Parasite Economy Latches onto New Host

Perhaps the biggest success story of the American economy in the past decade is the Microsoft Corp., which made a profit of $3.5 billion in fiscal 1997. Founder Bill Gates and a lot of other people in Redmond, Washington, got rich the only way you can in a free market: by producing something other people wanted.

Hundreds of brilliant people worked long hours producing computer software that millions of people chose to buy, in a highly competitive market that offered lots of other options.

But in our modern politicized economy—which Jonathan Rauch dubs the "parasite economy"—no good deed goes unpunished.

The federal government launched a Federal Trade Commission investigation, later compounded by a Justice Department investigation, of whether Microsoft has monopolized the software market. Microsoft capitulated, agreeing to restrictions on its contracting and pricing policies in order to avoid long and costly litigation. That wasn't enough for the government, which went on to launch more antitrust investigations.

Whether Microsoft behaved monopolistically, however (the facts cast a lot of doubt on this claim), is less important than the way the government lured the software company into the political sector of the economy.

For more than a decade the company went about its business, developing software, selling it to customers and innocently making money. Then in 1995, after repeated assaults by the Justice Department's Antitrust Division, Microsoft broke down and started playing the Washington game—entirely defensively, it appears.

It hired 4 former members of Congress, 32 former congressional staffers or government officials, and the former chairman of the Republican Party. It spent $1.9 million on lobbying in 1997, up 67 percent from 1996.

Of course, numbers like that still don't make it a big political player. IBM spends more than $3 million a year on lobbying, and General Motors more than $5 million.

Indeed, Washington politicians and journalists have been sneering at Microsoft's political innocence.

A congressional aide says, "They don't want to play the D.C. game, that's clear, and they've gotten away with it so far. The problem is, in the long run they won't be able to." Journalists ask, what makes Microsoft think it can stick to its programming and stay out of politics? Politicians tell Bill Gates, "Nice little company ya got there. Shame if anything happened to it."

And Microsoft gets the message: If you want to produce something in America, you'd better play the game. Contribute to politicians' campaigns, hire their friends, go hat in hand to a congressional hearing and apologize for your success.

The tragedy is that the most important factor in America's economic future—in raising everyone's standard of living—is not land, or money or computers; it's human talent. And some portion of the human talent at one of America's most dynamic companies is now being diverted from productive activity to protecting the company from political predation. The parasite economy has sucked in another productive enterprise.

The slowdown of our economic growth rate since about 1970 can be blamed in large measure on just this process—the expansion of the parasite economy into the productive economy. The number of corporations with Washington offices increased 10-fold between 1961 and 1982. *Congressional Quarterly* reports show that the number of people lobbying in Washington at least doubled and may have tripled between the mid-1970s and the mid-1980s.

Of course, all this investment in Washington reflected Willie Sutton's observation about robbing banks: "That's where the money is." The federal budget has grown steadily over the past 60 years or so.

Even if you don't want to get a piece of that $1.7 trillion, the long arm of the government reaches out to affect you. The number of pages in the Federal Register, where new regulations are printed, doubled between 1957 and 1967, tripled between 1970 and 1975, and grows by about 60,000 every year. No wonder so many corporations have opened Washington offices.

In his online diary in *Slate* magazine, Bill Gates wrote, "It's been a year since the last time I was in D.C. I think I'm going to be making the trip a lot more frequently from now on."

And that's what Janet Reno's Justice Department is costing America: Bill Gates is going to waste his mind on protecting his company instead of thinking up new products and new ways to deliver them.

Dragging Microsoft into the political swamps is a tragic example of the diversion of America's productive resources into the unproductive world of political predation.

Orange County Register, May 10, 1998

Prisoner Held for Ransom

Now that the government's case against Microsoft is on appeal, the discussion will revolve around arcane matters of law. But the essence of the earlier Microsoft ruling hasn't changed: They're stealing Bill Gates's company.

Judge Thomas Penfield Jackson ordered that the company be split into two separate companies, as the Justice Department had proposed. Mr. Gates will be allowed to run either the operating systems company or the applications company. But half of the company he has built will be taken away from him.

And that's not all. Microsoft has been ordered to share with its competitors its application programming interfaces—the asset it has spent billions of dollars to create. According to the *Washington Post,* "The judge found that Microsoft used access to the code to hurt its competitors and help its allies."

It's a strange kind of free enterprise in which companies that create useful products have to give their competitors access to those products.

All the economic debates and legal arguments are important. But the real issue is that 25 years ago a couple of college dropouts moved to New Mexico and started writing BASIC software for the primitive Altair computer. In 1975 they had three employees and revenues of $16,000. Over the next 25 years, they grew to 36,000 employees and revenues of $20 billion by obsessively figuring out what computer users needed and delivering it to them. Bill Gates, Paul Allen and eventually thousands of other people put their minds, their money and their selves into building the Microsoft Corp. What they achieved is now being taken away by Bill Clinton, Janet Reno and Joel Klein. What is being taken is not just money, not just a company, but the product of their minds.

The term "theft of intellectual property" hardly conveys the enormity of the process.

Over the years Mr. Gates and his colleagues made a lot of people mad, especially their competitors. Some of those competitors delivered a 222-page white paper in 1996 to Joel Klein, head of the Justice Department's antitrust division, and urged him to do to Microsoft in court what they couldn't do in the marketplace. Justice worked closely with the competitors for four years, often showing them sentences or paragraphs in drafts of the department's plans and soliciting their approval. The politics of the case is a far cry from the Platonic ideal of rigorous economists devising the best possible antitrust rules and wise, disinterested judges carefully weighing the evidence.

What lessons will Americans draw from the Microsoft case?

Don't be too successful. Success creates envy and attracts government regulators, who seem driven to attack the most productive people in our society. Bill Gates draws praise from the cultural elite when he gives away his money—and he has given away more than $20 billion—but he has done far more good for the world by creating and marketing something useful than by giving away some of the profits he earned.

Hire a lobbyist. For about 20 years Mr. Gates and his colleagues just sat out there in "the other Washington," creating and selling. As the company got bigger, Washington politicians and journalists began sneering at Microsoft's political innocence. In 1995, after repeated assaults by the Federal Trade Commission and the Justice Department, Microsoft broke down and started playing the Washington game. It hired lobbyists and Washington PR firms. Its executives made political contributions. And every other high-tech company is getting the message, too, which is great news for lobbyists and fundraisers.

What lesson should they draw?

The antitrust laws are fatally flawed. When our antitrust laws are used by competitors to harm successful companies, when our most innovative companies are under assault from the federal government, when lawyers and politicians decide to restructure the software, credit card and airline industries, it is time to repeal the antitrust laws and let firms compete in a free marketplace.

Janet Reno didn't send a SWAT team to Redmond, Wash., in the middle of the night. But the bottom line is the same: She is using the power of government to steal what the people at Microsoft created.

The Washington Times, June 30, 2000

The High Price of Regulation

The Food and Drug Administration, which banned the artificial sweetener cyclamate 20 years ago, plans to reapprove it, possibly this year. Once accused of causing everything from bladder cancer to birth defects, cyclamate is now widely thought to be harmless.

"I have no reluctance in saying that with cyclamate we made a mistake," Robert Scheuplein, acting director of the Office of Toxicological Sciences at the FDA's Center for Food Safety and Applied Nutrition, told the *Washington Post.* The irony of the agency's mistake is that until aspartame was approved a few years ago, Americans who use artificial sweeteners were forced to buy products containing saccharin, which might well be harmful, rather than cyclamate, which is not.

This cyclamate episode is a dramatic but hardly unique example of the failure of government regulation. For about 100 years Americans have tried to solve perceived problems in the marketplace by creating federal regulatory agencies. In the past 20 years scholars have built up an impressive body of literature demonstrating the failure of most of those agencies.

The economic problem in every society is how to use the scattered bits of knowledge that billions of consumers and producers possess to bring about the best possible allocation of resources. The market process, which involves competition, free exchange, and freely determined prices, enables its participants to identify each other's abilities and desires called supply and demand in the economist's parlance. Market competition is what F. A. Hayek called a discovery procedure. The desire for profit motivates entrepreneurs to discover the best possible allocation of resources.

Attempts by government regulation to improve market outcomes are likely to block or distort that subtle and complex discovery process. There is no way to know the "correct" price or quantity of any resource, and controls may prevent activities that have not yet been envisaged. Intervention in the market process can only bring about a result that differs from the one desired by consumers.

Consider a few examples of regulation failures. By 1977 a number of scholars had concluded that regulation had raised trucking rates by 40 percent or more; the Congressional Budget Office estimated that deregulation would lead to annual savings of $5 billion to $8 billion. But in 1987, after about seven years of deregulation, Robert V. Delaney estimated in a Cato Institute study that the annual savings had been $56 billion to $90 billion. Why the huge discrepancy? Delaney found that improved trucking practices had allowed companies to make massive reductions in their logistics and inventory costs—savings that even advocates of deregulation had not anticipated.

In 1962 Congress instructed the FDA to approve new drugs only if they had been proven effective as well as safe. Sam Peltzman of the University of Chicago found that the consumer costs of that law had been four times as great as the benefits. The 1962 amendments had halved the number of new drugs introduced each year and delayed approval by an average of four years. Only a one-year average delay in new-drug approval can cost 3,000 to 76,000 lives in a decade—several times the worldwide total of new drug-related fatalities. The delay of the heart drug TPA alone may have cost 3,000 lives.

The AIDS crisis has dramatized this issue, as FDA bureaucrats claim the right to forbid terminally ill patients from using drugs of unknown safety and efficacy. Given the subjectivity of values, the diversity of medical circumstances, and the difficulties of assessing medical risks, drug safety can be meaningfully defined only in terms of individual choice, not societywide mandates.

A final example shows that as part of its response to the energy crisis, the government required each car company to increase the average fuel economy of the cars it sells by a set amount each year. One way that companies have met the Corporate Average Fuel Economy standards is by making large cars more expensive. A recent study by Robert Crandall of the Brookings Institution and John Graham of Harvard University found that CAFE has cost Americans $4 for every gallon of gas saved, forced them to pay up to $1,200 more for a big car, and eliminated 130,000 jobs. But the most striking—and surely unanticipated—consequence is that traffic fatalities have increased because people have been forced to buy smaller cars. Crandall and Graham estimated that there are 2,200 to 3,900 more fatalities every year, along with 10,000 to 20,000 additional serious injuries.

To make informed choices, consumers need to be able to identify the products that have proved safe and effective, the products that have proved unsafe and ineffective, and the products whose safety and efficacy are unknown. The market process, along with a court system that enforces contracts, provides that information. Regulation simply forces consumers to purchase products they do not want.

And regulation has moral implications as well. Dry and academic terms such as "public policy," "market failure," "social costs," and "regulation" don't convey the full reality of this discussion. When government uses its coercive power to tell us whether we may enter a given occupation, what wages we may contract for, how much of our compensation must be in the form of safety and fringe benefits, whether we may hire or fire an employee, whether we may sell all the oranges we grow, what medicines we may use to treat life-threatening illnesses, and what we may broadcast on our radio and television stations, we are that much less free.

Cato Policy Report, July/August 1989

Junking Jobs: The War on Sidewalk Sales

New York Mayor Ed Koch calls them a "Hydra-headed" menace, but says "we have them on the run." A Boston merchants' association derides them as "a hodgepodge" giving the city a "negative image." A Washington, D.C., businessman calls them "unsightly." Are they referring to a plague of locusts? Child pornographers? Teenage gangs?

No, the objects of their wrath are small-business men out to make a living for themselves in a time of high unemployment—street vendors. Since Mayor Koch announced a crackdown a year ago, some 25,000 summonses have been issued to general vendors and almost as many more to food vendors. Goods were confiscated from vendors more than 20,000 times.

The consequences of this policy are tragic for individuals, deprived of the opportunity to make a living, and expensive for taxpayers. When the crackdown began, police confiscated goods that were displayed in front of some 14th Street discount stores. "A lady came by crying and told me she'd just been fired because they won't need anyone to work the outside tables any more," Joe Veseco of the Hollywood Discount Center told reporters. "Well, that's one more on welfare."

Mayor Koch isn't alone in his policies, of course. In Washington, the anti-vendor effort is being led by the Board of Trade. It has tried to get the City Council to outlaw most general-merchandise vending, severely restrict vending locations, impose strict record-keeping rules and make vendors pay $1,000 up front for a license. In Boston, Cincinnati, Philadelphia and Orlando, similar obstacles have been proposed or put in place.

Vendors have a long tradition in America. Early settlements and frontier towns would have been even more isolated if not for traveling peddlers. Peddling has been the road out of poverty for many ethnic groups, particularly Jews in the 19th century—including such now-famous names as Gimbel, B. Altman and Levi Strauss. J. C. Penney, Richard Sears and Marshall Field all started on the street. If Mayor Koch and Washington's Board of Trade had been around in earlier times, those people would never have had the chance to develop their entrepreneurial skills.

Perhaps the most ironic example of the war on vendors occurred last August at the March for Jobs, Peace, and Freedom in Washington. The march had been called because black leaders wanted to focus national attention on the unemployment problem by coming together on the 20th anniversary of the historic March on Washington led by Martin Luther King Jr. Most if not all of the speakers called on government to provide jobs for blacks and other unemployed Americans.

Out in the crowd, however, hundreds of blacks were providing their own jobs, not waiting for government to come to their aid. In classic entrepreneurial fashion, they made their best guesses about consumer demand: Expecting that several hundred thousand people would be marching in the hot sun to honor King, they came prepared to sell food, cold drinks, and mementos. Like all entrepreneurs, if they guessed wrong about consumer desires, they would lose money; but they stood to profit handsomely if they were right.

There were very few arrests for violence or robbery that day, but dozens of vendors were arrested for vending without a license or in an unauthorized area. Of the vendors booked at the nearby First District Police Headquarters (33 of 34 were black), not one was the subject of a complaint from a customer. Every arrest was initiated by a policeman. Indeed, some of the marchers protested vehemently as they tried to make purchases from vendors who were being hustled off to the police station. Yet not a single prominent public figure—including the rally's main speaker, Jesse Jackson—uttered a word of protest. If they really cared about black unemployment and black enterprise, why not?

The Wall Street Journal, April 2, 1984

Felix Rohatyn Reconstructs America

It isn't often that a businessman makes the cover of *Newsweek*, and when one does, it's a pretty good bet that he didn't get there by making a better product available to consumers at a lower price. More likely he's there because he's an "enlightened" businessman who understands the need for a "partnership of business and government."

That prediction is borne out by the *Newsweek* of May 4, which features "The Cities' Mr. Fixit," Felix Rohatyn. Rohatyn didn't achieve such prominence by his success in the marketplace; he did it by becoming the leading advocate of corporate liberalism—the corporate state—in the United States.

Rohatyn first achieved a national reputation as the chairman of New York's Municipal Assistance Corporation ("Big MAC"), which is alleged to have saved New York City from bankruptcy. What it in fact did was manage a partial default on the city's debt by calling it a "stretchout" from short-term to long-term debt. In other words, creditors who had expected payments on a certain day did not get them, but through some financial wizardry and good media relations Rohatyn avoided the term "default." In addition, New York State's credit was put on the line for the city, thus guaranteeing that when the city eventually does go bankrupt, it will take the state government with it.

This was regarded as such a success that other cities are now coming to Rohatyn and his firm, Lazard Freres, to engineer similar arrangements for them—a sign of the increasing desperation and lack of ideas in governments at all levels.

Now Rohatyn is everywhere—writing in the *Christian Science Monitor* and the *New York Times*, appearing on the cover of *Newsweek*, featured in the *National Journal* and the *Economist*. But interestingly, he is perhaps most inescapable in the *New York Review of Books*, that bastion of liberal intellectuals. He has had at least three articles in the *Review* in the last six months. It is there that he has laid out his ideas, under such titles as "The Coming Emergency and What Can Be Done About It" and "Reconstructing America." What are those ideas? Just what you'd expect state capitalism to be: a stiff gasoline tax to reduce consumption, subsidies to coal and nuclear power, "compromise" on environmental issues, government-subsidized jobs, wage and price controls, tax rebates and credits to direct investment in specific industries, and a military draft (to get the unemployed young out of the unemployment statistics?).

But the real centerpiece of Rohatyn's economic program is "a genuine partnership of business and labor in government." This would be accomplished primarily through a new Reconstruction Finance Corporation established to bail out failing corporations and bankrupt city governments. After we bailed out Chrysler, you see, it would be unfair not to bail out other large corporations. And a refusal to bail out a failing company would produce severe "dangers to the economy" and "untold human suffering." It would also, of course, produce major losses for New York banking houses and financiers who would prefer to be protected from the consequences of their own mistakes. What the American economy needs is not government funds to bail out corporate dinosaurs or to "pick the winners." Mismanaged companies ought to fail; that's how a free market retains its vitality. And "winners" don't need government help—if they really are winners and not some politician's favorite. What the economy needs are real tax cuts, across-the-board rather than targeted to achieve a specific end, and a freeing up of the economic system to allow real competition.

Rohatyn knows his plans will not be popular with everyone. "The specter of socialism will be raised by the conservatives and the cry of 'big business bail-out' by the liberals." For once, it seems, they'll both be right. For what Rohatyn is proposing is big business socialism.

Interestingly, a strong echo of Rohatyn's ideas could be heard in an article in the *Wall Street Journal* last December, an article not by a businessman but by Tom Hayden, the ex-New Leftist who now heads California's Campaign for Economic Democracy. His article argued, "America needs a revitalization program as new and farreaching as the New Deal was in its time. There must be a new social contract drawn between government, business, labor, minorities, and the general voting public." His specific proposals include energy conservation, "an industrial recovery plan," government help for renewable resources and high technology, corporate accountability, and more money for health, the cities, and other projects.

Thus do the establishment left and right come together: An investment banker writing in the *New York Review of Books* and an advocate of "economic democracy" in the *Wall Street Journal* propose essentially the same program. One gets the eerie feeling that Hayden's and Rohatyn's worlds would be remarkably similar, except that everybody on Rohatyn's planning board would wear a three-piece suit, while some on Hayden's would have open shirts and gold chains around their necks.

In a more honest age, we'd have called this by its right name: economic fascism. Today we call it "an activist agenda for liberals" or "reconstructing America," but it doesn't smell any sweeter.

Cato Policy Report, June 1981

Capitalism and Change

The harsh words passing between David Stockman and his adversaries have illuminated one of the basic issues of our time: the dynamism of a capitalist economy and the stultifying effects of government. In discussing the disinvestment going on in farming, as well as in such other industries as automobiles and thrift institutions, Stockman argued:

> That is the way a dynamic economy works. . . . And if you want
> an economy that's productive, that maximizes growth, income,
> opportunity over time, you've got to encourage both investment
> and disinvestment. You've got to have adjustment.

> Government basically is a reactionary institution that tries to foster
> one and retard the other, and usually makes a botch of both. So
> that's why we want to have a kind of hands-off adjustment policy.

In response, members of Congress and interest-group leaders have made eloquent appeals to stability, tradition, and a "threatened way of life." Defenders of the family farm ranging from the South Dakota legislature to the Widow Doonesbury have denounced Stockman's view that farmers are businessmen who should compete for profits in the marketplace.

Farmers are not alone in their resistance to economic change. The autoworkers and steelworkers unions have been eager to embrace any program that would retard the flow of capital out of their industries.

In many ways the entire program of the American left today is a reactionary opposition to change. Leftists organize to save basic industries, restrict plant closings, impose price controls, and resist technological change. They even wax nostalgic over the decline of the world's largest monopoly, AT&T. As the intellectual appeal of the left declines, they find support for their campaigns of resistance among the out-of-work autoworkers and steelworkers of the rustbelt, who would prefer not to go elsewhere to find work.

But change is part of, indeed the distinguishing characteristic of, capitalism. The process of creative destruction means that new products and services are constantly being created and thus that others are constantly being outmoded. Every new development, from the cotton gin to the computer chip, has created thousands or millions of new jobs and destroyed other thousands or millions.

As James Fallows wrote recently in the *Atlantic Monthly*,

> Capitalism is one of the world's more disruptive forces. It can call
> every social arrangement into question, make cities and skills and
> ranks merely temporary. To buy into it is to make a commitment
> to permanent revolution that few political creeds can match.

This permanent revolution disrupts not only jobs but lifestyles, and it is here that, ironically, the right often joins the left in reaction. Much of the "moral decay" decried by the New Right is a result of a dynamic, affluent capitalist economy. Capitalism means choice, and the affluence produced by capitalism gives people the wherewithal to take advantage of those choices. When the unprecedented affluence of the 1950s led to unprecedented lifestyle choices in the 1960s, many Americans reacted strongly. Like the steelworkers faced with the end of their jobs in the 1980s, these Americans just wanted things to stay the same. But as David Stockman says, change—of many sorts—is "the way a dynamic economy works." Or, as Samuel Brittan wrote in "Capitalism and the Permissive Society": "Competitive capitalism is the biggest single force acting on the side of what is fashionable to call 'permissiveness,' but what was once known as personal liberty."

The benefits of capitalism are many: a high and rising standard of living, of course, but also freedom of choice, the opportunity to be creative, to choose one's own lifestyle, even to opt out of "materialist" society and work as a nun or on a communal farm. (Try that in a society where a planning board chooses your occupation, or where every person must work from sunup to sundown just to eat.) But this dynamism has costs: the disruption of jobs and of traditional ways of life.

Ultimately, however, James Fallows and David Stockman are right: Capitalism is a permanent revolution, and government is reactionary. Which vision we will choose is what we are really debating when we talk about farm subsidies, protectionism, plant-closing restrictions, or using government to protect traditional lifestyles.

Cato Policy Report, March/April 1985

PART 4

The Politics of Left and Right

Left and Right in the Same Sorry Rut

The country is polarized, we're told. Bush-haters versus Clinton-haters. Mel Gibson versus Michael Moore. Red states versus blue states. Liberals and conservatives read different books, watch different networks, go to different churches.

But liberals and conservatives have more in common than you might think.

Both believe in government magic. And they want you to believe in it too. They want you to believe the president can be Superman, Santa Claus, and Mother Teresa all rolled into one and that he can cure poverty and racism, keep kids off drugs and keep families together. Magical thinking is cute among children. But adults should know that the world is complicated and that legislative actions often fail, or backfire, or have unintended consequences or disappear into bureaucratic sinkholes.

Both ignore history. Liberals look at the 20th century's grand experiment of capitalism versus socialism—the United States versus the Soviet Union, Western Europe versus Eastern Europe, China versus Hong Kong—and somehow conclude that what the United States needs today is more socialism. National health insurance, a more centralized educational system, government regulation for our most dynamic industries—in every case ignoring the historical triumph of competition and freedom. Conservatives think government can restore the world of the 1950s, ignoring the most basic lesson of history: Things change.

Both respond to special interests. Look at the Bush administration: an energy bill designed by energy companies, a steel tariff on imports for the steel industry, a Medicare drug entitlement that will shift costs from big business to the taxpayers, the proposed Federal Marriage Amendment for religious-right supporters. Meanwhile, liberal administrations never forget the trial lawyers, the feminists, the civil rights lawyers and the other groups that help them gain power.

Both involve the nation in unnecessary wars. Conservatives think the United States should send troops anywhere our vital interests are threatened, and they have a very expansive definition of our "vital interests." Liberals take a different tack: They like to send troops anywhere our interests are not threatened—it seems less greedy and Republican. That's why liberals get excited about sending U.S. troops to Somalia, Liberia and Bosnia.

Both will forgive anything a member of their team does. Remember when conservatives thought President Clinton's dalliance with Monica

Lewinsky was a national scandal, and liberals thought conservatives were a bunch of prudes? Then Arnold Schwarzenegger was accused of groping women, and suddenly the liberals wanted to hang him and the conservatives said Democrats should lighten up.

Conservatives sued to make Hillary Rodham Clinton report who was on her healthcare task force; liberals sued to make Dick Cheney tell us who was on his energy task force.

The red team/blue team mentality applies even to trivia: Liberals are shocked that Cheney said a bad word to a senator, but uber-liberal Hillary Clinton said, "You go, girl!" when Teresa Heinz Kerry told a reporter to "shove it!" Conservatives, outraged about Heinz Kerry's rudeness, had defended Cheney's vulgarity on the Senate floor.

And the No. 1 way liberals and conservatives are alike: Both think they can run your life better than you can.

Liberals want to raise taxes because they can spend your money better than you can. They don't believe in school choice because you're not capable of choosing a school for your children. They think they can handle your healthcare, your retirement, and your charitable contributions better than you can.

Conservatives want to censor cable television because you're too dumb to decide what your family should watch. They want to ban drugs, pornography, gambling, and gay marriage because you just don't know what's good for you.

The reality is, Americans aren't as polarized as the pundits say. Most want government out of their pocketbooks and personal lives. They want civil liberties and lower taxes. And they feel free to reject both liberals and conservatives when their ideas don't make sense.

Los Angeles Times, August 3, 2004

George Will and the Ideological Switcheroo

George Will has a thoughtful column in the *Washington Post* titled "The Case for Conservatism." You might say that it demonstrates that George Will has accepted modernity, because his definitions of liberalism and conservatism are thoroughly modern, not historical. Consider:

> Today conservatives tend to favor freedom. . . . Liberalism increasingly seeks to deliver equality in the form of equal dependence of more and more people for more and more things on government.

Traditionally, of course, it was liberals who favored freedom and minimal government. The *Encyclopedia Britannica* defines liberalism as a "political doctrine that takes the abuse of power, and thus the freedom of the individual, as the central problem of government." Wikipedia is similar: "Liberalism refers to a broad array of related doctrines, ideologies, philosophical views, and political traditions which advocate individual liberty. . . . Broadly speaking, liberalism emphasizes individual rights."

Conservatism, on the other hand, according to *Britannica*, is a "political philosophy that emphasizes the value of traditional institutions and practices." In many societies, of course, freedom is not a traditional practice. George Will may be talking strictly about American conservatism, in which case it is plausible to say that a conservative should want to preserve the traditional American institutions and practice of liberty and limited government. I have often wondered, What does it mean to be a conservative in a nation founded in libertarian revolution? If it means preserving the values of the Declaration of Independence and the Constitution, then a conservative is a libertarian—or what used to be called a liberal.

But what if one wants to conserve something else? Who's to say that the principles of 1776 are the right thing to conserve? What if you wanted to conserve Southern plantation society? Or the rights and privileges of the British monarchy? Or the institutions of the Dark Ages? Or the traditional Indian practice of suttee, in which widows are expected to immolate themselves on their husband's funeral pyre?

That is why Hayek said that he was not a conservative—because conservatism is essentially a philosophy of "opposition to drastic change," but without any fundamental principles of its own other than serving as a brake on change.

But that's not the conservatism that Will describes. In his view conservatism is about freedom and a sober recognition of the limits of power. "Liberalism's core conviction [is] that government's duty is not to allow social change but to drive change in the direction the government chooses. Conservatism argues that the essence of constitutional government involves constraining the state in order to allow society ample scope to spontaneously take unplanned paths."

If that's the case, then there's been almost a complete switch of the philosophies of liberalism and conservatism. Indeed, it's intriguing to switch the words in Will's article. Try the quotation above with the words reversed: "*Conservatism*'s core conviction [is] that government's duty is not to allow social change but to drive change in the direction the government chooses. *Liberalism* argues that the essence of constitutional government involves constraining the state in order to allow society ample scope to spontaneously take unplanned paths." It still works, right? That's the liberalism of John Locke, Adam Smith, John Stuart Mill, and F. A. Hayek.

And if it's not the conservatism of Maistre or Shelley—who wanted government to resist change, not drive it—it might be the conservatism of those in contemporary society who want government to actively instill virtue in the citizens.

One might alternatively try substituting "liberalism" for "conservatism" in Will's essay, and "illiberalism" for "liberalism." Then we might get, for instance, "*liberals* tend to favor freedom, and consequently are inclined to be somewhat sanguine about inequalities of outcomes. *Illiberals* are more concerned with equality, understood, they insist, primarily as equality of opportunity, not of outcome." Or:

> This reasoning is congruent with *liberalism's* argument that excessively benevolent government is not a benefactor, and that capitalism does not merely make people better off, it makes them better. *Illiberalism* once argued that large corporate entities of industrial capitalism degraded individuals by breeding dependence, passivity and servility. *Liberalism* challenges *illiberalism's* blindness about the comparable dangers from the biggest social entity, government.
>
> *Liberalism* argues, as did the Founders, that self-interestedness is universal among individuals, but the dignity of individuals is bound up with the exercise of self-reliance and personal responsibility in pursuing one's interests. *Illiberalism* argues that equal dependence on government minimizes social conflicts. *Liberalism's* rejoinder is that the entitlement culture subverts social peace by the proliferation of rival dependencies.

Maybe I'm dreaming of a golden age of liberalism that no longer exists, an age when liberals stood for freedom and limited government, for, in the words of Wikipedia, "a society characterized by freedom of thought for individuals, limitations on power (especially of government and religion), the rule of law, the free exchange of ideas, a market economy that supports free private enterprise, and a transparent system of government in which the rights of all citizens are protected." Maybe.

But then maybe George Will is dreaming of a Platonic vision of conservatism, a conservatism committed to freedom and limited government, a conservatism that certainly isn't classical conservatism and isn't the conservatism of the contemporary conservative movement. But it was the conservatism of Barry Goldwater and of Ronald Reagan's speeches, and often of William F. Buckley, Jr. And maybe, just maybe, if George Will and a few of his conservative soulmates prevail, the conservatism of the future. If I can dream of a liberalism that once again seeks to liberate the individual from the constraints of power, then Will can dream of a conservatism that actually favors freedom.

Britannica Blog, June 1, 2007

Filibuster Flip-Flops

It could be a Dr. Seuss story: Red team, blue team, my team, your team. Both Democrats and Republicans have flip-flopped on the use of the filibuster because the once solidly Democratic Senate now looks to be firmly Republican.

Republicans who once extolled the virtues of divided power and the Senate's role in slowing down the rush to judgment now demand an end to delays in approving President Bush's judicial nominees. President Bush says the Democrats' "obstructionist tactics are unprecedented, unfair, and unfaithful to the Senate's constitutional responsibility to vote on judicial nominees."

Democrats who now wax eloquent about a "rubber stamp of dictatorship" replacing "the rights to dissent, to unlimited debate and to freedom of speech" in the Senate not too long ago sought to eliminate the filibuster altogether.

In 1993 the distinguished Democratic lawyer Lloyd Cutler, counsel to President Jimmy Carter and later to President Bill Clinton, argued that the Senate could change the cloture rule by majority vote, just as Republicans argue today. In 1994 leading liberal ex-politicians launched the "Action, Not Gridlock!" campaign to stop filibusters against Clinton's legislative agenda and nominees. In 1996 nine current Democratic senators sought to declare that all filibusters unconstitutionally infringe on majority rule.

When Republicans balked at some of President Clinton's nominees, Democrats spoke forcefully about the injustice of it all. "An up-or-down vote, that is all we ask," said Sen. Tom Daschle in 1999. "Our institutional integrity requires an up-or-down vote," said Sen. Dianne Feinstein the same year. "If our Republican colleagues don't like them, vote against them. But give them a vote," said Sen. Edward M. Kennedy in 1998.

It's not just partisan politicians who switch sides. The *New York Times* editorialized in 1995, "Now is the perfect moment . . . to get rid of an archaic rule that frustrates democracy and serves no useful purpose." Nine years later the *Times* discovered that useful purpose: "The filibuster . . . is a rough instrument that should be used with caution. But its existence goes to the center of the peculiar but effective form of government America cherishes." The *Times* did have the good grace to note, "To see the filibuster fully, it's obviously a good idea to have to live on both sides of it. . . . We hope that acknowledging our own error may remind some wavering

Republican senators that someday they, too, will be on the other side and in need of all the protections the Senate rules can provide."

Likewise, E. J. Dionne Jr. of the *Washington Post* and the Brookings Institution groused about the "anti-majoritarian filibuster rules" that were preventing needed action in 1998 but warned in 2005 that ending the filibuster would be "a radical departure" that "would be disastrous for minority rights." Immediately after her election to the Senate in 2000, Hillary Rodham Clinton said she was proud "to be on the side of the democratic process working" by calling for an end to the anti-majoritarian Electoral College. Today she staunchly supports the Democrats' effort to prevent "the democratic process" from working in the Senate.

Back in 1993, Cutler wrote, "A strong argument can be made that its requirements of 60 votes to cut off debate and a two-thirds vote to amend the rules are both unconstitutional." Former Senate Republican leader and Reagan White House chief of staff Howard Baker responded, "Doing away with super-majority votes ... would topple one of the pillars of American democracy: the protection of minority rights from majority rule. The Senate is the only body in the federal government where these minority rights are fully and specifically protected. It was designed for that purpose by America's Founders."

Republicans were right in those days. They should take advantage of the Democrats' being right today and return to protecting the rights of the minority. No party holds a majority forever, and some day Republican senators will need to use the filibuster again to stop big-government legislation and slow down a Democratic president's most liberal nominees.

American Spectator, April 25, 2005

The Budget Two-Step

There's a conspiracy afoot to convince American taxpayers that President Bush has submitted a lean, mean budget for Fiscal Year 2006. The funny thing is, Democrats and Republicans are both in on it, and journalists are going along. A reality check is in order.

In announcing his budget, Bush proclaimed, "It is a budget that is lean and effective and says we'll spend money on programs that work." At the Detroit Economic Club, he called it "the most disciplined proposal since Ronald Reagan was in office." He added that "Congress needs to join with me to bring real spending discipline to the federal budget" and that "spending discipline requires difficult choices."

Vice President Cheney joined the chorus: "We are being tight. This is the tightest budget that has been submitted since we got here."

Journalists took him at his word. Google the phrase "Bush budget," and the first titles are "Bush budget seeks deep cutbacks," "Bush to outline 'toughest' budget," "Bush budget to call for spending cuts," and "Dramatic cuts part of Bush budget."

Many newspapers agreed. *The Wall Street Journal*: A "Lean" Budget from Bush Cuts Mainly at Home. *USA Today*: Bush budget calls for big cuts. *Los Angeles Times*: Bush to Propose Billions in Cuts. *New York Times*: President Offers Budget Proposal With Broad Cuts. *Washington Post*: Previously Untargeted Programs at Risk. And the Democrats chimed in. They agreed with Bush that his budget was lean and tight, though they denounced him for it. Senate Minority Leader Harry Reid called it "irresponsible," House Minority Leader Nancy Pelosi raised the stakes to "immoral." Sen. Edward M. Kennedy warned of "three million children left behind." Sen. Hillary Rodham Clinton denounced Bush for "slashing funding," and Rep. Pete Stark decried "massive cuts." Sen. Charles Schumer may have won the Senate contest by condemning "a meat-ax budget" that would be "devastating" and "brutal" for New York.

He couldn't quite match Baltimore mayor Martin O'Malley, who compared the president's budget to the 9/11 attacks. "Back on September 11, terrorists attacked our metropolitan cores, two of America's great cities. They did that because they knew that was where they could do the most damage and weaken us the most," O'Malley said. "Years later, we are given a budget proposal by our commander in chief, the president of the United States. And with a budget ax, he is attacking America's cities. He is attacking our metropolitan core."

Now for that reality check. President Bush proposes that the federal government spend $2.57 trillion, or $2,570 billion, in the next fiscal year. That's 38 percent more than the federal government was spending in the last year of President Bill Clinton's term. Spending on programs for the poor is up even more, about 45 percent. Annual spending has risen by $700 billion since President Bush took office. The proposed 2006 budget is $80 billion higher than the 2005 budget, though both can be expected to rise before the books are closed.

You'd have to be Jabba the Hutt to see that as a lean budget. So why does everybody seem to agree that it is? Well, to be fair, two journalists did see the reality. Janet Hook's article in the *Los Angeles Times* was headlined "President Putting 'Big' Back in Government." And Jim Vande-Hei reported on the budget in the *Washington Post* under this headline: "Blueprint Calls for Bigger, More Powerful Government."

But Democrats, Republicans, and journalists mostly agree that President Bush has submitted a lean, tight $2.57 trillion budget. Why? I think we have what dancers call a pas de deux going on here. Or maybe in honor of our Texas president and his aversion to all things French, we should just call it a Texas Two-Step: The president pretends to cut the budget, and Democrats pretend to believe him.

Both sets of politicians appeal to their bases that way. President Bush's voters want to hear that he's cutting the budget and saving tax dollars. The Democrats' base of government employees and federal grant recipients want to see Democratic senators fighting budget cuts. When Kennedy and Clinton denounce Bush's "devastating" budget cuts, their supporters become outraged at Bush. Meanwhile, Republican voters respond to such charges by becoming more supportive of Bush. They may have had some doubts about Bush's commitment to fiscal conservatism, but the denunciations from Pelosi and her colleagues assuage those doubts.

For taxpayers, though, the bottom line is this: This is indeed President Bush's tightest budget yet, but that's like being the slimmest sumo wrestler in the ring.

Washington Times, February 20, 2005

Bush, Kerry, and Partisan Hypocrisy

Republicans are criticizing a decorated Vietnam veteran, Democratic presidential candidate John F. Kerry, while liberals are denouncing President Bush for avoiding service in what liberals called an illegal and immoral war. That sort of reversal might seem odd if it wasn't so reminiscent of other partisan battles over the past decade. Washington has become mired in a Red Team-Blue Team battle that leads partisans on both sides into rank hypocrisy.

Just think back to the Clinton years: Conservatives used to think that sexual harassment laws were a good example of big government trying to regulate everything under the sun. Feminists, they thought, wanted to criminalize normal flirting and dating. Feminists pushed a law through Congress that allowed plaintiffs in a sexual harassment suit to examine the defendant's personal life in search of examples of similar behavior. It was the sort of thing that led Rush Limbaugh to call them femi-Nazis.

Then Bill Clinton—who perhaps unwisely had signed that law—was accused of making sexual advances to a low-level employee of the Arkansas state government when he was governor. Suddenly the conservatives were born-again femi-Nazis. Hang him, they said. It just can't be lawful for a powerful man to make a vulgar advance at a woman who works for him, however distantly. And then when the legal pursuit of that accusation uncovered a case of actual sexual involvement with a young woman in the White House, they were ready to lynch him.

And the feminists? Suddenly they discovered the virtues of laissez-faire. Consenting adults, they said. Intrusive regulation, they cried. No one should be asked such questions, they insisted—the questions they had earlier insisted powerful men must be asked in investigations of sexual harassment charges.

Would the switch be permanent? Would conservatives become the new avenging angels of shocked young ladies? Would feminists learn to say "lighten up, flirting can be fun, women like sex, too, you know"?

It didn't take long to find out. When Arnold Schwarzenegger was accused of serial groping in 2003, conservatives and feminists resumed their old positions. Feminists were shocked, shocked to discover that a powerful and testosterone-laden movie star had touched women without their consent. Republicans, meanwhile, tossed aside both their old traditional values and their newfound quasi-feminism to dismiss the charges. The allegations were old, they said, and they were just the women's word against Arnold's, and the women were Democrats, and besides, lighten up—movie sets aren't Grandma's parlor.

Now we're seeing another example of the same Red Team-Blue Team partisanship on the issue of draft dodging in the 1960s. A dozen years ago Bill Clinton was the first Vietnam-era candidate for president. He famously evaded the draft, and conservatives and Republicans hammered him mercilessly for it.

But Democrats like wounded Vietnam veteran Sen. Bob Kerrey defended Clinton, saying that Bush should "put the Vietnam memory behind us" and that politicians like Bush were responsible for the system that allowed privileged young men to duck military service. Voters didn't seem to mind whatever Clinton had done in his youth, as he defeated George Bush in 1992 and Bob Dole in 1996, both of whom had served honorably in World War II.

But this year providence has delivered the Democrats a presidential candidate who had a sterling record in Vietnam—three purple hearts, a Bronze Star, and a Silver Star. So liberals are badgering the younger George Bush about his own avoidance of Vietnam. For good measure, they've noted that Vice President Cheney and other leading Republicans also managed to avoid the military when it counted. They're hammering away at the question of whether Bush showed up for National Guard duty in Alabama.

And the Republicans? They're not just dismissing Bush's service record as old news. With amazing chutzpah, they've gone on the attack against *Kerry:* was he really wounded all that seriously? Did he leave Vietnam earlier than he should have? Did he lie about throwing away his medals when he got back?

It's Red Team-Blue Team time again. Liberal Democrats and conservative Republicans throw away their principles and policies at a moment's notice to help a particular candidate. Politics ain't beanbag, and I have nothing against attack ads. But such rapid switches of position make it hard to take these charges seriously.

Milwaukee Journal Sentinel, May 23, 2004

Does Anybody Believe in Federalism?

If conservatives don't want federalism any more, will liberals pick up the banner?

Federalism has always been a key element of American conservatism. In his 1960 book *The Conscience of a Conservative*, Barry Goldwater called for "the federal government to withdraw promptly and totally from every jurisdiction which the Constitution reserves to the states." That same year, the founding document of Young Americans for Freedom declared "That the genius of the Constitution—the division of powers—is summed up in the clause that reserves primacy to the several states, or to the people, in those spheres not specifically delegated to the Federal government." Ronald Reagan ran for president promising to send 25 percent of federal taxes and spending back to the states. As Republicans took control of Congress in 1995, Newt Gingrich stressed that "we are committed to getting power back to the states."

Lately, though, conservatives—at last in control of both the White House and both houses of Congress—seem to have forgotten their long-standing commitment to reduce federal power and intrusiveness and return many governmental functions to the states. Instead, they have taken to using their newfound power to impose their own ideas on the whole country.

Conservatives once opposed the creation of a federal Education Department. Congressional Republicans wrote, "Decisions which are now made in the local school or school district will slowly but surely be transferred to Washington. . . . The Department of Education will end up being the Nation's super schoolboard. That is something we can all do without." But President Bush's No Child Left Behind Act establishes national education testing standards and makes every local school district accountable to federal bureaucrats in Washington.

President Bush and conservative Republicans have been trying to restrain lawsuit abuse by allowing class-action suits to be moved from state to federal courts. The 2002 election law imposed national standards on the states in such areas as registration and provisional balloting. A 2004 law established federal standards for state-issued driver's licenses and personal identification cards. President Bush's "Project Safe Neighborhoods" transfers the prosecution of gun crimes from states to the federal government. The administration is trying to persuade federal courts to block implementation of state initiatives on medical marijuana in California and assisted suicide in Oregon.

Perhaps most notoriously, President Bush and conservatives are pushing for a constitutional amendment to ban gay marriage in all 50 states. They talk about runaway judges and democratic decision-making, but their amendment would forbid the people of Massachusetts, Connecticut, California, or any other state from deciding to allow same-sex marriage. Marriage law has always been a matter for the states, and it is strikingly centralist to impose one uniform marriage law on what conservatives used to call "the sovereign states."

Most recently we have the specter of the Republican Congress seeking to override six Florida court decisions in the tragic case of Terri Schiavo, intruding the federal government into yet another place it doesn't belong. Asked on Fox News about the oddity of conservatives seeking to override states' rights, *Weekly Standard* editor Fred Barnes responded passionately: "Please! States' rights? Look, this is a moral issue."

Which is what liberal Democrats always said, of course, as they spent 50 years eroding federalism and expanding the power of the federal government at every turn. They had a point when it came to the civil rights laws; Southern states were violating the constitutional rights of black citizens. But that was no excuse for federalizing everything from the minimum wage to the speed limit to environmental regulations. For decades liberals scoffed at federalist arguments that the people of Wisconsin or Wyoming understood their own needs better than a distant Congress. They brought more and more power to Washington, overriding state legislatures and imposing mandates on every nook and cranny of governance.

Now those chickens have come home to roost. Republicans run Washington, and they're using the federal power that liberals built in ways that liberals never envisioned.

Some liberals are rediscovering the virtues of federalism. They dimly recall that Justice Louis Brandeis called the states "laboratories of democracy" and are seeking to pursue their own policies at the state level when they fail in Washington. The prospect of a constitutional amendment banning gay marriage has made some liberals appreciate the virtues of having 50 states, each free to make its own marriage law. Some have even come to appreciate the value of diversity: Virginia and Vermont may have different marriage laws, and that's OK. Maybe it would even be OK for Los Angeles and Louisiana to have different environmental regulations.

But most liberals can't give up their addiction to centralism. Even as they rail against federal intervention in the Schiavo case—archliberal Eleanor Holmes Norton, the District of Columbia's delegate in Congress, discovers for the first time in her life that "the bedrock of who we are" is the "Founders' limited vision of the federal government"—they push for stricter regulations on pesticides and painkillers, a higher national minimum wage, and federal gun control laws.

No one really supports federalism these days except libertarians. And the American people, who oppose the congressional intervention in the Schiavo case by 82 percent and believe by 78 percent that the federal government has too much power.

Only one modern political party has a history of taking federalism seriously, but Republicans have decided to abandon this principle to pander to small but vocal constituencies. The nation will be poorer for it.

Cato Policy Report, May/June 2005

True Patriotism

Accusations of insufficient patriotism keynoted the 1988 presidential campaign. The candidates and their supporters may have generated more heat than light on the subject, but they gave us an indication of just how liberals and conservatives perceive the individual's relationship to the state.

Vice President Bush, of course, managed to get the most mileage out of the patriotism issue. He repeatedly criticized Gov. Michael Dukakis for refusing to force Massachusetts teachers to lead the recitation of the Pledge of Allegiance every day, and he said in his acceptance speech that Dukakis "sees America as another pleasant country on the UN roll call, somewhere between Albania and Zimbabwe." Though Bush denied that he was questioning Dukakis's patriotism, his supporters were not hesitant to impugn the patriotism of Dukakis and other liberal Democrats.

Dukakis countered that "the highest form of patriotism is a dedication and commitment to the Constitution of the United States and the rule of law"—a dignified and thoroughly American sentiment for which he was roundly criticized by neoconservative guru Irving Kristol.

Kristol seemed to be suggesting that patriotism consisted of loving one's country and supporting every action of one's government—unless "the patriotic commitment had been nullified" as a result of "extreme circumstances." The example he gave was Hitler's Germany. But surely a true German patriot in the Nazi era would not have ceased to love his country; he would simply have decided that patriotism required him to be disloyal to his government. Indeed, it has been said that—even under less extreme circumstances—a true patriot loves his country and hates his government.

Liberals had great fun mocking the flag-waving, Pledge-reciting brand of patriotism peddled by Bush and his conservative supporters. But Dukakis also resorted to unsavory forms of patriotism in an attempt to win votes. After a primary campaign in which he had courageously resisted joining the protectionist bandwagon, he took a leaf from Rep. Richard Gephardt's xenophobic script. He visited a red-blooded American factory and denounced foreign ownership of U.S. assets—only to discover that the factory was owned by an Italian firm, whereupon he limply explained that he had no objection to "that kind of foreign ownership!" What kind? White?

One Dukakis ad warned of the dangers of foreign ownership and featured a huge Japanese flag. But the British own the most American assets, followed by the Dutch and then the Japanese. Why didn't the ad feature a Union Jack? Could it be that Dukakis was appealing not only to xenophobia but to racism? (Of course, Japan doesn't own any American companies; various people who are citizens of Japan do.) It seems that liberal nationalism is no more high-minded than the conservative variety.

And consider a related issue in the campaign: both candidates proclaimed, "I'm on your side!" What did they mean? Dukakis used the line first, and he was much praised for getting back to the bedrock of the Democratic party: class hatred. "I'm on your side" was meant to imply that the GOP was the party of big business, of Wall Street, of yuppie investment bankers and plutocratic landlords—and that if we all got together, there'd be enough of us to outvote the rich and take their money.

Being on the rich side of a rich-poor battle line is not a good idea in an electoral contest, so Bush had to look for an alternative way to frame the debate. He went out the next day and proclaimed, "*I'm* on your side." In his formulation, the divide was cultural, not economic, and "they" were the Harvard elitists, the busers and social planners, the intellectuals. Both candidates' attempts to rally the masses against a nefarious "other" recall Henry Adams's observation that "politics, as a practice, whatever its professions, has always been the systematic organization of hatreds."

When a liberal talks about patriotism, it's a good idea to watch your wallet. *New Republic* editor Michael Kinsley, for instance, criticized both

Bush and the Democratic Leadership Council for invoking patriotism without demanding higher taxes or any other sacrifice from the average citizen. Aside from the question of whether increasing taxes would be good economic policy, why should loving a free country require one to be taxed more, or to be drafted?

Despite political candidates' abuse of the concept, there is a sound basis for patriotism in American tradition. Patriotism, properly understood, isn't a matter of loving a piece of land or hating foreigners but rather an attitude that Abraham Lincoln summed up in his eulogy of Henry Clay. Lincoln said that Clay "loved his country partly because it was his own country, but mostly because it was a free country; and he burned with a zeal for its advancement . . . because he saw in such, the advancement . . . of human liberty, human right, and human nature."

Cato Policy Report, January/February 1989

Liberals, Conservatives, and Free Speech

Libertarians sometimes say that they are "liberal on free speech but conservative on economic freedom," or that "liberals believe in free speech and personal freedom, while conservatives believe in economic freedom." That proposition got another test in the Supreme Court yesterday. Conservatives and liberals split sharply on two free-speech cases.

And let's see . . . in two 5-4 decisions, the Court's conservative majority struck down some of the McCain-Feingold law's restrictions on campaign speech and upheld a high-school principal's right to suspend a student for displaying a "Bong Hits 4 Jesus" banner. Liberals disagreed in both cases.

So the liberals strongly defend a student's right to engage in nonsensical speech that might be perceived as pro-drug, but they approve a ban on speech criticizing political candidates in the 60 days before an election.

Now I'm for free speech in both these cases. But if you had to choose, which is more important—the right of a high-school student to display silly signs at school-sponsored events, or the right of citizen groups to criticize politicians at the time voters are paying attention? Political speech is at the core of the First Amendment, and conservatives are more inclined to protect it than are liberals. That's a sad reflection on today's liberals.

Maybe libertarians should try to describe their philosophy by saying "libertarians believe in the free speech that liberals used to believe in, and the economic freedom that conservatives used to believe in."

Cato@Liberty, June 26, 2007

PART 5

Big-Government Conservatives

The Bush Betrayal

In 2000 George W. Bush campaigned across the country telling voters: "My opponent trusts government. I trust you."

Little wonder that some of his supporters are now wondering which candidate won that election.

Federal spending has increased by 23.7 percent since Bush took office. Education has been further federalized in the No Child Left Behind Act. Bush pulled out all the stops to get Republicans in Congress to create the biggest new entitlement program—prescription drug coverage under Medicare—in 40 years.

He pushed an energy bill that my colleague Jerry Taylor described as "three parts corporate welfare and one part cynical politics . . . a smorgasbord of handouts and subsidies for virtually every energy lobby in Washington."

It's a far cry from the less-government, "leave us alone" conservatism of Ronald Reagan.

Conservatives used to believe that the U.S. Constitution set up a government of strictly limited powers. It was supposed to protect us from foreign threats and deliver the mail, leaving other matters to the states or to the private sector—individuals, families, churches, charities and businesses.

That's what lots of voters assumed they would get with Bush. In his first presidential debate with Al Gore, Bush contrasted his own vision of tax reduction with that of his opponent, who would "increase the size of government dramatically." Gore, Bush declared, would "empower Washington," but "my passion and my vision is to empower Americans to be able to make decisions for themselves in their own lives."

Bush was tapping into popular sentiment.

In fact, you could say that what most voters wanted in 2000 was neither Bush nor Gore but smaller government. A *Los Angeles Times* poll in September 2000 found that Americans preferred "smaller government with fewer services" to "larger government with many services" by 59 to 26 percent.

But that's not what voters got. Leave aside defense spending and even entitlements spending: In Bush's first three years, nondefense discretionary spending—which fell by 13.5 percent under Ronald Reagan—has soared by 20.8 percent. His more libertarian-minded voters are taken aback to discover that "compassionate conservatism" turned out to mean social conservatism—a stepped-up drug war, restrictions on medical research, antigay policies, federal subsidies for marriage and religion—and big-spending liberalism justified as "compassion."

When they're given a chance to vote, Americans don't like big government.

Last November 45 percent of the voters in the most liberal state in the Union, Ted Kennedy's Massachusetts, voted to abolish the state income tax.

In January, Oregon's liberal electorate rejected a proposed tax increase, 55 percent to 45 percent.

In September Alabama voters rejected Gov. Bob Riley's $1.2 billion tax hike by 2 to 1.

California voters tossed out big-spending Gov. Gray Davis, and 62 percent of them voted for candidates who promised not to raise taxes to close the state's deficit.

Bush and his aides should be worrying about the possibility that libertarians, economic conservatives and fed-up taxpayers won't be in his corner in 2004 in the same numbers as 2000.

Republican strategists are likely to say that libertarians and economic conservatives have nowhere else to go. Many of the disappointed will indeed sigh a deep sigh and vote for Bush as a lesser evil.

But Karl Rove, who is fascinated by the role Mark Hanna played in building the post-1896 Republican majority, should remember one aspect of that era: In the late 19th century, the Democratic Party of Jefferson, Jackson, and Cleveland was known as "the party of personal liberty." More so than the Republicans, it was committed to economic and cultural laissez-faire and opposed to Prohibition, protectionism, and inflation.

When the big-government populist William Jennings Bryan claimed the Democratic nomination in 1896, many assumed he would draw industrial workers from the Republicans and bring new voters to the polls. Instead, Bryan lost in a landslide, and turnout declined for the next few elections. As the more libertarian Democrats found less reason to go to the polls, the Republicans dominated national politics for the next 36 years.

It could happen that limited-government voters decide to stay home, or vote for an independent candidate in the mold of Ross Perot or Jesse Ventura or vote Libertarian.

They could even vote for an antiwar, anti-Patriot Act, socially tolerant Democrat.

Given a choice between big-government liberalism and big-government conservatism, the leave-us-alone voters might decide that voting isn't worth the trouble.

Washington Post, November 30, 2003

Franklin Delano Bush

It wasn't a fireside chat on the radio. No, it was different. President Bush stood in front of a church and addressed the nation by television. But otherwise, we're back in the days of President Franklin Delano Roosevelt and his big-spending, big-government New Deal. Except the New New Deal costs a lot more.

Franklin Delano Bush promised a gigantic federal relief effort—one that would go far beyond the traditional idea of disaster relief. He didn't just promise to clean up debris, or provide temporary housing, or even rebuild New Orleans and coastal Mississippi. He promised that federal taxpayers would pay for the education of displaced children in both public and private schools. And that Medicaid would pay for health care for evacuees. And that taxpayers would give displaced workers cash grants of $5,000 each.

Sweeping streets of debris is one thing. Sweeping promises are another. Bush promised that rebuilt communities "must be even better and stronger than before the storm." Oh, and he promised to cure poverty, inequality, and racism along the Gulf Coast.

The president didn't tell us what all this would cost, but experts have been suggesting a figure of $200 billion. That would be about twice what American taxpayers spent (adjusted for inflation) on the Marshall Plan to rebuild all of Western Europe after the devastation of World War II. As Stephen Moore wrote in the *Wall Street Journal*, with $200 billion you could give each of the 500,000 evacuated families $400,000. That would surely be the largest cash transfer program in history. And it raises the question: What's the federal government going to do that costs $400,000 per family?

Bush's speech came just two weeks after Hurricane Katrina swept through Louisiana and Mississippi, revealing the incompetence of federal, state, and local governments. Clearly no serious thought has been given to what ought to be done for the future.

Have President Bush and his advisers even considered whether it makes sense to rebuild a city below sea level on a hurricane path? Maybe New Orleans should return to being the "Crescent City," so named because it originally sat on a narrow crescent of high land on the bank of the Mississippi River.

Only 51 percent of Americans think it makes sense to rebuild New Orleans, even without asking them if they'd be willing to pay for it. Don't expect them to be asked, either.

Because the politicians know that when they're given a chance to vote, Americans don't like big government. Federal taxpayers never get a chance to vote on taxes and spending. If they did, we might see a resounding rejection of President Bush's massive increase in the federal budget.

Voters know that politicians tend to spend money to get votes, not to solve problems.

Consider that Congress passed a $51.8 billion Katrina relief bill on the very day the Associated Press released a study of where the $5 billion small-business relief money after 9/11 went. It found that the funds went to a South Dakota country radio station, a Virgin Islands perfume shop, a Utah drug boutique, and more than 100 Dunkin' Donuts and Subway shops—"companies far removed from the devastation." Fewer than 11 percent of the loans went to companies in New York and Washington.

Bush and the new Republican Party are turning their backs on Americans who want smaller government. They're delivering big-government conservatism across the board. But we already have a big-government party. The voters deserve a debate over the size and power of government. They deserve a debate right now on whether it is the responsibility of people in New York and Illinois and Colorado to pay for the education, health care, housing, and business investments of people in Louisiana and Mississippi.

Chicago Sun-Times, October 2, 2005

Conservatives Warm Up to Majoritarian Tyranny

Republicans and conservatives are in high dudgeon over Senate Democrats' refusal to let the Senate vote on some of President Bush's judicial nominations. "This filibuster is nothing less than a formula for tyranny by the minority," says Senate Majority Leader Bill Frist.

Frist speaks for many conservatives who want to change the rules of the Senate on a simple majority vote, to eliminate the filibuster for judicial nominations. Fifty-five Republicans, 55 votes to change the Senate's rules, case closed.

But those conservatives are being ahistorical, short-sighted, and unconservative. Judicial nominations are important, but so are our basic constitutional and governmental structures.

Conservatives aren't simple majoritarians. They don't think a "democratic vote" should trump every other consideration.

The Founders were rightly afraid of majoritarian tyranny, and they wrote a Constitution designed to thwart it. Everything about the Constitution—enumerated powers, separation of powers, two bodies of Congress elected in different ways, the electoral college, the Bill of Rights—is designed to protect liberty by restraining majorities.

The Senate itself is apportioned by states, not by population. California has 53 members of the House to Wyoming's one, but each state gets two senators. If each senator is assumed to represent half that state's population, then the Senate's 55 Republicans represent 131 million people, while its 44 Democrats represent 161 million. So is the "democratic will" what the 55 senators want, or what senators representing a majority of the country want?

Furthermore, the Senate was intended to be slower and more deliberative. Washington said to Jefferson, "We put legislation in the senatorial saucer to cool it."

The Founders didn't invent the filibuster, but it is a longstanding procedure that protects the minority from majority rule. It shouldn't be too easy to pass laws, and there's a good case for requiring more than 51 percent in any vote. And supermajorities make more sense for judicial nominations than they do for legislation. A bill can be repealed next year if a new majority wants to. A judge is on the bench for life. Why shouldn't it take 60 or 67 votes to get a lifetime appointment as a federal judge?

Throughout the 20th century, it was liberal Democrats who tried to restrict and limit filibusters, because they wanted more legislation to move faster. They knew what they were doing: they wanted the federal government bigger, and they saw the filibuster as an impediment to making it bigger.

As Norman Ornstein of the American Enterprise Institute writes, the filibuster "is a fundamentally conservative tool to block or retard activist government."

Conservatives know this. For decades they have resisted liberal efforts to grease the Senate's wheels. In the 19th century, Senate debate was unlimited. In 1917, at Woodrow Wilson's prodding, the Senate adopted Rule 22, which allowed 67 senators to invoke cloture and cut off a filibuster.

In 1975 that quintessential big-government liberal Walter Mondale moved in the post-Watergate Senate to cut off debate with a simple majority, to make it that much easier to advance the Democrats' legislative agenda. Conservatives resisted, and the Senate compromised on 60 votes to end a filibuster.

Conservatives may believe that they can serve their partisan interests by ending filibusters for judicial nominations without affecting legislative filibusters. But it is naïve to think that having opened that door, they won't walk through it again when a much-wanted policy change is being blocked by a filibuster—and naïve in the extreme to think that the next Democratic Senate majority won't take advantage of the opening to end the filibuster once and for all.

In the play *A Man for All Seasons* that great conservative St. Thomas More explained to his friend Roper the value of laws that may sometimes protect the guilty or lead to bad results. Roper declared, "I'd cut down every law in England ... to get at the Devil!" More responded, "And when the last law was down, and the Devil turned 'round on you, where would you hide?"

American constitutional government means neither majoritarianism in Congress nor acquiescence to the executive. If conservatives forget that, they will rue the day they joined the liberals in trying to make the Senate a smaller House of Representatives, greased to make proposals move quickly through the formerly deliberative body. The nuclear option will do too much collateral damage.

Sun-Sentinel, May 6, 2005

Libertarians, Beware the Rigid Reign of Rudy

Behind Rudy Giuliani's impressive lead in the polls is one fact that puzzles the pundits: Many cultural conservatives are backing a pro-choice, pro-gun control candidate. But what should be equally surprising is the strong support Giuliani is finding among libertarian-leaning Republicans, who also make up a big slice of the GOP base.

Here's why: Throughout his career, Giuliani has displayed an authoritarian streak that would be all the more problematic in a man who would assume executive powers vastly expanded by President Bush.

As a U.S. attorney in the 1980s, Giuliani conducted what University of Chicago Law Prof. Daniel Fischel called a "reign of terror" against Wall Street. He pioneered the use of the midday, televised "perp walk" for white-collar defendants who posed no threat to the community—precisely the sort of power play for which conservatives reviled former state Attorney General Eliot Spitzer. And Giuliani's use of federal racketeering statutes was so disturbing that the Justice Department changed its guidelines on the law.

As mayor, Giuliani had many successes. Crime came down. He cut taxes and held down spending. But his prosecutorial personality sometimes threatened personal freedoms. He cracked down on jaywalkers and street vendors. His street crime unit used aggressive tactics to confiscate guns from city residents, resulting in wholesale searches and detentions of citizens, especially young minority males, and occasional tragedies like the shooting of the unarmed Amadou Diallo.

When a police officer fatally shot another unarmed black man, Patrick Dorismond, Giuliani had police release Dorismond's sealed juvenile arrest record. The city later settled with Dorismond's family for $2.25 million.

And it should distress many conservatives that Giuliani took umbrage at affronts to his dignity, perhaps most notoriously when he tried to stop city buses from carrying a New York magazine ad saying the publication was "possibly the only good thing in New York Rudy hasn't taken credit for." The First Amendment lawyer Floyd Abrams notes in his book, *Speaking Freely*, that "over 35 separate successful lawsuits were brought against the city under Giuliani's stewardship arising out of his insistence on doing the one thing that the First Amendment most clearly forbids: using the power of government to restrict or punish speech critical of government itself."

As a presidential hopeful, Giuliani's authoritarian streak is as strong as ever. He defends the Bush administration's domestic surveillance program. He endorses the President's power to arrest American citizens, declare them enemy combatants and hold them without access to a lawyer or a judge. He thinks the President has "the inherent authority to support the troops" even if Congress were to cut off war funding, a claim of presidential authority so sweeping that even Bush and his supporters have not tried to make it.

Giuliani's view of power would be dangerous at any time, but especially after two terms of relentless Bush efforts to weaken the constitutional checks and balances that safeguard our liberty.

In 1964, Barry Goldwater declared it "the cause of Republicanism to resist concentrations of power." George W. Bush has forgotten that; Rudy Giuliani rejects it.

New York Daily News, May 30, 2007

Why Do Conservatives Like Bush?

Why do conservatives like Bush? After all, even his defenders call him a "big-government conservative," which was once an oxymoron. He's increased federal spending 48 percent in six years, further centralized education, inaugurated the biggest expansion of entitlements since the profligate President Lyndon B. Johnson, lured 17 percent more people onto the welfare rolls during five years of economic growth, and declared that "When somebody hurts, government has got to move."

So why do conservatives who grew up on Reagan like Bush? I can think of several reasons:

1. Tax cuts. Defying the establishment media and the class warfare of the Democrats, he has persisted in the Reaganite mission of cutting taxes, especially income tax rates.
2. The war. He stands up to the Islamo-fascists, as Reagan stood up to the evil empire. And as long as conservatives believe that the war in Iraq is part of the war on terrorism, they will support Bush there.
3. Religion. Conservatives like his willingness to talk about his born-again faith and to bring conservative Christian values (as he defines them) to political issues such as abortion, gay marriage, stem cell research, and government funding for religious charities.

And finally,

4. As a nominating speech for President Grover Cleveland once put it, "They love him most for the enemies he has made." Conservatives love Bush because the left hates him. If the *New York Times* would run a front-page story headlined "Bush Delivers the Big Government Clinton Never Did," and the lefty bloggers would pick it up and run with it, maybe conservatives would catch on.

So here's your challenge, lefty bloggers: If you don't like the tree-chopping, Falwell-loving, cowboy president—if you want his presidency fatally wounded for the next three years—then start praising him. One good Paul Krugman column taking off from that *USA Today* story on the surge in entitlements recipients under Bush, one *Daily Kos* lead on how Clinton flopped on national health care but Bush twisted every arm in the GOP to get a multi-trillion-dollar prescription drug benefit for the elderly, one cover story in the *Nation* on how Bush has acknowledged federal responsibility for everything from floods in New Orleans to troubled teenagers, and maybe, just maybe, *National Review* and the *Powerline* blog and Fox News would come to their senses. Bush is a Rockefeller Republican in cowboy boots, and it's time conservatives stopped looking at the boots instead of the policies.

Comment Is Free, March 16, 2006

The Rise of Big-Government Conservatism

In 1994 the American people resoundingly expressed their concern about big government and deteriorating families. Unfortunately, both Democrats and Republicans seem to find it more appealing to offer yet more government programs that would ostensibly strengthen the family than to downsize the federal government.

Take Secretary of Housing and Urban Development Henry Cisneros, one of the most accomplished politicians in the Clinton administration, for instance. He can talk the talk. In a new essay written with National Park Director Roger Kennedy, Cisneros says the first step toward civic reform is to "decentralize with a vengeance." He points out that many churches, neighborhood groups and small businesses "know at least as much and are better positioned than the organizationally encumbered government in Washington" to improve their own communities.

But Cisneros can't walk the walk. His latest HUD program would put classrooms in public housing developments. According to the *Post*, "Cisneros said he envisions housing developments modeled after college campuses, with units wired for computers and *all residents required to attend classes each day*—in prenatal training, educational day care, high school equivalency sessions or seminars for the elderly" (emphasis added).

Does he think that is what Americans voted for in 1994? Welfare creates dependency and fatherlessness; government schools graduate students who can't read and write; government housing projects are wracked by crime; and Cisneros proposes to have the federal government extend even further its control over the lives of the hapless poor.

Perhaps this sort of breathtaking expansion of government is to be expected of Democrats, even "new Democrats" who promise to "end welfare as we know it" and "decentralize with a vengeance." Like alcoholics returning to the bottle, they can promise to lay off the hard stuff, but one whiff of a government program and they are hooked again.

But it seems Republicans suffer from the same weakness. The latest example is the Project for American Renewal, launched Sept. 6 by William Bennett and Sen. Dan Coats (R-Ind.). Bennett and Coats endorse "devolution of federal authority and funding to state governments" but go on to argue that Republicans "need to offer a vision of rebuilding broken communities—not through government, but through those private institutions and ideals that nurture lives." They stress that "even if government undermined civil society, it cannot directly reconstruct it."

They talk the anti-big government talk even better than new Democrats, which is why the 1994 election saw a historic shift toward GOP. But look at the "be it enacted" clauses that follow Bennett and Coats's libertarian whereases.

As part of the Project for American Renewal, Coats has introduced 19 bills. They include:

- The Mentor Schools Act, to provide grants of $1 million to school districts to develop "same gender" schools.
- The Role Model Academy Act, to establish an innovative residential academy for at-risk youth.
- The Kinship Care Act, to create a $30 million demonstration program for states to use adult relatives as the preferred placement option for children separated from their parents.
- The Restitution and Responsibility Act, to provide grants to states for programs to make restitution to victims of crime.
- The Assets for Independence Act, to create a four-year, $100 million demonstration program to establish 50,000 Individual Development Accounts, to be used for the purchase of a home, college education, or small business.
- The Community Partnership Act, to institute demonstration grants for programs to match communities of faith with welfare recipients and nonviolent criminal offenders.

And on and on it goes. Most of the goals are good: Some students do better in all-boys or all-girls schools; children who lose their parents should ideally live with other adult relatives; restitution is a valuable aspect of dealing with a crime. But why does the federal government need to do any of those things? If the 10th Amendment and the new-found commitment to devolution of power mean anything, they mean that residential academies, victim restitution and welfare reform should be undertaken by state governments—if not local communities or even nongovernment groups.

And surely the First Amendment would recommend that such a worthy goal as matching "communities of faith"—that is, churches—with people in need should be undertaken without government support. As for 50,000 Individual Development Accounts, I'd like one—wouldn't you?

Like the Democrats, the Republicans just don't get it. They're still living in the Washington that Roosevelt built, the Washington where if you think of a good idea you create a government program. But conservative social engineering, like liberal social engineering, will fail. Worse, it will create new problems.

The message of 1994—like the message of 1776 and 1789, one might add—is not that the federal government should rebuild families and communities. It is that the federal government should get out of our lives.

Washington Post, September 27, 1995

Welcome to Our Side

Ralph Reed, executive director of the Christian Coalition, says in a speech distributed by Hillsdale College that America is held together by "a vision of a society based on two fundamental beliefs. The first belief is that all men, created equal in the eyes of God with certain unalienable rights, are free to pursue the longings of their heart. The second belief is that the sole purpose of government is to protect those rights." It would be hard to express the libertarian credo better. Dr. Reed isn't dumb, so he knows that the longings of men's hearts vary widely. Some men's hearts long for the wide-open spaces, others for the densely crowded cities. Some long for Jesus, some for Mohammed, others for Reason. Some long for a pot of tea, others for a pot of coffee, others just for the pot. Some men's hearts, indeed, long for the hearts of other men. It's good to know that, whatever moral objections Dr. Reed may have to some longings, as a good Jeffersonian he is committed to defending all men's rights to pursue happiness in their own way.

Liberty, July 1996

PART 6

Big-Government Liberals

Hillary Hates Freedom

Maybe that's a bit strong. Let's just say, Sen. Hillary Rodham Clinton operates with reckless disregard for individual freedom and the limited government that protects and sustains it.

In her latest salvo, she dismisses the great promises of the Declaration of Independence, the founding principles of the United States, as rhetorical flourishes, mere garnishes on the real stuff of life. "We can talk all we want about freedom and opportunity, about life, liberty, and the pursuit of happiness, but what does all that mean to a mother or father who can't take a sick child to the doctor?" she asked.

In her senatorial activities and her presidential campaign, Clinton has tended to propose modest, moderate programs. Even her new health care proposal is being hailed as more modest than her 1993 plan (though it would in fact impose a new government mandate on every person in the United States). But at her core, Hillary Clinton rejects the fundamental values of liberalism, values like individual autonomy, individual rights, pluralism, choice, and yes, life, liberty, and the pursuit of happiness. She seems to see no area of life that should be free from the heavy hand of government. And to her the world of free people seems a vast nothingness. When a few Republicans proposed to eliminate the National Endowment for the Arts, which spends about $125 million of the $63 billion spent on arts in the United States, she declaimed that such a move "not only threatens irrevocable damage to our cultural institutions but also to our sense of ourselves and what we stand for as a people."

After her first attempt at nationalizing and bureaucratizing American health care, she told the *New York Times* that her next project would be "redefining who we are as human beings in the post-modern age." I'd say 300 million Americans can do that for themselves.

Her hostility to freedom is not just a left-wing attitude. In the Senate, she's been adding the paternalistic agenda of the religious right to her old-fashioned liberal paternalism. Clinton has called for federal legislation to prohibit the sale of "inappropriate" video games to children and teens. She's introduced a bill to study the impact of media on children, a likely prelude to restrictions on television content, and she touts the V-Chip regulation that President Bill Clinton signed. She supports federal legislation to outlaw flag desecration (though not a constitutional amendment).

In her book *It Takes a Village*, she insisted that 300 million free people could somehow come to "a consensus of values and a common vision of what we can do today, individually and collectively, to build strong families and communities." She told *Newsweek*, "There is no such thing as other people's children," a claim that ought to frighten any parent. She promised to inflict on free citizens government videos running constantly in every gathering place, telling people "how to burp an infant, what to do when soap gets in his eyes, how to make a baby with an earache comfortable"—all the things that no one knew how to do until the federal government came along.

Hillary Clinton is no socialist. But when she makes her rejection of liberal values as explicit as she did on Monday—dismissing "freedom and opportunity [and] life, liberty, and the pursuit of happiness" as irrelevant to people's real lives—she is far too reminiscent of some of the most authoritarian figures of the 20th century. Lenin, for instance, wrote, "Bourgeois democracy is democracy of pompous phrases, solemn words, exuberant promises and the high-sounding slogans of freedom and equality."

And maybe it's no surprise that Clinton cosponsored her videogame ban with Sen. Rick Santorum, who is also an articulate and determined opponent of individualism. In his book *It Takes a Family* and in various media appearances, he denounced "this whole idea of personal autonomy." At least once he rejected "the pursuit of happiness" explicitly, saying, "This is the mantra of the left: I have a right to do what I want to do" and "We have a whole culture that is focused on immediate gratification and the pursuit of happiness . . . and it is harming America." Not the mantra of the Hillary Clinton left, obviously.

We know that societies that reject bourgeois freedom—the freedom of individualism, civil society, the rule of law, and yes, you guessed it, life, liberty, and the pursuit of happiness—in favor of collectivism and economic goods end up with neither freedom nor prosperity. The United States has the most advanced medical care in the world—the rate of death from heart disease in the U.S. was cut in half between 1980 and 2000, for instance—because we have a mostly free and capitalist economy. Mandates and regulations make medical care more costly than it needs to be, and Hillary Clinton now proposes to pile on yet more mandates and regulations. But the really scary prospect of another Clinton presidency is not what she would do to our medical care but what she would do to the "life, liberty, and the pursuit of happiness" that is the foundation of our free society.

Cato@Liberty, September 18, 2007

Hillary Moves Right in All the Wrong Directions

Conventional wisdom says Sen. Hillary Rodham Clinton is moving to the political center as she prepares to run for president in 2008. When, in June, she was booed by a roomful of liberal activists for repeating her support for the war in Iraq, some even suggested she had engineered a "Sister Souljah moment" to dramatize her newfound centrism.

At first blush, such positioning would make sense. A rightward shift seems to be just what Hillary, who is broadly perceived as a liberal, needs in order to broaden her appeal.

But there's a problem: Senator Clinton is sliding right in all the wrong directions. Rather than countering the perception that she's a big government left-winger, she's simply adding pieces of the agenda of the big government right to her portfolio.

Consider some stances she's taken over the past year or so. In July 2005, Clinton called for federal legislation to prohibit the sale of "inappropriate" video games to children and teens. She has supported federal legislation to outlaw flag desecration (though not a constitutional amendment). She has declined to back same-sex marriage.

And of course, she voted to give President Bush a blank check to invade Iraq and has consistently opposed a hard timetable for withdrawal ever since.

Yet as Senator Clinton moves right in these ways, she continues to embrace nearly every big government cure-all imaginable. In the 108th Congress, she introduced 211 bills to increase spending—more than any other senator—and only three bills to cut spending.

Clinton voted against the Central American Free Trade Agreement and for a windfall profits tax on oil companies. And in an attempt to do for education what the country wouldn't let her do for health care, she wants the federal government to guarantee "every student with seven fundamental resources needed to learn, including: instruction from a highly qualified teacher, rigorous academic standards, small class size, up-to-date facilities and textbooks and updated computers."

Such positions are unlikely to appeal to the millions of Americans who want more personal freedom and a less powerful federal government— like the 28 million Bush voters who, according to the University of Michigan's National Election Studies, support gay marriage or civil unions, or the 17 million Kerry voters who think "the less government the better."

It looks like Hillary Clinton aims to run for president as a big-government centrist. It's not clear there's a market for that combination.

New York Daily News, August 9, 2006

The Man with the Plan

Better sell your export stocks. Ira Magaziner's got a new project.

The architect of Hillary Clinton's health care debacle is now busily working on increasing American exports. If this project is as successful as his previous endeavors, we'll be importing grain from Russia by Election Day.

Magaziner is one of those baby boomer idealists, inspired by President Kennedy's soaring rhetoric, who decided that smart young Ivy Leaguers could solve all the world's problems if only people had to obey them. His generational hubris has led him into a string of disastrous attempts to remake the world.

His best-known effort was the 1993 task force to reconstruct the American health care system. It was a heady time for a policy wonk suddenly given a taste of power. He organized 500 bureaucrats into 15 committees and 34 working groups to redesign in 100 days an industry as big as the economy of France. What they came up with was a Rube Goldberg scheme of agencies, alliances, boards, commissions, and gatekeepers that would effectively nationalize one-seventh of the American economy.

Fortunately, Americans retain some of the good sense our Founders had, and the plan was ignominiously rejected after much national debate.

Magaziner must have been disappointed, but it wasn't his first experience with people who don't have his appreciation for complex, government-run plans. In 1984, he produced a 1,000-page report for a Rhode Island industrial policy to be called the Greenhouse Compact. It proposed a $250 million, seven-year plan, including a state venture-capital fund, grants for job training, day care, and modernization, and four technology research centers. Brown University economist George Borts pointed out that a $250 million plan in Rhode Island was the equivalent of $60 billion on a national level.

The Rhode Island establishment loved it. And why wouldn't they? It promised lots of jobs for the boys. It had to be approved by the voters before it could be put in place, but the politicos were too greedy to restrain themselves before the referendum. Both the two leading Democrats and the two leading Republicans in the legislature appointed themselves to the supposedly nonpolitical oversight commission for the plan.

The national media converged on Rhode Island, celebrating this concerted revival of activist government. They made Magaziner a minor national hero. Then the voters got their turn, and the Greenhouse Compact got a resounding vote of confidence from 20 percent of them.

Never one to be discouraged, Magaziner moved on. In March 1989, two Utah scientists announced that they had achieved nuclear fusion at room temperature. Within a month Magaziner was testifying before a congressional committee that it should invest $25 million of taxpayers' money in cold fusion, because the Japanese were working through the night on it. The committee should gamble with other people's money, Magaziner said, "for the sake of my children and all of America's next generation." The taxpayers were saved four days later, when major newspapers reported that leading scientists called cold fusion "scientific schlock" and "maybe fraud."

The next year he worked with Hillary Rodham Clinton on a report on workforce skills for the National Center for Education and the Economy. The report called for national performance standards, "a comprehensive system of technical and professional certificates," and federally assisted state centers to guide students. Work permits, contingent on meeting federal standards of workforce preparation, would be required for those up to age 18. All companies would be required to spend at least 1 percent of their payrolls on certified, accredited, union approved skills training. On-the-job training would not count. Overseeing the program would be—you guessed it—"a system of employment and training boards."

That plan turned up again in 1992, in Bill Clinton's campaign platform, except he raised the mandated cost to 1.5 percent of payroll. Economist Larry L. Orr told Jonathan Rauch of the *National Journal* that "it would be a fairly monstrous thing" to monitor business compliance with the mandate. And small businessman David Flowers said that his auto-parts company trained all of its new hires, but in ways that wouldn't qualify for Clinton's mandate. Because of Labor Secretary Robert Reich's opposition, the plan was shelved early in the Clinton administration.

The biggest of Clinton's Magaziner Mandates, though, was one that got little attention. In a little-noted comment during the 1992 campaign, Clinton offered a breathtaking view of government's ability and obligation to plan the economy:

> We ought to say right now, we ought to have a national inventory of the capacity of every . . . manufacturing plant in the United States: every airplane plant, every small business subcontractor, everybody working in defense.
>
> We ought to know what the inventory is, what the skills of the work force are and match it against the kind of things we have to

produce in the next 20 years and then we have to decide how to get from here to there. From what we have to what we need to do.

Since five-year plans didn't work, Clinton and Magaziner decided to plan more long-term. After the election Magaziner fleshed out this sweeping vision: defense conversion would require a 20-year "detailed organizational plan . . . to lay out how, in specific, a proposal like this could be implemented."

In all of these schemes, Magaziner displays a failure to appreciate the natural working of the market process; he can't see the order that emerges out of its undirected and apparently chaotic workings. He has the mind of an engineer. A GE executive recalls Magaziner, as a business consultant, taking "apart a television set, component by component," to understand GE's problems. Magaziner named his consulting firm Telesis, allegedly from the Greek for "well-planned progress."

That sort of planning and attention to detail makes sense for an individual or a firm. What Magaziner and his kind don't understand is that a society is not an enterprise. We're not all working for the same goal; indeed, our plans conflict all the time. They get sorted out in the marketplace. Competing for the hard-earned money of consumers and investors is a better way to find the best firms and the best ways of producing goods and services than having a board of experts spend other people's money.

Just imagine if an older Ira Magaziner had been asked by President McGovern to draw up a 20-year plan for, say, the computer and telephone industries. Could he possibly have envisioned—much less brought about—today's world of personal computers 100 times more powerful than the mainframes of 1975 and telephones that do things we never dreamed of then?

Adam Smith identified Magaziner's problem 200 years ago:

> The man of system . . . seems to imagine that he can arrange the different members of a great society with as much ease as the hand arranges the different pieces upon a chess-board; he does not consider that the pieces upon the chess-board have no other principle of motion besides that which the hand impresses upon them; but that, in the great chess-board of human society, every single piece has a principle of motion of its own, altogether different from that which the legislature might choose to impress upon it.

Ivy League intellectuals like Magaziner and the Clintons are so smart, they think they can solve society's problems as they would arrange chess pieces. They're just not smart enough to see the spontaneous order all around them that gives us everything from milk and bread in the morning to the highest-quality health care in the world to computers that bring the world's supply of knowledge to our desktops.

So, following the Washington principle of failing upward, Magaziner's record of disaster qualifies him to take on trade policy. Here he runs into a factual difficulty and a conceptual problem. The annoying fact is that American exports are booming, so why do we need a special export task force headed by a White House planner? Well, the *Washington Post* says it's because "imports are still a great deal higher."

That's a misconception, as a real understanding of economics would tell you. In the first place, exports are a cost; they're what we have to give other people to get imports. Sadly, firms in other countries will not ship us oil, cars, or fresh fruit in the winter without getting something in return. And not for long will they settle for those green pieces of paper that we can churn out on demand. "Balance-of-trade" figures often leave out services, where the United States has a surplus, and suffer from other conceptual difficulties. The fact that both exports and imports are booming means that more of our economy is devoted to foreign trade, which is generally a good thing, because it means more specialization in the world marketplace.

No doubt Rhode Island's economy could have benefited from better public policies, but not what Magaziner proposed. Health care could use some reforms, such as Medical Savings Accounts, but not Magaziner's nationalization. And we could certainly use better trade policies, but somehow it's hard to imagine Magaziner's latest task force proposing to repeal U.S. trade barriers and let international commerce develop.

Liberty, July 1996

Hash Brownies and Harlots in the Halls of Power

Eight British Cabinet ministers have admitted that they smoked marijuana in their youth, most of them "only once or twice" in college, which would be an atypical pattern. The revelations began with Jacqui Smith, the new Home Secretary, the equivalent of the attorney general. They also include the police minister and the Home Office minister in charge of drugs. The eight have been dubbed the "Hash Brownies," in acknowledgment of Prime Minister Gordon Brown.

On Wednesday Brown announced that Smith would lead a government review of the laws on marijuana, specifically with reference to whether simple possession should be again grounds for arrest. (The law was eased in 2002.) Several leading Conservatives in the Shadow Cabinet have also acknowledged using drugs, and party leader David Cameron has emulated President Bush in saying that he's not obligated to discuss every detail of his private life before he entered politics.

In the United States many leading politicians including Al Gore, Newt Gingrich, Bill Bradley, and Barack Obama have admitted using drugs, while Bush and Bill Clinton tried to avoid answering the question.

In both Britain and the United States, all these politicians support drug prohibition. They support the laws that allow for the arrest and incarceration of people who use drugs. Yet they laugh off their own use as "a youthful indiscretion."

These people should be asked: Do you think people should be arrested for using drugs? Do you think people should go to jail for using drugs? And if so, do you think you should turn yourself in? Do you think people who by the luck of the draw avoided the legal penalty for using drugs should now be serving in high office and sending off to jail other people who did what you did?

And the same question applies to Sen. David Vitter, who has acknowledged employing the services provided by the "D.C. Madam." Many people have compared Vitter to other politicians who engaged in adultery, or have mocked his commitment to "family values"—he has said that no issue is more important than protecting the institution of marriage from the threat of gay couples getting married. But the other politicians usually cited were not breaking the law when they had affairs, and Vitter's hostility to gay marriage while cheating on his own is a matter of simple political hypocrisy. The more specific issue, as with the pot-smoking drug warriors, is that Vitter (presumably) supports the laws against prostitution. Yet he himself, while a member of the United States Congress, has broken those laws and solicited other people to break them.

Vitter should be asked: Do you think prostitution should be illegal? If so, will you turn yourself in? Or will you testify for the defense in the D.C. Madam case, asking the court not to punish Deborah Jeane Palfrey if it's not punishing you?

I hope that Jacqui Smith, Barack Obama, and David Vitter will engage in some introspection and conclude that if they didn't deserve to go to jail, then neither do other pot smokers, prostitutes, and their customers. They might decide that not every sin or mistake should be a crime. But they should not sit in the halls of power, imposing on others the penalties they don't think should apply to them.

Our Friend, the State

Review of Garry Wills, *A Necessary Evil: A History of American Distrust of Government*. New York: Simon & Schuster, 1999.

What a remarkable book this is. Garry Wills has managed to categorize and rebut more "anti-government myths" than most of us could identify. By the time he's finished, everyone from Thomas Jefferson, Thoreau, Brook Farm, and H. L. Mencken to Martin Luther King Jr., the NRA, and Timothy McVeigh has been assigned a place in his classification system.

Wills gives us two "revolutionary" myths, six "constitutional" myths, and then six kinds of people who challenge or resist the authority of the national state: nullifiers, seceders, insurrectionists, vigilantes, withdrawers, and disobeyers. Most of these categories are a bit arcane and moss-covered in the twenty-first century, but occasionally they fit contemporary politics. He counts as "insurrectionists," for instance, academics who find an individual right to keep and bear arms in the Second Amendment.

Oddly, although the book purports to be a defense of government against Americans who prefer liberty to government power, Wills hardly ever cites a modern libertarian or conservative. Criticisms of Daniel Shays, John Taylor of Caroline, John C. Calhoun, John Brown, clinic bombers, and McVeigh are all well and good, but where is any serious engagement with F. A. Hayek, Milton Friedman, Harvey Mansfield, Robert Nozick, Randy Barnett, or Richard Epstein—people who in different ways have defended the wisdom of limited government and the Founders' vision? Where even is a consideration of the arguments of Barry Goldwater, Ronald Reagan, or Rush Limbaugh?

Because Wills doesn't consider the arguments of any actual advocates of limited government, he spends a surprising amount of time rebutting claims that don't seem very important. Other times his rebuttals just seem odd. He declares, for instance, that "Nowhere . . . does the Constitution mention checks, or balances, or separation of powers." Well, no. It just checks, balances, and separates the powers.

A major theme of the book is that throughout American history we find contrasting sets of principles held by advocates and critics of central government. Those opposed to government power believe government should be "provincial, amateur, authentic, spontaneous, candid, homogeneous, traditional, populist, organic, rights-oriented, religious, voluntary, participatory, and rotational." Government's advocates think it should be "cosmopolitan, expert, authoritative, efficient, confidential, articulated in its parts, progressive, elite, mechanical, duties-oriented, secular, regulatory, and delegative, with a division of labor." I hardly know what to make of this alleged dichotomy. I disagree with the author's argument that we find these various priorities opposing each other in all the central conflicts of our history, from the Revolution to the 1960s.

As an advocate of limited government, I would not want to be forced to pick one group or the other. Part of the problem, of course, is that Wills has chosen words that tilt the debate. Government close to the people, rather than in distant capitals, is called "provincial." Citizen control of government is called "amateur."

In his final section, "A Necessary Good," Wills briefly lays out a positive case for government. But who in modern America is opposed to government per se? Wills is trying to smuggle in an expansive central government, virtually unconstrained by the Constitution, in a plain brown wrapper marked merely "Government."

Like so many opponents of liberty, he triumphantly uses traffic laws to prove the necessity of government. He begins by writing, "I know men who feel they have lost their liberty if they are obliged to wear a seat belt or a motorcycle helmet. It is odd that they cavil at this while they submit to far more stringent restrictions." What sort of restrictions? "What could be more arbitrary . . . than the order to drive only on the right side of the road?" After further philosophical reflection on the rules of the road, Wills writes, "I have deliberately taken something rather trivial to illustrate the blessings of government."

Actually, his example proves a great deal. Of course we need rules to be able to use the roads with other drivers, and of course we want roads to give us mobility and prosperity. To oppose stop signs and assigned lanes is not to be a libertarian, or even an anarchist. It is to be a nihilist, or a child, or a Unabomber. The purest libertarian understands that humans need to cooperate in order to achieve their goals, and that cooperation requires some agreed-upon rules. The key distinction is between rules that prevent harm to others and enable cooperation, and rules that are designed to prevent harm to ourselves. The reason people "feel they have lost their liberty if they are obliged to wear a seat belt" is that that rule is designed not to make social activity possible but to tell us how to run our lives. And anyone who cannot understand that distinction cannot understand the American heritage of freedom and the American distrust of government.

After all of Wills's efforts to prove that the Founders did not really distrust government—they set one up, after all—and that all the Americans who have challenged the national state are somehow unfaithful to the system, we are left with the reality that the United States was created by people who loved liberty, feared power, and set up a government of delegated, enumerated, and thus limited powers.

Wills makes his own, quite different goals clear when he writes, "The real victims [of our ingrained fear of government] are the millions of poor or shelter-less or medically indigent who have been told, over the years, that they must lack care or life support in the name of their very own freedom. Better for them to starve than to be enslaved by 'big government.'" This is not the place for a discussion of whether limited or unlimited government creates more wealth, shelter, and medical care. Suffice it to say that the countries with the biggest governments do not have very good records in that regard.

I'll stick with Thomas Paine, who bequeathed to America the notion that "society in every state is a blessing, but government even in its best state is but a necessary evil."

American Enterprise, June 2000

Taking Marxism to China

Marxism is a bore in China, but tie-dyed American socialists are trying to revive it. Apparently it's easier to believe in socialism if you haven't actually tried to live under it. The *Los Angeles Times* reports:

> It isn't easy teaching Marxism in China these days.
>
> "It's a big challenge," acknowledged Tao, a likable man who demonstrates remarkable patience in the face of students more interested in capitalism than "Das Kapital." The students say he isn't the problem.
>
> "It's not the teacher," said sophomore Liu Di, a finance major whose shaggy auburn hair hangs, John Lennon-style, along either side of his wire-rim glasses. "No matter who teaches this class, it's always boring. Philosophy is useful and interesting, but I think that in philosophy education in China, they just teach the boring parts."
>
> Classes in Marxist philosophy have been compulsory in Chinese schools since not long after the 1949 communist revolution. They remain enshrined in the national education law, Article 3 of which states: "In developing the socialist educational undertakings, the state shall uphold Marxism-Leninism, Mao Tse-tung Thought and the theories of constructing socialism with Chinese characteristics as directives and comply with the basic principles of the Constitution."

Chinese students are forced to learn the official ideology—or, I should say, they are forced to sit in classes where the official ideology is expounded—few of them seem to be listening any more. And yet, students say, it's still hard to find anyone who will openly criticize communism—partly because it's still very helpful to be a member of the Communist Party and partly because it's dangerous to criticize the official ideology of an authoritarian government.

Fortunately, just as China's Marxists begin to deal with their terminal despair at the decline of Mao's Good Old Cause, a couple of "veteran Vermont activists" are riding to the rescue. Ellen David-Friedman and Stuart Friedman—she's a self-described Marxist, an organizer for the Vermont teachers' union, and vice-chair of the Progressive Party, he's a clinical social worker at Central Vermont Hospital—are leaving their jobs in the People's Republic of Vermont to teach the Chinese about the horrors of capitalism. Communist Party apparatchiks and overseers at Guangzhou University have never attempted to censor her or Stuart's teaching, David-Friedman tells the Vermont weekly *Seven Days*. "We can say anything we want to in the classroom," she notes—perhaps because these radicals are in fact teaching the official ideology, and it's so hard to find people who want to do that these days!

Communism is always such a disappointment in practice. You'd think by now even romantic communists would have given up on it. But no—neither the activists nor the *Seven Days* reporter is ready for that:

> China's communist revolution has gone off the rails, David-Friedman adds. The party "has divorced itself, tragically, from allowing itself to be led by the needs of workers," she adds. But maybe, in some small measure, these Vermont Progressives can help put the world's largest country back on the track toward socialism.

The *Los Angeles Times* concludes,

> Talking over tea at the Education Ministry's modern offices in central Beijing, education official Zhou laughed a bit about today's students.
>
> "They don't believe in God or communism," he said. "They're practical. They only worship the money."

That sounds a lot like the French philosopher Jean-Francois Revel's 1971 book *Without Marx or Jesus: The New American Revolution Has Begun*. Has the liberal-capitalist revolution begun in China?

Comment Is Free, July 5, 2007

PART 7

Civil Rights and Wrongs

Don't Forget the Kids

As conservatives gear up for the fall elections, many are pinning their hopes on attacking gay rights. Self-styled "pro-family" groups, seeking to build on the success on five local and state anti-gay initiatives in 1993, have been working to get similar measures on the November ballots in several states.

These organizations are correct in saying that America faces some real social problems, and that many can be attributed to the deterioration of families. What is upsetting, however, is the extent to which they focus on gay issues almost to the exclusion of real problems.

Children need two parents, for financial and emotional reasons. Children in fatherless homes are five times as likely to be poor as those in two-parent families. Single mothers also find it difficult to control teenage boys, and such boys have made our inner cities a crime-ridden nightmare. Conservatives have taken note of this problem, and many of them have correctly indicted the welfare state. But with a few exceptions—notably Dan Quayle—they seldom put a high enough priority on condemning single parenthood.

And they pay almost no attention to the effects of divorce—every year more children experience divorce or separation than are born out of wedlock. These children are nearly twice as likely as those from intact families to drop out of high school or to receive psychological help.

Conservatives overlook this because they are too busy attacking gay men and lesbians. Consider the leading conservative journals. The *American Spectator* has run 10 articles on homosexuality in the past three years, compared with two on parenthood, one on teen-age pregnancy and none on divorce. *National Review* has printed 32 articles on homosexuality, five on fatherhood and parenting, three on teenage pregnancy and just one on divorce.

The Family Research Council, the leading "family values" group, is similarly obsessed. In the most recent index of its publications, the two categories with the most listings are "Homosexual" and "Homosexuals in the Military"—a total of 34 items (plus four on AIDS). The organization has shown some interest in parenthood—nine items on family structure, 13 on parenthood and six on teen pregnancy—yet there are more items on homosexuality than on all of those issues combined. There was no listing for divorce. (Would it be unfair to point out that there are two items on "Parents' Rights" and none on "Parents' Responsibilities"?)

As for the Christian Coalition, despite Executive Director Ralph Reed's vow not to "concentrate disproportionately on abortion and homosexuality," its current Religious Rights Watch newsletter contains six items, three of them on gay issues. The July issue of the American Family Association's newsletter, Christians and Society Today, contains nine articles, five of them on homosexuality.

Cobb County, Ga., a major battle ground in the conservatives' culture war, is a microcosm of this distorted focus. In 1993 the county commission passed a resolution declaring "gay life styles" incompatible with community standards. Cobb County is a suburb of Atlanta; its residents, 88 percent white, are richer and better educated than the national average. Yet it had a 20 percent illegitimacy rate in 1993, and there were two-thirds as many divorces as marriages. Surely the 1,545 unwed mothers and the 2,739 divorcing couples created more social problems in the county than the 300 gay men and women who showed up at a picnic to protest the county commission's assault on their rights.

When teenage girls wear sexually explicit T-shirts, when teenage boys form gangs to tally their sexual conquests, when eighth graders watch twice as much television as their European counterparts, when 10-year-olds on bicycles dart in front of my car at 1 A.M., when students take guns to class—where are the "family values" conservatives, and why aren't they calling on parents to take their responsibilities more seriously?

Perhaps they fear that making an issue of divorce would alienate middle-class supporters, including divorced conservatives. Perhaps they fear that putting welfare at the top of their agenda would seem racist, or worry that calling for parental responsibility would be a hard sell politically. They may be right, but that's no excuse for ducking crucial family issues. Their scapegoating of gay men and lesbians may get them some votes and contributions, but it's not going to solve any of American families' real problems.

New York Times, September 10, 1994

Legal Immigrants?

As millions of Hispanics march against restrictive immigration laws and the U.S. Senate compromise bill collapses, Kate O'Beirne writes in the conservative magazine *National Review* that "America is a nation of legal immigrants."

True enough. But that's largely because for most of our history all immigrants were legal immigrants; there were no restrictions on immigration. When Thomas Boaz arrived on these shores from Scotland via Ireland in 1747, he and his family became instant Americans. In the 19th century, when millions of Irish came to America—maybe even the O'Beirnes—there were no restrictions on immigration and thus no "illegal immigrants." There were rules governing naturalization and citizenship, but anyone who could get here could live and work here.

Immigration expert Stuart Anderson writes: "Immigration to the United States can be described as openness punctuated by periods of restriction. During the 17th, 18th, and 19th centuries, immigration was essentially open without restriction, and, at times, immigrants were even recruited to come to America."

The first restrictive immigration law was the Chinese Exclusion Act of 1882. (Ah, for the days when Congress gave laws honest names. These days, a tax scheme is called Social Security and a grab bag of civil liberties violations is dubbed the USA Patriot Act. Back in 1882, when Congress wanted to exclude the Chinese, they called it the Chinese Exclusion Act.) In 1917 a literacy test was imposed on immigrants, and in 1921 the Temporary Quota Act first imposed numerical limits on immigration based on "national quotas." Since then we have had both legal and illegal immigrants.

If Hispanics were coming here under the rules that welcomed my Scottish and Irish ancestors, we'd still be a nation of legal immigrants.

Comment Is Free, April 11, 2006

Enlightenment Values

The Anglican Archbishop of South Africa, Njongonkulu Ndungane, says his church should abandon its "practices of discrimination" and accept the gay Episcopal bishop V. Gene Robinson of New Hampshire. That makes him unusual in Africa, where other Anglican bishops have strongly objected to the ordination of practicing homosexuals.

The Nigerian primate, for instance, Archbishop Peter Akinola, condemned the consecration of Robinson as bishop, calling it a "satanic attack on the church of God." According to the *San Francisco Chronicle*, "He even issued a statement on behalf of the 'Primates of the Global South'—a group of 20 Anglican primates from Africa, the West Indies, South America, India, Pakistan, and Southeast Asia—deploring the action and, along with Uganda and Kenya, formally severed relations with Robinson's New Hampshire diocese."

So what makes Ndungane different? He's the successor to Nobel laureate Desmond Tutu, one might recall. And they both grew up in South

Africa, where enlightenment values always had a foothold, even during the era of apartheid. Ndungane studied at the liberal English-speaking University of Cape Town, where Sen. Robert F. Kennedy gave a famous speech in 1966.

Ndungane didn't hear that speech, alas, because he was then imprisoned on Robben Island. But after he was released he decided to enter the church and took two degrees at King's College, London. The arguments of the struggle against apartheid came from western liberalism—the dignity of the individual, equal and inalienable rights, political liberty, moral autonomy, the rule of law, the pursuit of happiness.

So it's no surprise that a man steeped in that struggle and educated in the historic home of those ideas would see how they apply in a new struggle, the struggle of gay people for equal rights, dignity, and the pursuit of happiness as they choose.

Comment Is Free, May 16, 2006

Yellow Peril Reinfects America

The House is expected to vote this month on Rep. John Bryant's Foreign Ownership Disclosure Act, which would require foreign investors with a "significant interest" in any business or property to register with the U.S. government.

The growing support for such legislation, which already has passed the House twice, parallels the growth of Japanese companies as significant buyers of American properties alongside traditional investors from Britain, Canada and the Netherlands. Yet discussion of foreign interest always focuses on Japan, which is only the third-largest foreign investor in the U.S., behind Britain and Canada. Could it be that the idea of British and Canadian investors owning American buildings just doesn't frighten Americans because . . . well, because they're white?

It wouldn't be the first time. Racism directed against Asians and Asian-Americans has a long history in this country. In 1882, the Chinese Exclusion Act made the Chinese the first nationality specifically banned from immigrating to this country. It worked. Chinese immigration fell from some 30,000 that year to less than 1,000. Labor leader Samuel Gompers argued, "The superior whites had to exclude the inferior Asiatics, by law, or, if necessary, by force of arms."

From 1854 to 1874, a California law prevented Chinese from testifying in court against white men. The 1879 California constitution denied suffrage to all "natives of China, idiots, and insane persons."

Some harassment was more subtle. For instance, as economist Thomas Sowell points out in *Ethnic America*: "License fees in nineteenth-century San Francisco were higher for laundries that did not deliver by horse-and-buggy, and it was made a misdemeanor to carry baskets suspended on a pole across the shoulder—the way the Chinese delivered."

After the turn of the century, the rising sun of Japan became the focus of American hostility. During World War II, the U.S. engaged in a massive propaganda campaign against Japan. As historian John Dower demonstrates in *War Without Mercy: Race and Power in the Pacific War*, the enemy in Europe was the madman Hitler, and the enemy in Asia was "the Japs."

The most egregious example of anti-Japanese racism, of course, was Executive Order 9066 by which President Franklin D. Roosevelt ordered more than 110,000 Americans of Japanese ancestry interned in 10 camps. Though there was never a single instance of sabotage or disloyalty by a Japanese-American, the incarceration was upheld by the Supreme Court and endorsed by such opinion-molders as the *Los Angeles Times*, which editorialized: "A viper is nonetheless a viper wherever the egg is born— so a Japanese-American, born of Japanese parents, grows up to be a Japanese, not an American."

After the war such hostilities seemed to fade. Japan became a staunch American ally and trading partner, and Asian-Americans prospered here. By 1969, Japanese-American and Chinese-American family incomes were, respectively, 128 percent and 109 percent of the incomes of white families.

Perhaps they prospered too much. By the 1970s there was a revival of anti-Asian prejudice touched off by several factors, including the influx of Indochinese refugees after the Vietnam War, the academic success of Vietnamese-American students a few years later, and a feeling of U.S. economic decline in the face of the success of the Japanese and Korean economies.

The resurgence of protectionism has often been tinged with racism. In 1980, presidential candidate John Connally warned the Japanese they had "better be prepared to sit on the docks of Yokohama in your little Datsuns and your little Toyotas while you stare at your own little television sets and eat your mandarin oranges, because we've had all we're going to take!" Two years later, Walter Mondale was echoing Connally: "We've been running up the white flag, when we should be running up the American flag! . . . What do we want our kids to do? Sweep up around Japanese computers?" Around the 40th anniversary of the bombing of Hiroshima and Nagasaki, former Sen. Howard Baker pointed out "two facts": "First, we're still at war with Japan. Second, we're losing."

The recent hysteria over foreign investment in the U.S. has an even clearer racist aspect. *Los Angeles Times* cartoonist Paul Conrad satirized former President Reagan's "Morning in America" theme by showing the

White House surrounded by skyscrapers topped by Japanese flags. A TV ad for presidential candidate Michael Dukakis about the dangers of foreign investment featured a Japanese flag. Martin and Susan Tolchin's book *Buying Into America* contains 15 index references to Japanese investment and a total of one to British, Canadian and Dutch investment.

U.S. liberals frequently accuse conservatives of racism or racial insensitivity. Evidence for such a charge might be found in Sen. Jesse Helms's (R.-N.C.) comments during last year's debate over providing compensation to the Japanese-Americans who had been incarcerated in the World War II camps. Mr. Helms suggested such compensation be considered only when the Japanese government compensated the victims of Pearl Harbor—clearly implying Japanese-Americans bore some sort of racial guilt for the misdeeds of the Japanese government.

But there's at least as much anti-Asian prejudice on the left as on the right: Witness Messrs. Mondale, Dukakis, and Conrad. Writing in the *Nation*, Gore Vidal warns we are entering an era in which "the long-feared Asiatic colossus takes its turn as a world leader" and calls for a U.S.-Soviet alliance in order to have "an opportunity to survive, economically, in a highly centralized Asiatic world."

Perhaps the most alarming example of the new racism—because of the stature and sobriety of both author and publication—was the late Theodore H. White's 1985 *New York Times Magazine* article, "The Danger from Japan." Mr. White warned that the Japanese were seeking to create another "East Asia Co-prosperity Sphere"—this time by their "martial" trade policies, and that they would do well to "remember the course that ran from Pearl Harbor to the deck of the USS *Missouri* in Tokyo Bay."

Along with the resurgence of Asian-bashing by pundits and politicians has come an increase in reports of physical Asian-bashing. The Justice Department says incidents of violence against Asians jumped 62 percent between 1985 and 1986, accounting for 50 percent of all racial incidents in Los Angeles and 29 percent in Boston. Much hostility against Asian entrepreneurs has developed in black communities.

In 1982, two unemployed auto workers followed a young Chinese-American man down a Detroit street and beat him to death with a baseball bat—because they thought he was Japanese and thus somehow responsible for their unemployment. A judge at the original sentencing, noting the stress that Japanese imports had caused the men, gave them each three years' probation and an approximately $3,700 fine.

Like anti-Semitism, much of the prejudice against Asian-Americans is based on resentment of the academic and economic success of the group. Rather than admire or emulate the characteristics—hard work, self-discipline, stable families, respect for education—that have made Jews and Asians so successful in America, some Americans convince themselves the alien groups must have somehow "cheated" and deserve to be punished.

This resentment seems to have motivated Patrick Purdy, whose jealousy of the success of Asian immigrants led him to open fire in a Stockton, Calif., schoolyard, killing five Asian-American children. It was elucidated in a series of "Doonesbury" cartoons last year, in which neighbors complained to the parents of an Asian-American student that teaching her "the value of discipline, hard work, and respect for elders" gave her an unfair advantage.

Besides the costs of protectionism and the ugliness of racism, one more aspect of anti-Asian prejudice is even more ominous. Various Western leaders have taken to declaring the Cold War over. Should events justify that optimistic prediction, there is a possibility Americans will seek a new national adversary. Why? First, because throughout history people have seemed to need an enemy. And second, because at least some American interest groups—possibly including the federal government itself—benefit from the existence of a national enemy. As Thomas Paine wrote in *The Rights of Man*, governments do not raise taxes to fight wars, they fight wars to raise taxes.

Who might be America's new enemy? Iran, Libya, South Africa, and Nicaragua might all qualify as devil figures, but none poses a plausible threat to the U.S. It seems entirely likely that those who thrive on fighting enemies will conjure up a new Yellow Peril. Already Japan's eagerness to sell us quality products at good prices is described in military terms: "aggressive" investors, an "invasion" of Toyotas, "an economic Pearl Harbor." Jack Anderson quotes "some strategists" who "fear World War III is an economic war, which we are losing."

Home-grown racism is bad enough. Let's hope it doesn't turn into a race war.

Wall Street Journal, April 7, 1989

Marriage Measure Is an Amendment Too Far

There's never been a same-sex marriage in Virginia, and they've been outlawed by statute for more than 30 years. So why are Virginia voters being asked to vote on a constitutional amendment to ban gay marriage?

Mostly because it's a bait-and-switch game. The proposed Ballot Question No. 1 is far broader than a simple ban on gay marriage.

Supporters say the amendment is needed in order to prevent activist judges from unilaterally changing the definition of marriage. But no liberal activists have yet been sighted in the Virginia judiciary. And that's no surprise because judges in Virginia are selected by the same legislature that has repeatedly passed bans on gay marriage, civil unions and domestic partnerships, including this proposed amendment.

In fact, Virginia is one of only two states where the legislature directly appoints judges to the state courts, including the state Supreme Court. It is inconceivable that Virginia judges, including four members of the Supreme Court, are going to impose gay marriage on the state. Virginia is not Massachusetts nor Vermont or New Jersey, and our judges are certainly more conservative than those in New York, where the high court recently upheld the state's ban on gay marriage.

The irony in Virginia is that conservatives fearful of an out-of-control judiciary are in fact inviting the judiciary to get involved in micro-managing family law. Take a look at the actual text of what journalists are inaccurately calling "the proposed ban on gay marriage."

The first sentence of the amendment reads: "That only a union between one man and one woman may be a marriage valid in or recognized by this Commonwealth and its political subdivisions." That sentence is what amendment supporters want you to read.

But read the rest of it: "This Commonwealth and its political subdivisions shall not create or recognize a legal status for relationships of unmarried individuals that intends to approximate the design, qualities, significance, or effects of marriage. Nor shall this Commonwealth *or* its political subdivisions create or recognize another union, partnership, *or* other legal status to which is assigned the rights, benefits, obligations, qualities, or effects of marriage."

Note the italicized words. The use of the word "or" makes this a very broad law.

Supporters of the amendment rely on the assurance of Virginia Attorney General Robert McDonnell that passage "will not affect the current legal rights of unmarried persons."

But lawyers disagree. The firm of Arnold and Porter issued a 71-page analysis of the amendment coming to starkly different conclusions. Their lawyers concluded that the amendment could be interpreted by Virginia courts to invalidate rights and protections currently provided to unmarried couples under domestic violence laws, block private companies from providing employee benefits to domestic partners, and prevent the courts from enforcing child custody and visitation rights, as well as end-of-life arrangements, such as wills, trusts and advance medical directives, executed by unmarried couples.

The firm went on to say: "This exceedingly broad and untested language is the most expansive such proposal ever to have been put before the voters of any state."

We should not pass constitutional amendments whose effects are so uncertain. A simple ban on gay marriage would be redundant, but it would have the virtue of clarity for the courts. The actual amendment invites judges to review every private contract, every employee benefit, every legal arrangement between unmarried partners.

That should be anathema to opponents of judicial activism. It should also be a frightening prospect to Virginia businesspeople. A growing number of companies are offering benefits to the domestic partners of gay employees, and they will want to locate in states where those benefits are clearly legal.

This amendment goes too far. But even its first sentence—the ban on gay marriage—is unworthy of a state that was the birthplace of American freedom. It is a cruel irony that this amendment to restrict contract rights and exclude loving couples from the institution of marriage is to be added to Virginia's Bill of Rights, a document originally written by the great Founder George Mason.

Mason's eloquent words inspired Thomas Jefferson in writing the Declaration of Independence and James Madison in writing the Bill of Rights for the U.S. Constitution. We should not add language to Virginia's Bill of Rights that would limit rights rather than expand them.

Gay marriage is not legal in Virginia, and there's no prospect of changing that in the foreseeable future, whether by legislative or judicial action. Ballot Question No. 1 is unnecessary and will create legal uncertainty.

Washington Examiner, October 30, 2006

Domestic Justice

New York's new governor, George Pataki, plans to reverse Mario Cuomo's policy of granting health benefits to the domestic partners of all unmarried state employees. Mr. Pataki is part of a rising political tide that includes Gov. Pete Wilson of California, who said in vetoing his state's domestic partnership bill that "government policy ought not to discount marriage by offering a substitute relationship that demands much less." That's legitimate, but it overlooks that there are two kinds of domestic partnerships—heterosexual and same-sex. Although the most vocal opposition to domestic partnerships is aimed at gay couples, giving them benefits doesn't undermine marriage. Rather, it remedies the injustice that homosexuals can't marry the people with whom they share their lives, and it creates financial incentives for stable relationships. Is this not the goal we seek in encouraging marriage?

Giving domestic partnership benefits to unmarried heterosexual couples, on the other hand, does undermine marriage. They give people who can marry all the financial benefits of a legal union without demanding commitment. "If two heterosexuals are going to shack up together, then they ought to get married," said the Rev. Charles Bullock, who fought successfully to overturn a partnership law in Austin. "If they're not going to make that commitment to each other, why should the city?"

Although the voters' shift to the right in 1994 has imperiled domestic partnership laws, the trend toward giving benefits remains strong in the workplace—most recently at Microsoft, Time Inc., and Capital Cities/ABC. Even Coors, perhaps America's most famously conservative company, is studying the issue.

But many politicians, upset by rising illegitimacy and divorce rates, say that such policies fly in the face of concern about family stability. As Senator Trent Lott, Republican of Mississippi, said in seeking to overturn the District of Columbia's domestic partnership law, "We must begin to take a stand for the family." Gay leaders haven't helped themselves in this debate. They invariably urge that heterosexual couples be included in legislation and corporate policies. Many have even denounced the traditional family as a stifling, patriarchal institution, thereby fueling a middle-class backlash.

Gay leaders would be better off making a pro-family case, playing up their commitment to their partners and their desire for a legal union. This argument has found sympathy in the private sector. In 1992 Stanford University extended benefits to domestic partners of homosexuals (but not heterosexuals) because "their commitment to the partnership is analogous to that involved in contemporary marriage," said Barbara Butterfield, a university vice president.

Governments invariably get this wrong, while businesses usually get it right. Every city that has adopted domestic partnership laws has included both same-sex and heterosexual couples, and in almost every case more heterosexuals than homosexuals have filed for partnership status.

But many private organizations—including Stanford, Montefiore Medical Center, Lotus Development Corporation and the Public Broadcasting Service—have extended benefits only to same-sex couples. Most of these companies have said that if homosexual couples are allowed to legally marry, these policies would be ended—which is as it should be.

"This policy discriminates against heterosexuals who choose not to marry," an embittered heterosexual employee at Lotus said. Exactly. And that's a point that Governor Pataki and sensible gay activists ought to be able to agree on: commitment should be encouraged, while relationships without commitment should not expect social recognition or financial benefits.

New York Times, January 4, 1995

Virginia Is for (Homoracial, Heterosexual, Mentally Adequate) Lovers

By a razor-thin vote (49-48), the Virginia State House passed a bill in late February that would allow private companies to extend health insurance coverage to members of employees' households other than spouses or dependent children. The measure was surprisingly controversial, given that it included no legal requirement for companies to cover anybody and that every other state in the union already allowed private firms to offer such coverage. Why was the Republican-dominated State House so reluctant to allow greater freedom of private contract?

In a letter circulated to colleagues, delegate Richard H. Black (R–Loudoun) framed the issue in terms that are becoming all-too-familiar to gay Virginians. Black acknowledged that the bill did not "mandate same-sex benefits" but he warned that the "ultimate objective is to mandate such benefits for same-sex partners," so legislators should not push the state down this slippery slope.

The state of Virginia has been busy shoring up its footing for the past several years. Not content to trust that the federal Defense of Marriage Act would allow the state to refuse to recognize gay marriage, the state in 2004 passed a law prohibiting civil unions with the Orwellian title the "Marriage Affirmation Act."

The language of the Marriage Affirmation Act is incomprehensibly broad. Does its ban on "partnership contract or other arrangement" include wills, custody agreements, medical powers of attorney, or joint bank accounts? Is my mortgage, for instance, shared with my partner, an "arrangement . . . purporting to bestow the privileges of marriage"? This session the legislature moved to make the marriage and civil union bans immune to legal challenge by passing them as a constitutional amendment. If the same body approves the bill again next year, it will go to voters to decide in 2006 whether to write this blatant discrimination against a class of people into the state constitution.

By my conservative estimate, the effort to circumscribe gay relationships is not the Virginia legislature's first attack on private, contractual relationships in the past century; it's the third. The first two efforts are now almost universally condemned, if not always well remembered.

The first push occurred in 1924. At the urging of "progressive" advocates of eugenics, Virginia enacted a law requiring the sterilization of people in state institutions "who shall be found to be afflicted with a hereditary form of insanity or imbecility." Only three months after the bill took effect, Virginia officials found a good case to test the validity of the law. Carrie Buck had been committed by her foster father to the State Colony for Epileptics and the Feeble-Minded after she gave birth to an illegitimate child at the age of 17. The superintendent of the facility asked a state board to order her to be sterilized because she was a "moral delinquent . . . of the moron class."

As William E. Leuchtenberg writes in *The Supreme Court Reborn*, Buck had been "branded as wayward because of her allegedly licentious behavior though, in fact, she had become pregnant because she had been raped by a relative of her foster parents." Her biological mother had also been committed to the same institution, and a representative of the Eugenics Record Office submitted the results of a test supposedly showing that Carrie's seven-month-old daughter Vivian was mentally below average— thus showing a hereditary pattern of mental defectiveness. (In fact, Vivian made the honor roll in public school before she died of a childhood ailment at the age of seven.)

The head of the Eugenics Record Office, who never met Carrie or any of her family, testified that she suffered from hereditary feeble-mindedness. He relied on a nurse who had said, "These people belong to the shiftless, ignorant, and worthless class of anti-social whites of the South." Virginia's Supreme Court of Appeals eventually found that Buck, "by the laws of heredity, is the probable potential parent of socially inadequate offspring likely affected as she is."

It took three years for the case to reach the U.S. Supreme Court, which ruled in favor of the state. Justice Oliver Wendell Holmes, the country's most respected jurist, wrote that there is a state interest in preventing "those who are manifestly unfit from continuing their kind." In conclusion, he wrote, "Three generations of imbeciles are enough." Carrie Buck was sterilized. And thanks to the case of *Buck v. Bell*, so were another 8,000 Virginians and more than 60,000 other Americans. They were forcibly deprived of the chance to have children based on flimsy evidence of their low intelligence.

More than 30 years later, Virginia's longstanding law against interracial marriage—dating back to colonial times and reaffirmed in the Racial Integrity Act of 1924—came under fire. Mildred Jeter, who was black, and Richard Loving, who was white, grew up near each other in Caroline County, Virginia. Eventually, barred from marriage in Virginia, they went to Washington, D.C. to marry. They then returned to Caroline County and lived together.

The Lovings were indicted for violation of the anti-miscegenation law and pled guilty. They were sentenced to a year in jail; the state's law didn't just ban interracial marriage, it made such marriage a criminal offense. However, the trial judge suspended the sentence on the condition that they leave Virginia and not return together for 25 years. He stated in an opinion that "Almighty God created the races white, black, yellow, malay, and red, and he placed them on separate continents. And but for the interference with his arrangement there would be no cause for such marriages. The fact that he separated the races shows that he did not intend for the races to mix."

The Lovings moved to Washington, but in 1963 they filed suit to have their sentences overturned under the Fourteenth Amendment. They didn't expect an easy time of it; a Gallup Poll indicated in 1965 that 42 percent of Northern whites supported bans on interracial marriage, as did 72 percent of Southern whites. The case found its way to the Supreme Court, which unanimously overturned the law against interracial marriage in 1967. Chief Justice Earl Warren wrote for the majority, "The freedom to marry has long been recognized as one of the vital personal rights essential to the orderly pursuit of happiness by free men. Marriage is one of the 'basic civil rights of man,' fundamental to our very existence and survival."

Neither of these now-derided laws is a perfect match with the predicament facing gays in Virginia, but both flowed from an arrogant desire by the state to control private relationships. The state is schizophrenic about such things, but if the past is any indicator, things do not look good for gay Virginians. In the 1995 case of Sharon Bottoms, the Virginia high court took a two-year-old child away from his lesbian mother, because of her sexual orientation. If voters pass the amendment against gay marriage and civil unions next year, it would have real teeth. Already, many gays in Virginia are talking about moving to Washington or Maryland if what they view as an anti-gay crusade doesn't recede. If things continue on their present course, the state might have to amend its slogan, "Virginia is for lovers," to include the caveat, "some exceptions apply."

Reason.com, April 28, 2005

Don't Put Slavery in the Flag

On April 17 Mississippi voters will decide whether to remove the Confederate battle flag from the state flag. As in other states where this controversy has flared, emotions are running high. An activist who wants to keep the flag says, "We'll lose our heritage [and] our history." A black state legislator says, "When I see that flag, it tells me that Mississippi still cherishes and honors a time when my great-grandmother was marched all the way from Selma, Alabama, to Ebenezer, Mississippi, and sold as a slave."

Strong feelings. Irreconcilable demands. Different views of history. What's a voter to do?

It would seem that I have every reason to side with the defenders of the flag: I grew up in the South during the centennial of the Civil War—or, as we called it, the War Between the States, or in particularly defiant moments, the War of Northern Aggression. My great-grandfather was a Confederate sympathizer whose movements were limited by the occupying Union army. I've campaigned against political correctness and the federal leviathan. I think there's a good case for secession in the government of a free people. I even wrote a college paper on the ways in which the Confederate Constitution was superior to the U.S. Constitution.

Much as I'd like to join this latest crusade for Southern heritage and defiance of the federal government, though, I keep coming back to one question: What does the flag mean?

The spin doctors of the South would have us believe that the flag just stands for a part of history. Yet Mississippi was once part of France, and nobody's proposing to put the fleur de lis on the state flag. Not all our history demands official commemoration.

More broadly, the spinners say that the Civil War was about states' rights, or taxes, or tariffs or the meaning of the Constitution. Indeed, it was about all those things. But at bottom the South seceded, not over some abstract notion of states' rights, but over the right of the Southern states to practice human slavery. As Gov. James S. Gilmore III of Virginia put it in his proclamation commemorating the Civil War, "Had there been no slavery, there would have been no war." Mississippi didn't go to war for lower tariffs or for constitutional theory; it went to war to protect white Mississippians' right to buy and sell black Mississippians.

Given that, the Confederate emblem in the state flag can't be separated from slavery. So is it legitimate for a majority of the voters of Mississippi to endorse a state flag that seems to celebrate slavery?

The political philosopher Jacob T. Levy of the University of Chicago points out that official state symbols are very different from privately displayed symbols. The First Amendment protects the right of individuals to display Confederate battle flags, Che Guevara posters and vulgar bumper stickers. But official symbols—flags, license plates, national parks—are a different matter. As Levy writes: "When the state speaks . . . it claims to speak on behalf of all its members. . . . Democratic states, especially, claim that their words and actions in some sense issue from the people as a whole."

The current Mississippi flag—three bars of red, white and blue along with the Confederate cross—cannot be thought to represent the values of all the people of the state. Indeed, it doesn't just misrepresent the values of Mississippi's one million black citizens; it is actively offensive to many of them. As Levy writes, "Citizens ought not to be insulted or degraded by an agency that professes to represent them and to speak in their name." Can we doubt that black Mississippians feel insulted and degraded by their state flag?

As long as the violence and cruelty of slavery remain a living memory to millions of Americans, symbols of slavery should not be displayed by American governments. Those who want to honor their brave ancestors who fought for Southern independence should fly the Confederate flag themselves, tend to Confederate graves and hold Southern Heritage picnics. They should not ask their fellow citizens to walk into a state capitol under a banner that proclaims the superiority of some citizens to others.

City News (Newark, N.J.), April 25, 2001

PART **8**

Down the Drain

At Least Eight Good Reasons to Pass a Tax Cut

Advocates of high taxes have denounced President Bush's preferred tax-cut argument, it will help the economy, as outmoded Keynesianism. They have a point.

In his first address to Congress, Bush said, "To create economic growth and opportunity, we must put money back into the hands of the people who buy goods and create jobs."

That sounds like the old Keynesian idea made popular during Franklin Roosevelt's New Deal: Cut taxes and increase government spending to "prime the pump" during a recession; raise taxes and reduce spending to slow down an "overheated" economy. Keynesianism seemed to have been finally laid to rest in the 1980s when President Ronald Reagan argued for a tax cut on supply-side grounds, and even liberal economists now agree that such fine-tuning has little effect on the economy.

But one weak argument doesn't mean we shouldn't cut taxes. Here are eight good reasons for a cut in income tax rates:

- In a free country, money belongs to the people who earn it. The most fundamental reason to cut taxes is an understanding that wealth doesn't just happen, it has to be produced. And those who produce it have a right to keep it. We may agree to give up a part of the wealth we create in order to pay for such public goods as national defense and a system of justice. But we don't give the government an unlimited claim on our money to use as it sees fit.
- Private individuals and businesses use money more efficiently than governments do. People with their own money at risk spend or invest it carefully. You don't find many $600 hammers or insolvent retirement programs in the private sector. Money will do more good for more people in private hands than in government hands.
- High taxes discourage work and investment. Taxes create a "wedge" between what the employer pays and what the employee receives, so some jobs don't get created. High marginal tax rates also discourage people from working overtime or from making new investments. It's true, as some critics say, that our current marginal rates of 39.6 percent (somewhat higher when combined with other taxes) do not depress economic output as much as the 70 percent rates that taxpayers faced in 1980. But most economists now agree that a reduction in marginal tax rates will increase output to some degree.

- Income taxes should be cut because the overall tax burden is quite high right now. As of the third quarter of 2000, federal revenues as a share of the gross domestic product hit a peacetime high of 20.8 percent. Prosperity has made Americans more accepting of the rising tax burden, but the current economic slowdown will make high taxes harder to bear.
- If we don't cut taxes, Congress will spend the money. If one thing is certain in Washington, it is that Congress will spend every dollar it can get its hands on. Every interest group wants something, a road, a dam, a social program, more teachers, more policemen, more corporate welfare, and members of Congress want to be liked. The only way to "put the surplus in a lockbox" is to let the taxpayers keep it.
- Lower taxes are the only real check on the expanding size and scope of the federal government. If we want smaller government, our best strategy is to reduce the amount of money Congress has to play with.
- Elected officials should keep their promises. As a candidate, Bush promised to cut income taxes. As president, he should keep that promise.
- For Bush and Republicans in Congress, this may be the most important reason of all: Republicans win when they cut taxes. Tax cuts unite the Republican base. The tax consumers in our society are well organized; the taxpayers need to be organized, too, around a tax cut program. In 1980, 1984 and 1988, Ronald Reagan and George Bush won three presidential elections by promising to cut taxes and then cutting them. George Bush raised taxes and lost the next election. I wager this is a lesson not lost on George W. Bush.

There you have it: one bad reason to cut taxes, eight good ones. President Bush should drop his weak argument and focus on those that work.

Houston Chronicle, March 2, 2001

The Transportation Boondoggle Bill

Question: How is a museum like a highway?
Answer: Both get lots of money in the "highway bill" that Congress is currently debating.

And not just one museum, either. The massive $284 billion spending bill includes $3 million for the National Packard Museum in Warren, Ohio, where the Packard automobile was first produced. There's also $1.5 million for the Henry Ford Museum in Dearborn, Mich., and $400,000 for the Erie Canal Museum in Syracuse, N.Y.

At least those museums have something to do with transportation, though that doesn't quite explain why they should be paid for by federal income taxpayers. But there's money for three children's museums in the bill, as well, including $14 million for the Children's Museum of Indianapolis. Why are taxpayers in California and Texas and Massachusetts paying for a museum in Indianapolis?

The pork-barrel projects in this bill don't stop with museums, of course. Members of Congress have loaded the bill with 4,000 special projects for their states and districts free money, it seems, that the senators and representatives can boast about back home. It's Christmas in April.

Even the transportation projects don't seem to have much national purpose. Perhaps the most egregious item is $125 million for a bridge linking Gravina Island to the town of Ketchikan in Alaska. According to Taxpayers for Common Sense, federal taxpayers will eventually pay $315 million for this bridge. Here's the deal: Ketchikan is a town of 8,000 people (13,000 in the whole county, and population is declining). Its airport is on the nearby Gravina Island. Right now you have to take a seven-minute ferry ride from the airport to the town. To save people that seven-minute ride, Alaska wants to build a $315 million bridge.

But even if Alaska wants to do it, why should Congress pay for it? Maybe because Alaska's congressman, Don Young, is chairman of the House Transportation and Infrastructure Committee. Young managed to squeeze $722 million for Alaska into the bill.

But he's not alone. The bill also includes the following:

- $2 million to construct a garage on the campus of Lipscomb University, a college in Nashville affiliated with the Churches of Christ.
- $4 million for a graffiti-elimination program in Queens and Brooklyn.
- $500,000 for sidewalks and landscaping in Glennville, Ga.
- $1.5 million for horse trails in High Knob, Va.
- $850,000 for a bike and trolley path in Hattiesburg, Miss.
- $2 million for a parking facility in Bozeman, Mont.
- $14 million for reconstruction of a crosstown expressway in Oklahoma City.

Now you might say that if every state and city gets something out of the bill, then what's the problem? But of course not every state gets an equal amount, or an amount equal to the taxes paid by its citizens. States with powerful congressmen like Don Young get more.

But even if it were fairly divided, why send the money on a round trip to Washington? Why not let city councils and state legislatures decide how best to spend their taxpayers' money?

Local museums, parking garages, and crosstown expressways ought to be paid for locally. Last year's budget bill included money for the construction of an additional lane to the off-ramp of the northbound Ventura Freeway at Van Nuys Boulevard in the San Fernando Valley. A better example of a local project might be hard to imagine. Though the Gravina Island Bridge might top it.

Rep. Jeff Flake (R-Ariz.) has introduced a bill to turn over responsibility for highways and transportation to the states. He would also roll the federal gasoline tax back from 18 cents a gallon to 2 cents, allowing the states to raise gas taxes if necessary to fund projects locally. Some state legislatures have endorsed the idea, though many local politicians like getting free money from Washington to build local projects.

As transportation economist Gabriel Roth writes in a Cato Institute study, "States fully responsible for their own roads would have stronger incentives to ensure that funds paid by road users were spent efficiently. For example, in the absence of federal grants for new construction, some states could prefer to better manage and maintain their existing roads rather than build new ones. Others might find ways to encourage the private sector to assume more of the burden of road provision—for example, by contracting with private firms to maintain their roads to designated standards or to provide new roads."

If Congresses passes the transportation boondoggle bill, President Bush should veto it and tell Congress to consider new ideas that would be better for taxpayers and better for transportation.

San Gabriel Valley Tribune, April 11, 2005

Budget Cuts: Less Than Meets the Eye

The Education Department's budget is $33.5 billion, so abolishing the department would save the taxpayers $33.5 billion right? Wrong. Under House Republican legislation, taxpayers would save only about 10 percent of that sum. Many programs would be transferred to other Cabinet departments, and the legislation would provide $11 billion in block grants to states.

Energy Secretary Hazel R. O'Leary recently told a House subcommittee that abolishing the Energy Department would save only $3.5 million—the budget for her office and support staff. She obviously assumed that the department's functions would remain in the federal bureaucracy.

Pointing to proposals to kill departments and shift their programs to others, the director of the Office of Management and Budget, Alice M. Rivlin, said that "little would be gained by moving the boxes around."

No wonder the Clinton administration insists that Republican legislation to abolish the Commerce, Education and Energy Departments is a waste of time.

Some Republicans in Congress seem to have forgotten the lessons of the Reagan administration, the message of the 1994 elections and the real reasons to abolish agencies.

Ronald Reagan took office in 1981 promising to abolish two Cabinet departments, Energy and Education. Instead, he created a new one, Veterans Affairs. His administration did squeeze financing for a lot of agencies. But rather than put them on a track to elimination, the bureaucrats bided their time—and came back strong in the Bush administration.

Take the Small Business Administration, a classic candidate for elimination by a free-market administration. As David Frum pointed out in his book *Dead Right*, the Reaganites managed to reduce its budget from $2 billion to $85 million. But the agency stayed in business and by 1993 it was back to $785 million.

Examples abound: The Export-Import Bank, down from $1.2 billion to $67 million in the Reagan administration, back up to $613 million by 1995. The Department of Education, $17 billion in 1981; down to about $14 billion in the middle of the Reagan years, at $33.5 billion in 1995.

The Senate Republicans propose to halve the budgets of the National Endowment for the Arts and the National Endowment for the Humanities, and to cut financing for the Legal Services Corporation by 65 percent. Defenders will fight the cuts with every weapon at their disposal. So why not make the abolition of the agencies the real goal of the fight so that the battle might not have to be fought every year?

Voters did not end the Democrats' 40-year grip on Congress in order to move boxes on an organizational chart. Many Republicans in Congress still have not grasped how much real change the nation wants.

The real reason to abolish departments like Energy and Education is not to promote efficiency, nor even to save the taxpayers' money. It is that many agencies perform functions that are not federal responsibility.

The Founders delegated to the government only strictly defined authority in Article I, Section 8, of the Constitution. Search the entire Constitution, and you will find no authorization for Congress to subsidize the arts, finance and regulate education, or invest tax revenues in energy research. So the programs should be ended—including block grants for education—and not transferred.

Abolishing departments is an appropriate response to the failure of Big Government. But while a smaller Cabinet table would be a visible symbol of limited government, it must be more than a symbol: it must reflect a real change in the leviathan.

New York Times, July 6, 1995

What Does It Mean to Abolish an Agency?

Many advocates of the free market are skeptical that any president will ever really "get the government off our backs." The more federal agencies are reorganized, the less anything seems to change. So when candidates for president promise to streamline, to reorganize, or to coordinate agencies, these people take it with a grain of salt.

In 1980, however, Ronald Reagan didn't promise to reorganize. He promised to abolish agencies, particularly the Departments of Energy and Education. Those who thought the federal government had no business being involved in energy and education rallied to his cause. At last, they thought, we have a candidate who's promising something meaningful. When President Reagan appointed secretaries of those departments who were pledged to carry out his orders, things looked even better.

Since the Inauguration, Reagan has also promised to abolish the Council on Wage and Price Stability and has discussed abolition of the Bureau of Alcohol, Tobacco, and Firearms. To those who believe the federal government is far too big and involved in far too many areas, this is good news.

But what does it mean to abolish a government agency? To most observers, the answer is probably obvious. To abolish an agency is to do away with it, the presumed purpose being to end the government's involvement in that particular activity. Of course, one might close down an agency and transfer its functions to another office, but that would likely be characterized as "reorganization" rather than "abolition."

But consider the record so far of President Reagan's "abolition" proposals:

- One of his first acts was to announce the abolition of the Council on Wage and Price Stability. However, in the fine print we learned that most of the Council's staff, budget, and functions had been transferred to another department. Only a small (though important) part of COWPS had been eliminated.
- The *New York Times* reports, "President Reagan has approved a proposal to abolish the Department of Energy and transfer most of its surviving functions to the Department of Commerce, Administration officials said today."

- Late last year the administration was debating whether to turn the Education Department into a foundation or to disperse its programs throughout the bureaucracy.
- In September the administration was reported to be considering a plan to "eliminate" the Bureau of Alcohol, Tobacco and Firearms and shift its functions to other federal law-enforcement agencies.

In no case, apparently, is the administration actually planning to remove the federal government from any of these areas. The question then becomes not a serious debate over the role of the government but simply a power struggle between agencies. In the discussion of the Energy Department proposal, for instance, Interior Department officials struggled with the Commerce Department to inherit DOE's functions. Commerce won, apparently, and Interior Secretary James Watt was moved to assure his associates, "I lost on this one, but I support the President."

One would hope, of course, that dismantling a department would at least reduce expenditures. But in the case of the Education Department, the proposed foundation would retain $11 billion in education programs, transfer $1.5 billion to other departments, and eliminate only about $150 million worth of programs. Budget Director David Stockman's proposal for abolishing the Energy Department would result in a savings of only about $1.5 billion out of the agency's $13.8 billion.

It should be made clear that those people who supported President Reagan's call for abolishing the Energy and Education Departments— and other agencies—did so for two basic reasons. First, they believed that the federal government should not be involved in energy, education, wage-price control, or whatever. There are certainly strong arguments against federal government—or any government—involvement in these areas, and Reagan implicitly or explicitly cited such arguments during his campaign. Second, many people support abolition of such agencies as a cost-saving measure. There may be a federal role in these areas, they argue, but it is simply too expensive. Neither of these groups, of course, will get their wish from President Reagan's "abolition" proposals. They are almost entirely a triumph of form over substance.

The only way to reduce the size, cost, and power of the federal government is to abolish agencies and programs. Unfortunately, President Reagan is rarely taking this course. Those who would like to see a reduced federal government should read carefully any stories about the "abolition" of an agency. And they should let their elected officials know that abolishing an agency should mean just that.

Cato Policy Report, March 1982

Bush's Tiny Tax Cut

Just how big is President Bush's proposed tax cut? He wants to cut taxes by $1.6 trillion over 10 years, keeping a promise he made in his 2000 campaign. It sounds like a lot—$1.6 trillion—and that's how journalists have treated it. So, is that a big cut or a small one?

First, it's a total over 10 years. On average, it's a tax reduction of $160 billion a year. Big, but not in the trillions. If you use enough years, any number—tax cuts, tax hikes, spending on bananas—would seem immense.

Another way to look at it is to say: Compared to what? From where will the $1.6 trillion be cut? According to revised numbers from the Congressional Budget Office, the 10-year total revenue figure (including payroll taxes) for the federal government will equal $28.6 trillion. That is the largest amount of money collected by any government in history. The tax cut is about 5.6 percent of the government's projected revenue. That's hardly huge. "Modest," "small," or even "tiny" would be the reaction of most taxpayers.

Indeed, the National Taxpayers Union points out that the proposed Bush tax cut is smaller than either President Kennedy's 1963 tax cut proposal or President Reagan's 1981 tax cut. Kennedy proposed a cut that amounted to 12.6 percent of projected federal revenues, while Reagan cut 18.7 percent of projected revenues. Facing a gusher of tax revenue, Bush proposes a smaller cut.

Too much chatter in Washington focuses on what the tax cut will "cost" or on whether the government can "afford" a tax cut. Politicians and pundits seem to have forgotten that money is earned by individuals, who are taxed to pay for collective (i.e., government) goods. Any money not essential for authentically collective purposes should stay with the people who earned it. We talk about spending money on housing, education, medical care and the like—and that's what the people who earn it will do. The argument is over whether the money should be spent by individuals and their families or by elected officials and federal employees.

We know what Congress will do with the "surplus" if it doesn't cut taxes. It will spend the money. A day in the life of a member of Congress is a constant stream of appeals from individuals, interest groups and government agencies to spend more money on their favorite projects. It's a racket.

Economists call it the problem of "concentrated benefits and diffuse costs"—members of Congress hear from the small number of people who will benefit from each new spending program, but they almost never hear from the large number of people who will pay the bill for each program. A new farm program or education program might mean $10,000 for each beneficiary—so they will take the trouble to make their voices heard. But any one program might cost each taxpayer a few dollars, so they won't know about each new spending program.

The way for taxpayers to protect themselves is to put strict rules on the government's power to tax and spend. We should require the federal government to balance its budget so we never again run up deficits like those of the 1980s and 1990s. And we should reach that balance by slashing federal spending and closing certain federal departments. Also, we should cut taxes now, by more than the Bush administration proposes.

President Bush proposes to bring the top tax rate down to 33 percent. Polls show that most Americans think no one should pay more than a 25 percent tax rate. So one way to improve Bush's plan and let Americans keep more of their own money would be to drop the top rate to 25 percent. For the sake of simplicity there should be no more than two rates, perhaps 25 percent and 15 percent.

The federal government is proposing to collect $28,600,000,000,000 from us over the next 10 years. That's $5.6 trillion more than the biggest-spending Congress in history proposes to spend. We're overtaxed. It's the people's money. Congress should give it back. President Bush's tiny tax cut is a down payment on the tax cut we need.

New York Post, February 18, 2001

Bush: The Biggest Taxer in World History

The Treasury Department reported Friday that federal revenues reached $2.12 trillion ($2,120,000,000,0000) for the first 10 months of fiscal year 2007. In both current and inflation-adjusted dollars, that puts the federal government on course for the most revenue it's ever collected in a year. Indeed, it's the most revenue any government in the history of the world has ever collected. And yet it's not enough to satisfy the voracious appetites of the spenders in Congress and the administration. Spending was $2.27 trillion for the same 10 months.

It seems that the deficit problem in Washington is not a result of insufficient tax revenue but rather the inexorable growth of spending on everything from earmarks to entitlements to war.

To be sure, the U.S. economy is the largest national economy in history, and that's the main reason for record tax levels. And tax revenues are not at their peak in terms of percentage of GDP—though they're getting close. Earlier in the year OMB estimated that revenues as a percentage of GDP would reach 18.5 percent in 2007. But as of a month ago that figure had reached 18.8 percent, approaching the levels that typically produce popular demand for relief. But as spending interests become stronger and more widespread in Washington, popular demand for lower taxes faces more resistance. It seems safe to conclude that George W. Bush will go down in history as the biggest taxer and the biggest spender ever.

Cato@Liberty, August 12, 2007

PART 9

Let the Children Go

Let the Children Go

Aurelia Davis went to the Supreme Court in January to get justice for her daughter LaShonda. LaShonda was taunted by a boy in her fifth-grade class. He grabbed at her and whispered that he wanted to "get in bed" with her. Despite repeated complaints, school officials in Forsyth, Georgia, did nothing to stop the boy.

So Aurelia Davis sued the school district, claiming that under federal education laws, which prohibit sex discrimination, schools should be financially responsible for a student who sexually torments another student.

The Supreme Court justices seemed skeptical of creating what Justice Anthony Kennedy called "a federal code of conduct" for every classroom in the country. Indeed, it would be unwise for the federal courts to prescribe student conduct rather than let parents, teachers, and administrators handle those problems.

But another question was not raised before the Court: Why should a mother have to spend *six years* taking a case all the way to the Supreme Court to get her daughter a safe fifth grade? Why didn't she just put LaShonda in another school? (Of course, LaShonda has long since moved on to high school, and her accused harasser has moved to another town.)

We all know the answer. Students are assigned to schools by the government, and in most cases the only alternative to the assigned school—and even the assigned classroom—is to pay for a private school. If Georgia had a school voucher program, Mrs. Davis could have told the principal, "Get this problem fixed by the end of the semester, or we're out of here." Instead, she had to go to the Supreme Court, where she may still not get what she wants.

Under a voucher or scholarship plan, the state or local government undertakes the responsibility of paying for the education of every child in the district, but it doesn't require every student to attend a government-run school. Instead, each parent receives a scholarship (or voucher) that can be spent for a child's education at the local public school, a different public school, or a private school.

Newspapers are full of stories about education problems that could be solved by the implementation of a choice plan. In November, we read of Greg Nelson, who had recently moved to the Washington, D.C., area. He chose to live in a distant suburb because he preferred the smaller schools there. Research shows the benefits of smaller schools, and it's unfortunate that many school districts continue to build schools too large to provide the personal attention that children need. But if Virginia had a scholarship system, Nelson could live where he wanted to, and still choose the kind of school he wanted his children to attend.

Not long ago, the Baltimore *Sun* ran this headline: "It's a school, but the aura is of prison." The horrifying front-page article told how Southern High School in Baltimore keeps its doors and windows bolted to try to keep out intruders and control violence. But some students hide out in the stairwells, where guards rarely patrol and where the floors are covered in "cigarette butts, broken glass and chicken bones—muck enough to cause more than one student to fall." The principal says, "I'm sure there are streets in Baltimore you won't walk down. I ask my students not to go into Stairwells 5 and 6 for the same reason. It's about personal safety."

Student Sandy Pearce says, "Look at the words, 'lockdown,' 'work release'—it's like we go to a jail." Wouldn't it be good if Sandy could use her scholarship to go to another school? But under the current system, all she can do is circulate a petition for better conditions.

Critics of the voucher system say that we shouldn't "give up" on public schools, we should all pull together to make them better. That's fine rhetoric for a campaign speech. But a child will be six years old only once, and will be in elementary school for only a few years—while changing an unwieldy public school system takes much time and effort.

Why should Aurelia Davis have to spend years fighting a legal battle to get a safe school for her daughter? Why should Greg Nelson have to endure a long commute to find a school district he likes? Why should Sandy Pearce be stuck in a school where her life is literally in danger?

Parents and children suffer while politicians and school administrators say, "Give us just a little more time. We're setting up a task force that will devise a selection process for a comprehensive commission that will hold hearings to develop a master plan to implement a scheduled improvement in our community's schools."

Meanwhile, children suffer in schools that don't fit their values, don't nurture their intellectual and personal development, and may even be unsafe. Let the students get a better education. Let the families choose. Let the children go.

Cato Policy Report, January/February 1999

Congress Waves Good-Bye to Local Control of Schools

Say good-bye to local control of local schools. Liberals and conservatives in Washington have usurped the authority of local communities to run their own schools. The education bill now moving through Congress with bipartisan support involves unprecedented new federal mandates on local school districts.

Among the most notable requirements are:

- The bill would require states to test all students each year in reading and math in the third through eighth grades and once in high school.
- If test scores in a school don't improve enough to meet federal standards, the school would get extra federal aid but would have to change its curriculum and train its teachers.
- After another year of failure in federal eyes, the school would be required to let students transfer to other public schools.
- If the feds are still unhappy after three years, they could require the school to replace staff, turn over operations to the state, or restructure.

The bill also involves lots more taxpayer money, of course. To prove he cares about education and to compromise with Democrats, President Bush proposed $19.3 billion in additional federal spending. The Republican-controlled House then upped the ante to $24 billion, and the Democrat-controlled Senate's version of the bill sees the House and makes the total $33 billion.

There was a time when Republicans—and even some Democrats—complained about federal control of local schools. When the Education Department was created in 1979, many critics warned that a secretary of education would turn into a national minister of education. Rep. John Erlenborn (R-Ill.) for instance, wrote, "There would be interference in textbook choices, curricula, staffing, salaries, the make-up of student bodies, building designs and all other irritants that the government has invented to harass the population. These decisions which are now made in the local school or school district will slowly but surely be transferred to Washington."

Such concerns were not limited to Republicans. Then-Rep. Patricia Schroeder (D-Colo.) predicted, "No matter what anyone says, the Department of Education will not just write checks to local school boards. They will meddle in everything. I do not want that."

Richard W. Lyman, president of Stanford University, testified before Congress that "the 200-year-old absence of a Department of Education is not the result of simple failure during all that time. On the contrary, it derives from the conviction that we do not want the kinds of educational systems that such arrangements produce."

People even used to know that there is no authority in the Constitution for federal intervention in education. For example, an official government document made under the direction of President Franklin D. Roosevelt, the vice president and the Speaker of the House in 1941, contained this exchange in a section titled "Questions and Answers Pertaining to the Constitution":

Q. Where, in the Constitution, is there mention of education?

A. There is none; education is a matter reserved for the states.

But the absence of constitutional authority for a bill doesn't seem to bother many congressmen today.

Now that liberal Democrats have spent years using the lure of federal money to impose rules on local schools, conservative Republicans have decided to join the fun. This expansion of federal power over schools was sponsored by President Bush and introduced in the House by Rep. John Boehner (R-Ohio) with many leading conservatives as co-sponsors.

And then conservatives added their own micro-management of local schools. Sen. Jesse Helms (R-N.C.) and Rep. Van Hilleary (R-Tenn.) proposed an amendment to the education bill that would deny federal funds to school districts that exclude the Boy Scouts from meeting on school property. They're miffed at critics who challenge the Boy Scouts' exclusion of homosexuals. So much for conservatives' defense of local control of schools.

On the other side, Sen. Barbara Boxer (D-Calif.) never previously shy about federal mandates on local governments, complains that the Helms amendment is a "slap in the face" to local control of schools. Sen. Patty Murray (D-Wash.) likewise a backer of federal imperialism, complains that "this amendment is about imposing a federal mandate on local schools."

The most laughable aspect of this depressing tale is the pretentious titles that members of Congress gave to their bloated and meddlesome education bills: in the Senate, the Better Education for Students and Teachers Act; in the House, the No Child Left Behind Act. If only words could fix the schools.

Star-Ledger, June 21, 2001

California's $200 Billion Mistake

We goofed.

That's how a *Sacramento Union* headline writer summed up the past 10 years of math and reading "reforms" in California schools.

After state test results showed that the vast majority of California public school students could not read, write, or compute at levels considered proficient, Superintendent of Public Instruction Delaine Eastin appointed two task forces last April to investigate reading and math instruction.

The task forces found that there had been a wholesale abandonment of the basics—such as phonics and arithmetic drills—in California classrooms. According to newspaper reports, Eastin said there was no one place to lay the blame for the decade-long disaster. "What we made was an honest mistake," she said.

The reading task force found that for many years California's public colleges have trained teachers who do not know how to teach students to read. It urged state education officials to recognize that "reading is the highest priority in California schools."

What kind of school system has to be told to make reading a priority?

Some 450,000 students enter the first grade in California's public schools each year, so we can assume that about 4.5 million students suffered from the system's "honest mistake" of not teaching them to read, write, or compute. The mistake didn't come cheap for taxpayers, either. California spent about $201.7 billion on public schools during the "mistake" decade.

Unfortunately, this problem is not specific to California. About the same time Eastin made her confession, a bipartisan federal panel reported only modest progress toward the education goals set by the nation's governors five years ago. Reading achievement among high school seniors is down, drug use and classroom disruptions are up.

Another survey released this fall found that U.S. students are woefully ignorant of American history. Results of the 1994 National Assessment of Educational Progress showed that 57 percent of high school seniors scored below the "basic" level of history achievement. To achieve the "basic" level, students only had to answer 42 percent of the questions correctly.

Bad as the overall results were, some of the findings raise questions about just what our teachers are trying to teach. For instance, only 39 percent of fourth-graders knew who said, "This government cannot endure half slave and half free" (Abraham Lincoln), only 41 percent knew that the Pilgrims and Puritans came to America for religious freedom, but 69 percent knew that Susan B. Anthony was famous for helping women win the right to vote. Only 47 percent of high school seniors knew that containing communism was the most important goal of U.S. foreign policy between 1945 and 1990, but nearly 70 percent knew that infectious diseases brought by European settlers were the major cause of death among American Indians in the 1600s. One might suspect that our teachers are more determined to teach feminist history and the sins of America and its founders than the basic facts of American history and American achievements.

And what do school officials propose to do about our educational failures? They have just one answer. It's the one provided by Superintendent Eastin in her California press conference: more money. Give us more money, the education establishment says, and we'll start teaching reading and arithmetic. How much money does that take? Teachers in one-room schoolhouses with McGuffey's Readers taught children to read. Today California spends about $5,000 per pupil (which is actually less than the national average of $6,300 per pupil), or some $150,000 per classroom, and its top education official says that's not enough to teach reading and arithmetic.

The problem with U.S. schools is not lack of funding. The problem is that the schools are run by a bureaucratic government monopoly, which is increasingly isolated from competitive or community pressures. We expect good service from businesses because we know—and we know that they know—that we can go somewhere else if we're not happy. We instinctively know we won't get good service from the post office or the Division of Motor Vehicles because we can't go anywhere else.

So why, on the eve of the 21st century, are we still running our schools like the post office instead of Federal Express? We need to open up education to competition. Let parents choose the schools they think will be best for their children, without making them pay once for government schools and again for an independent school. Take that $5,000 or $6,000 the government spends on each child's education and give it to the parents as a scholarship. Then let the parents take the scholarship to any school, public or private, that they think will best meet their child's needs.

You can bet that if schools had to depend on satisfying customers, there wouldn't be many that decided to skip phonics and math for 10 years and then say, "We made an honest mistake." Long before 10 years had passed, the students and their families would be gone.

Cato.org, 1995

Can Government Put Values in the Schools?

Concerns about the quality of the public schools and a general moral decline in society have combined to produce a growing interest in teaching values in the schools. From the Rainbow Curriculum in New York City to the attempt in Lake County, Florida, to teach students that "American culture is superior to other foreign or historic cultures" to the Vista, California, school board's policy that teachers discuss the "scientific evidence" that challenges the theory of evolution, different groups are trying to impose their values on all students through control of the public schools.

An obvious problem, of course, is what values—or whose values—to teach. Many civil libertarians answer that question by declaring that no one's values should be taught in public schools, though they rarely seem to object to the schools' teaching students the values of racial tolerance, environmental responsibility, and safe sex. And critics point out that if it were possible to entirely strip the curriculum of values, children would get the message that values are not important.

Some people say that there must be values on which we can all agree-not political or religious values but a basic moral code. Congress recently debated adding character education to the latest education bill. Rep. George Miller (D-Calif.) proposed a national conference and demonstration projects to promote the teaching of such values as honesty, responsibility, and caring. A *Wall Street Journal* reporter was mystified at the failure in committee of Miller's amendment. "Only in Washington," he wrote, "could teaching children to refrain from lying, cheating or stealing be an issue." But Rep. Dick Armey (R-Tex.) correctly pointed out that we don't need bureaucrats in Washington deciding what to teach in millions of classrooms nationwide.

Many teachers object to even the most basic values teaching. According to Charles L. Glenn and Joshua Glenn, writing in *First Things*, a recent survey of undergraduates at one of the country's most selective schools of education found that nearly half would refuse to use a teaching method that relied on "a conscious effort to teach specific virtues and character traits such as courage, justice, self-control, honesty, responsibility, practicing charity, obeying lawful authority, etc." Take a look at that list. There's no mention of such controversial issues as religion or sexuality. Conservatives would criticize the list for being insipid and baseless, ignoring the roots of virtue and character. Yet almost half of our brightest future teachers would refuse to teach such values.

When schools do establish character-education programs, they are often laughably banal. In Tyler, Texas, many schools declare a value of the month, which businesses advertise on billboards or store-window signs. Police officers hand out baseball-style cards featuring their pictures on the front and their favorite value on the back. As Dave Barry would say, I'm not making this up.

Honesty, charity, and self-control are fine, but the fact is that we do want our children to learn certain political values. A free society needs a political and civic culture supportive of freedom and of constitutional republicanism. Students should leave school with a healthy understanding of the roles of private property, the rule of law, the Constitution, the Bill of Rights, the separation of powers, and the independent judiciary in securing freedom, as well as the basic liberal virtues of toleration, openness, independent thinking, and mutual respect. Theoretically, public schools transmit those values to the next generation.

Some advocates of public schools charge that private schools couldn't be trusted to do so, that they might instead teach a whole range of illiberal values from Ku Kluxism to Farrakhanism. If true, that would be a concern for those of us who advocate educational freedom. But at present, there seems to be no evidence that private schools inculcate values inimical to civil society. In fact, most private schools display a value-based sense of mission, unlike most public schools.

Education of course is closely associated with the concept of indoctrination, which should lead us to worry about putting the education of all children into the hands of the state. As John Stuart Mill warned, "A general state education is a mere contrivance for moulding people to be exactly like one another. . . . It establishes a despotism over the mind."

I think that we do not want politically correct activists imposing a Rainbow Curriculum on 1 million New York City children. Nor do we want Ralph Nader and the National Education Association imposing a new civics curriculum that requires children to participate in movements for social change. At the same time, we should not want rival groups of activists to impose an unscientific creationist curriculum on the schools or to teach that "family values" require intolerance toward gay families.

The fact that competitive markets produce better quality is a good argument for school choice. An even better argument is that the values our children are taught in schools should not be a political football. We will get stronger, more sensible values—and values that reflect the wishes of individual parents—from a diverse, competitive system of private schools than from a politically controlled, bureaucratically run, state monopoly school system.

Cato Policy Report, July/August 1994

The Big Flaw in School Reform

Secretary of Education Lamar Alexander is shaking the department out of its lethargy. He may even give the Bush administration a domestic policy. And, happily for the nation, he seems to understand that the quality of education is not measured by how much it costs.

But the contradictions that have marked conservatives' education policies for a decade are still evident in Mr. Alexander's plan. His two major proposals are to create a national student achievement test and to give parents more choice in where to send their children to school—to centralize and decentralize at the same time.

As the education consultant Lawrence Uzzell has pointed out, school reformers can generally be grouped into two camps: neo-pluralists and neo-centralists. Neo-pluralists believe decisions about education should be made by parents, teachers and principals, and they support plans for school choice like vouchers and tax credits. Neo-centralists, harking back to the Progressive Era of the early 20th century, believe the current system can be made to work with strong leadership and comprehensive reforms drawn up by state or federal officials.

Both camps were represented in the Reagan administration. It promised to reduce federal regulation—even to abolish the Education Department—and to encourage choice plans, but also to restore prayer to public schools and to promote a national curriculum. The confusion between the centralist and pluralist agendas may have been partly responsible for the lack of real progress in education in the 1980's.

Today, with growing recognition that American schools are operated as a bureaucratic monopoly, the neo-pluralists would seem to be in the stronger intellectual position. Dismay over the failures of public education has caused the spread of plans promoting school choice.

But the drive for national tests and a strengthened Education Department attests to the lingering attraction of the centralist model. Since the Progressive Era, the assumption has been that experts in centralized offices would design the best schools. The number of districts fell from 100,000 in 1946 to 18,000 by 1970, and most districts became far too large for any real parental involvement. Spending on education has soared—per-pupil expenditures have quadrupled in real terms since World War II—yet the declining quality of education has become a national scandal.

The public schools have failed because they are essentially socialist institutions: one system for the entire society, centrally directed and managed, with little use for competition or market incentives.

And, much like Soviet factories, the schools have become backward, over-staffed and unresponsive to consumer demand, operated instead for the convenience of bureaucrats. With every year, they become more incapable of keeping up with the needs of a dynamic, diverse society.

National achievement tests won't bring about the decentralization that schools need. Formal standards for what students should know would lead all schools to teach the same subjects at the same time, as early as the fourth grade. Children have varying abilities, and they naturally learn in spurts while focusing on subjects that interest them. Schools should accommodate their needs rather than create a one-size-fits-all curriculum.

But letting schools experiment doesn't fit the mechanistic models of the testers. Tests designed by experts are a relic of the era when intellectuals believed that centralization, professionalization and bureaucracy were the way to organize an extended society. Matching schools to the needs and interests of children will never be done by pilot programs directed by the Education Department, nor will diversity be encouraged by national tests. What is needed instead is the diversity and individualization engendered by a free market.

Conservative reformers need to make up their minds: do they want choice and decentralization, or national tests and standards?

New York Times, May 30, 1991

The Trouble with Compulsory Schooling

Rereading *The Twelve-Year Sentence* a quarter-century after it was first published is an interesting experience. By many measures it would seem that the time is even more ripe to discuss the problems with compulsory schooling. Not a week goes by without another report on the declining or inadequate quality of the government schools. Polls show that public dissatisfaction continues to grow. Even as the schools fail to teach children reading, writing, and arithmetic, they are expanding their warrant into new areas. Education theorists explain that we can no longer teach morality in the government schools because not all Americans hold the same moral values. Fair enough. But this turns out to be mere cover for a very different position: that the schools shouldn't teach *traditional* morality, that is, the values of patriotism, free enterprise, sexual restraint, and especially traditional religion. In fact, today's schools—especially in large metropolitan areas and university towns—vigorously push such politically charged moral values as anti-business environmentalism, welfare statism, multiculturalism, anti-racism, anti-sexism, "safe sex," victimology, and faith in big government. The schools have not in fact become value-neutral, as bad as that would be; they have simply changed the particular morality they seek to impose on impressionable young minds. In the 1990s, one of the latest educational innovations is to require "community service" for high school graduation. (The advocates have learned to avoid the Orwellian term "mandatory volunteerism.") So the compulsion is compounded; not only are children forced to attend school, ostensibly in order to prepare themselves for the adult world, now they are forced to labor on behalf of others.

The compulsion is also compounded now as a result of teachers' apparent inability to make their classes interesting. In the era of the therapeutic state, when children—especially young boys—are bored and restless in class, the solution is to declare them victims of attention deficit disorder (ADD) and drug them with Ritalin. It makes me think there may be a great deal of wisdom in the words of an experienced teacher profiled on television: "We don't need to get kids ready for school, we need to get schools ready for kids."

In response to many of these problems, much agitation for educational change has arisen. Parents in many cities and states have demanded the right to send their children to any school, government or independent, that they choose, without having to pay extra for non-government education. A handful of legislatures have responded with "voucher" or "school choice" programs, and more are likely to do so in the near future. Other activists have tried to create more diversity within the government school system, with charter schools, magnet schools, and "public school choice." For-profit companies have undertaken to run some government schools. An uncertain number of children—perhaps as many as a million—are being educated outside of any formal school, as "homeschooling" has caught the imagination of hundreds of thousands of parents. A movement has even arisen to make education as independent of government as religion is. Sheldon Richman published *Separating School and State: How to Liberate America's Families* in 1994, and about that time (but independently) the Separation of School and State Alliance was created.

But a few problems confront the enthusiast for educational freedom. First, despite all the agitation for reform, the government school system goes merrily on its way, collecting more tax dollars every year even in the face of swelling criticism. Second, few education reformers even think of challenging something as fundamental as compulsory schooling laws. To the writers in this book, today's reforms would seem like rearranging deck chairs on the Titanic. Third, and most disconcertingly, despite all the concerns about declining quality and moral values in the government schools, they continue to enroll about 88 percent of American children, with about 11 percent attending private schools and 1 percent being homeschooled.

Given everything we have heard about the quality of government schools, why do the overwhelming majority of parents continue to send their children to them? Yes, it's true that polls show most people think the nation's schools are bad but their own are pretty good. (But *why* do they think that?) And yes, people who are taxed to pay for a "free" service have less money available to purchase the service elsewhere. Even so, people who care about their children's education ought to be inclined to sacrifice for it. Instead, the percentage of parents using private schools has remained virtually stable for 30 years.

It seems that advocates of educational freedom—and indeed advocates of education—must do more than criticize the existing system and offer policy reforms. They must exhort parents to exercise their responsibility for their children's wellbeing. It can't be enough to send one's children to school, or even to move to a suburb with a reputation for good schools. Parents need to investigate whether the local schools are adequately preparing children for adulthood, and are well suited to their children's particular needs, and then consider other options if necessary. Along with "talk to your children about drugs," we need public service campaigns urging parents "talk to your children about their schools; are they learning anything?"

The papers in *The Twelve-Year Sentence* were prepared in 1972 and published in 1974, at the end of a heady decade of political and cultural turmoil. The prospects for radical change, even in such a pillar of the welfare state as compulsory schooling, must have seemed very real at the time. Today, in an era of peace and prosperity, radical change seems unlikely. But events have a way of surprising us, and economic and cultural changes often swamp mere politics. The globalization of the economy has forced new efficiencies on most of our industries, and it may yet demand that American workers and entrepreneurs find a decent education one way or another. Technology is revolutionizing every form of information transfer *except* schooling (and of course the U.S. Postal Service), and it's likely that the schools won't be impervious to change forever. In *School's Out: Hyperlearning, the New Technology, and the End of Education*, Lewis J. Perelman suggests that trying to improve the government school system in the 1990s is like a great national effort to improve horses in the 1890s: it completely misses the revolutionary changes that are going to make schools obsolete in the near future.

Still, there are important philosophical issues at stake in the debate over compulsory schooling that should not be simply ignored as technology and economic change make the laws increasingly irrelevant. There have always been those who regarded children as collective property, to be shaped and molded according to the state's needs. Benjamin Rush, a signer of the Declaration of Independence, is often quoted in this regard: "Let our pupil be taught that he does not belong to himself, but that he is public property. Let him be taught to love his family, but let him be taught at the same time that he must forsake and even forget them when the welfare of his country requires it." German thinkers from Luther to Fichte to the Prussian monarchs developed a theory and practice of compulsory government schooling to serve the state. Horace Mann and other architects of the American compulsory-schooling system were admirers of the Prussian approach.

Today one rarely hears educators being as blunt as Rush, but his theme is still there. In 1981 William H. Seawell, a professor of education at the University of Virginia, told a crowd that "public schools promote civic rather than individual pursuits" and that "each child belongs to the state." A Michigan school district recently objected to a child's being allowed to "escape" from his own district and attend a government school in a neighboring district.

And the will to power involved in the combination of compulsory schooling and government-run schools may have been summed up by Winnie Mandela, campaigning in 1994 in South Africa's first all-races election. She promised "free and compulsory education" for all, then added, "Parents not sending their children to school will be the first prisoners of the ANC [African National Congress] government." That would be a party-state that took indoctrination seriously.

Educational libertarians can easily reject the claim that "each child belongs to the state." But neither libertarianism nor any other political philosophy seems to have a well-thought-out theory of children's rights. Few would argue that children have *no* rights, that they can be ignored or abused at will by their parents or by any other party. But on the other hand few would argue that children have the same rights as adults. So for the purposes of our discussion here, there are some crucial questions to be answered: Do children have the right to decide whether to go to school? At what age? If they have such a right, should it require a positive check-off—that is, children go to school *unless* they assert their right not to? And conversely, do children have a right to be educated? If so, against whom is that right directed? Their parents? The state? And how much education are they entitled to?

A good philosophical case against compulsory education must rest on answers to such questions. Of course, many educational libertarians would point out that a good utilitarian case against compulsory schooling can be constructed without developing a full philosophical case. E. G. West has demonstrated, here and elsewhere, that almost all children in Great Britain and the United States were being educated privately before the introduction of free, compulsory education, and surely there is a presumption against state action when the need hasn't been proved. H. George Resch would point to the difficulty of designing an adequate one-size-fits-all education for myriad diverse children. Joel Spring would argue that state education will necessarily serve the state and its ruling elites. Economists would point out the dismal record of monopolies and captive customers compared with competitive markets and consumers who are free to choose. Many educational critics would agree that, theory aside, in practice compulsory schooling has by no means produced universal education. A very practical argument against compulsory schooling for teenagers has been raised recently by the sociologist Jackson Toby: keeping in school students who don't want to be there often leads to disruption and even violence, creating an atmosphere in which even the diligent students find it difficult to learn.

But perhaps the best argument against compulsory schooling is the one raised by Isabel Paterson in *The God of the Machine*, in the form of a question to educators who support compulsion: "Do you think nobody would *willingly* entrust his children to you or pay you for teaching them? Why do you have to extort your fees and collect your pupils by compulsion?"

foreword to *The Twelve-Year Sentence: Radical Views of Compulsory Schooling*, edited by William F. Rickenbacker (San Francisco: Fox & Wilkes, 1999)

A Right to Safer Schools

Two students were shot, one fatally, in D.C. schools during January. After the murder of 16-year-old Antar Hall at Cardozo High School, a *Post* headline reported, "D.C. Leaders at a Loss for Ways to Improve School Safety." That concession means that not only are children compelled to attend school until age 18, they are forced to do so in danger of their lives.

In a recent Justice Department study, more than one in five male high-school students reported owning a gun. Locally, the number of weapons confiscated in schools more than doubled in the past five years. It is horrifying that school authorities can't keep guns out of school, but it is unconscionable that we force students to spend six hours a day in such dangerous environments.

If Mayor Barry, the school board, and the police cannot keep children safe in school—and by their own testimony they cannot—then we should give children the legal right and the ability to choose safer schools. We could do that by employing a new twist on the hottest idea in education reform, school choice.

Under a classic school choice plan, the state or city would take some portion of the money it spends on schools and give it to the parents of every student as a voucher, or scholarship, which could be presented at any school, public or private, in the area. Instead of all school spending staying within the government system, school money would flow from the school board to the families to the schools chosen by individual parents.

The general argument for school choice is that American schools aren't working very well and that competitive systems work better than government monopolies. Let parents—not just rich parents, but all parents—choose the schools their children will attend, and several things would happen:

- Parents would take more interest in finding out which schools would be best for their children.
- More children would be able to attend non-government schools, which consistently demonstrate better results than government schools.
- New schools would be created in response to the increased demand for educational alternatives.
- And, ideally, public schools would improve in order to keep or attract families that had other options.

School choice proposals have been bitterly resisted by the educational establishment. School superintendents and teachers unions seem to be convinced that giving parents a choice about where to send their children would mean a mass outflow of students from the public schools.

But in Milwaukee, an alliance between state legislator Polly Williams and Gov. Tommy Thompson managed to get a small choice program implemented three years ago. The educational establishment fought it in the courts, but several hundred poor Milwaukee children now attend private schools on government-financed scholarships. Their parents universally report that they're satisfied with the new schools and would not want to return their children to the public schools.

The epidemic of violence in big-city schools provides an urgent reason to give poor and inner-city families an opportunity to escape dangerous schools. The D.C. school board should declare an educational emergency and offer a voucher good in any private or public school in the District to every student who is assigned to a school that has had a shooting or stabbing or more than one weapons confiscation in the past year, whether on school property or on school buses.

In the 1991–92 school year, D.C. spent $9,549 per student, more than any state spent and the highest amount spent by any of the country's 40 largest school districts. For that money the taxpayers of D.C. got a high-school graduation rate of 56 percent. Disadvantaged urban students in 38 states and the District participate in the National Assessment of Educational Progress tests; in 1992 D.C. students made the lowest scores.

For $9,000, students from Cardozo and other dangerous schools could get a better education in a safer environment at a number of Catholic and independent schools in the District. For instance, tuition at Archbishop Carroll High School is only $3,850 a year, while Gonzaga charges $7,100. For elementary school, a voucher worth only half what the public schools spend would get students into a number of safer and better schools.

No child should be forced to attend a dangerous school. Let's give students at such schools an alternative.

Washington Post, February 26, 1995

Five Myths about School Choice

School choice received another setback in Colorado on Election Day, but voucher plans will be back before legislators and voters in many states in the next two years. Conservatives in the Bush administration and elsewhere have made vouchers a key part of their education agenda, along with national standards for educational achievement, to be measured by state, regional, or national tests.

Few observers have pointed out the conflict between these proposals. National standards tend to create centralization and uniformity; choice tends toward decentralization, competition, and diversity. If the problem is that our schools are stagnant, bureaucratic, and unproductive, then the last thing we need is national tests demanding that every fourth-grader in America learn the same things at the same time. Parental choice is the remedy that will bring the benefits of competition and innovation into our school system.

Congress has been more receptive to the national-standards proposal—which tends to give the federal government more power—than to choice, which would tend to disperse power. But fortunately choice plans are spreading through states and cities, from East Harlem to Milwaukee to Minnesota and on to initiatives like the 1994 vote in California, which is as it should be in a federal republic.

In response to the growing demand for educational choice, defenders of the education monopoly have thrown up a smokescreen of charges against vouchers. Many of the charges are the same complaints that have always been made against competitive capitalism. In fact, if American history had evolved such that education was provided privately with school stamps for the poor, but food was sold in government-run grocery stores with assigned geographical areas and a Central Grocery Authority in every city and a State Department of Public Nourishment laying down the rules, the nourishment establishment would be telling us, "Of course private enterprise can provide education, but food is different."

There are several specific charges that will be hurled against any choice plan, none of which hold up under careful examination.

• *"Choice Won't Help Unaware Parents."* One of the most revealing criticisms of educational choice is that it won't help parents who are uneducated, unambitious, or unaware. There is a great deal of paternalism, if not outright racism, in this charge. It's not the parents in Scarsdale and Fairfax County who are said to be unable to choose their children's schools; it's the parents in the ghetto.

There is simply no evidence that most poor black parents cannot do an adequate job of finding good schools—if they have the wherewithal to do so and they know that their involvement in the decision will make a difference. *Education Week* has reported that suburban school districts are setting up elaborate programs to apprehend and expel the urban students who are sneaking into suburban schools in order to get a better education.

As for inner-city parents being able to choose among many different schools, it really isn't necessary for all or even most consumers to be well informed about market alternatives; a small number of educated consumers will force all suppliers to compete for *their* business, thereby providing reasonable combinations of price and quality for all their customers. For instance, my mother read the grocery ads carefully and compared the price and quality of meats and produce at different groceries. I just dash into the Safeway down the block and buy what's available. But because there are shoppers like my mother, I can be reasonably certain that Safeway and its competitors are attempting to offer the best value for the money possible. Certainly even an ignorant consumer like me is better off than if the government ran all the groceries in town.

• *"Choice Would Enhance Segregation."* Critics frequently charge that choice would lead to more racial segregation in the public schools. In large measure this argument stems from memories of the "segregation academies" set up in some Southern cities in response to the busing orders of the 1970s. But it reflects a misunderstanding of the situation in our schools today. In the first place, choice would have the greatest effects in our inner cities, where the public schools are already effectively segregated. In Manhattan, for instance, the public schools are nearly 90 percent black or Hispanic, while the private schools are more than 80 percent white. Nationally there is a smaller percentage of black students in private schools but less racial segregation *within* the private sector. By definition, the movement of children from the almost-all-black public schools to the less-black private schools would increase integration.

• *"Choice Means the Public Schools Won't Be a Melting Pot."* The traditional argument in favor of a unitary, near-monopoly school system is based on the myth of the American melting pot: Everyone goes to the same school and learns to get along with people of different races, different incomes, different cultures. In small towns this myth may still be reality. But most Americans now live in cities or suburbs, and there's much less social interaction in those schools. Inner-city schools are overwhelmingly poor and black. Suburban schools are heavily middle- and upper-middle-class. And even if they are racially integrated, almost all the students come from families of similar socioeconomic status. Charles Glenn, a long-time equal-opportunity advocate in the Massachusetts Department of Education, points out that "the student body of the elite boarding school Phillips Academy in Andover, Massachusetts, is more diverse than is that of Andover High School."

The melting pot theme emerged in the late 19th century as a rather un-American fear of diversity. The Progressive reformers wanted everyone to receive the same education designed by those elite reformers. One of the oft-stated goals of the reformers was to "Christianize the immigrants"—most of whom were Catholic. To do that they tried to discourage attendance at private and parochial schools, a campaign that was most pronounced in Oregon's attempt to ban nongovernment schools. What those reformers did not realize is that the United States thrives on diversity. Our common commitment is to political and economic freedom, not to a particular set of religious and moral values. We are most likely to produce students with the values of both individualism and respect for others by allowing parents to choose from a diverse array of schools.

• *"There Aren't Enough Schools."* Perhaps the most absurd criticism of educational choice is that students can't really benefit because there aren't enough private schools to absorb all the students who might want to transfer: In response to two lawsuits demanding voucher programs, the *Washington Post* editorialized recently, "But choice . . . is unlikely to help much. There aren't enough private or parochial schools in either Los Angeles or Chicago or anyplace else to help more than a relatively small number of carefully chosen kids. What of the rest? Who will 'liberate' them?" People who make such charges misunderstand the nature of the free market.

The market is constantly responding to changes in supply and demand. A few years ago there were no personal computer stores and no video stores. And there certainly wasn't enough poultry and seafood in the groceries a few years ago to satisfy today's demand for lower-fat foods. But when demand arose for such products—or when entrepreneurs perceived that there would be demand if the products were made available—stores were established to meet the demand. On every block, old stores are closing and new stores are opening to keep up with changing consumer demand. When every family has the ability to choose a private school, we can count on entrepreneurs—nonprofit and profit-seeking—to respond with a variety of teaching methods and new technologies.

A related objection is that there won't be enough alternative schools in poor neighborhoods. But when all parents in Harlem have $2,500—or $5,000—per year to spend on each child's education, we can expect schools to spring up in response (although many Harlem parents may well want to send their children to schools on the Upper East Side, in Scarsdale, or in New Hampshire). There are, after all, groceries and other stores in ghettos.

• *"Choice Means Giving Up on Public Schools."* This is the last-ditch defense of the education establishment: With educational choice, you're giving up on the public schools. Shouldn't we try to make the public schools work instead? The problem is that we've tried government monopoly for years, and it's just getting worse. Costs keep rising and test scores keep falling—despite a decade of high-priced reform. How many more generations of students should leave school unprepared while administrators say, "Give us just a little more time"? Teachers in government schools, who should know the state of those schools best, send their children to private schools at rates far in excess of other parents—46 percent in Chicago, 36 percent in Memphis, more than 50 percent in Milwaukee— yet they don't want to make it easy for other parents to choose alternatives.

Some defenders of the education monopoly boast that they send their children to the public schools: they say such things as, "When our children reached school age, we moved to Palo Alto, or Greenwich, so we could keep our children in the public schools." For parents who can afford a $500,000 mortgage in an elite suburb, we already have educational choice. It's time to make school choice a little more affordable.

Sometimes the claim is that educational choice would cause a wholesale flight from the government schools. But given the effort of finding a new school, quite possibly farther from home than the neighborhood government school, as well as the natural tendency to stick with the familiar, surely such a wholesale flight would indicate that the government schools are truly terrible. If that were the case, why should we want to force students to stay there? At least the mass exodus would give the government schools a strong signal that they need to reform.

As for the notion that a school-choice plan would allow the private schools to "skim the cream" of the students and leave the government schools with "the dregs," such an attitude reflects a bureaucratic mentality that treats students and parents as a caseload rather than as customers. Profit-seeking businesses rarely describe potential customers as dregs. Schools would develop to meet a variety of educational needs, and some of them would likely be able to motivate the students written off by the bureaucratic schools as unmotivated, undisciplined, or uneducable. Indeed, Marva Collins's Westside Prep in Chicago has a long tradition of teaching Shakespeare to elementary students tagged as "learning-disabled" by the public schools; those students weren't learning-disabled, they were schooling-disabled.

Every argument against choice made by the education establishment reveals the contempt that establishment has for its own product. School boards, superintendents, and teachers unions are convinced that no one would attend public schools if they had the choice. Like Fidel Castro and former postmaster general Anthony Frank, they have a keen sense of the consumer demand for their product and are fighting a rearguard action to protect their monopoly.

Education Week, January 27, 1993

PART 10

The Nanny State

The Republicans, Smaller Government, and Terrell Owens

The Bible tells us that not a sparrow falls but that God knows about it.

Congressional Republicans seem to have decided that the federal government should follow the same rule. Nothing should happen in America without Congress getting involved.

The latest example comes from Rep. Joe Barton (R-Texas) chairman of the House Energy Committee, who called a hearing to investigate the "deeply flawed" Bowl Championship Series that determines a national college football champion.

Where did Chairman Barton get the idea that a college football championship was a matter of federal concern? Well, he might have gotten it from all the other Republicans who have recently subjected all manner of sports to congressional meddling.

Take Sen. Arlen Specter (R-Pa.). He's suggested that the Senate Judiciary Committee, which he chairs, investigate the Philadelphia Eagles' treatment of wide receiver Terrell Owens, who was suspended for being a difficult teammate.

After all, the Senate Judiciary Committee has nothing else to do these days. Except, you know, Supreme Court nominations, rules for the war on terror, habeas corpus reform, grand jury reform, property rights, immigration and so on.

Today's Republicans hold three-ring-circus hearings on steroids in baseball, requiring top stars to testify under oath as if they were Mafia dons. They introduce bills to mandate steroid testing. They threaten to punish Major League Baseball if the owners allow left-wing billionaire George Soros to be a part owner of the new team in Washington.

When Major League Baseball owners suggested that Congress had no authority to investigate steroid use, committee chairman Tom Davis (R-Va.) and ranking Democrat Henry Waxman told baseball that the committee "may at any time conduct investigations of any matter." So much for James Madison's promise that "The powers delegated by the proposed Constitution to the federal government are few and defined."

Republicans have come down with a serious case of Potomac Fever. They believe that their every passing thought is a proper subject for federal legislation.

They vote for a federal investigation of the video game *Grand Theft Auto.* They sharply increase the fines for alleged indecency on television. They hold hearings on whether college textbooks are too expensive.

Last year and again this year, they held hearings into whether the TV industry's ratings czar, which faces little competition, needs government oversight.

"It's impossible to achieve a high quality of broadcasting if shoddy audience measurement practices are permitted to proliferate," charged Sen. Conrad Burns (R-Mont.).

Republicans used to accuse Democrats of setting up a nanny state, one that would regulate every nook and cranny of our lives. They took control of Congress in 1994 by declaring that Democrats had given us "government that is too big, too intrusive and too easy with the public's money." After 10 years in power, however, the Republicans have seen the Democrats' intrusiveness and raised them. They, too, use the powers of the federal government to lavish money on favored constituents, summon us before congressional hearings to explain ourselves, and intrude into our most local and personal decisions.

Federal meddling in football games and television ratings may be more ridiculous than ominous. But the busybody Republicans have taken on bigger matters as well. They have pushed the feds further into the local schools with the No Child Left Behind Act and tried to take marriage law away from the states with the Federal Marriage Amendment.

They overruled a series of Florida courts in the Terri Schiavo case, imposing the massive power of the federal government on a tragic family matter.

In a free society, citizens don't turn to the national government to solve every problem. Indeed, a free society is measured by the amount of life that remains outside the control of government.

We may all be tempted from time to time to say, "There oughta be a law!" when we're angry or frustrated. Indeed, that's why we write a Constitution—to protect us from our own temptations to turn our exasperation into laws, and to protect us from our fellow citizens yielding to the same temptation.

As citizens of a free society, we don't need government to be either Big Brother or a national nanny. We have the right and the responsibility to live our own lives without interference, so long as we don't infringe on the rights of others.

Neither our football teams nor our local schools need Congress's supervision.

Republicans who campaign on the promise of smaller government forget that at their peril.

The Beacon Journal, December 16, 2005

Obesity and "Public Health"?

Health and Human Services Secretary Tommy Thompson says, "Obesity is a critical public health problem in our country."

Wrong. Obesity is a problem for many people, but it is not a *public* health problem. By calling it one, however, Thompson can promise that we, the taxpayers, will pay for everyone's diet programs, stomach surgery, and behavioral counseling. Get out your wallet.

The meaning of "public health" has sprawled out lazily over the decades. Once, it referred to the project of securing health benefits that were public: clean water, improved sanitation, and the control of epidemics through treatment, quarantine, and immunization. Public health officials worked to drain swamps that might breed mosquitoes and thus spread malaria. They strove to ensure that water supplies were not contaminated with cholera, typhoid, or other diseases. The U.S. Public Health Service began as the Marine Hospital Service, and one of its primary functions was ensuring that sailors didn't expose domestic populations to new and virulent illnesses from overseas.

Those were legitimate public health issues because they involved consumption of a collective good (air or water) and/or the communication of disease to parties who had not consented to put themselves at risk. It is difficult for individuals to protect themselves against illnesses found in air, water, or food. A breeding ground for disease-carrying insects poses a risk to entire communities.

Plenty of people in Africa and Asia still need those basic public health measures. As Jerry Taylor writes in *Regulation* magazine: "Diseases associated with inadequate sanitation, indoor air pollution from biomass stoves and furnaces, and contaminated water occur mainly in developing countries and account for 30 percent of the total burden of disease in those nations. Diarrheal diseases, brought on by poor sanitation and contaminated water, alone kill more than three million children annually, and experts believe that two million of those deaths could easily be prevented with even minimal improvements in sanitation and water quality. Approximately seven million die each year from conditions like tuberculosis, cholera, typhoid, and hookworm that could be inexpensively prevented and cured and are virtually unknown as serious health problems in advanced countries."

In the United States and other developed countries those public health problems have been largely solved. For instance, in the 1920s there were 13,000–15,000 reported cases of diphtheria each year in the United States.

Only one case was reported each year in 1998, 1999, and 2000. Before 1963, there were about 500,000 cases of measles and 500 measles deaths reported each year. A record low annual total of 86 cases was reported in 2000. The last cases of smallpox on earth occurred in an outbreak of two cases (one of which was fatal) in Birmingham, England in 1978, almost 30 years after the last case in the United States.

But bureaucracies are notoriously unwilling to become victims of their own success. So, true to form, the public health authorities broadened their mandate and kept on going. They launched informational and regulatory crusades against such health problems as smoking, venereal disease, AIDS, and obesity. Pick up any newspaper and you're apt to find a story about these "public health crises." Those are all health problems, to be sure, but are they really *public* health problems?

There's an easy, perfectly private way to avoid increased risk of lung cancer and heart disease: Don't smoke. You don't need any collective action for that. Want to avoid AIDS and other sexually transmitted diseases? Don't have sex, or use condoms. (The threat to the blood supply did have public health aspects and was dealt with promptly.) As for obesity, it doesn't take a village for me to eat less and exercise more.

Language matters. Calling something a "public health problem" suggests that it is different from a personal health problem in ways that demand collective action. And while it doesn't strictly follow, either in principle or historically, that "collective action" must be state action, that distinction is easily elided in the face of a "public health crisis." If smoking and obesity are called public health problems, then it seems that we need a public health bureaucracy to solve them—and the Public Health Service and all its sister agencies don't get to close up shop with the satisfaction of a job well done. So let's start using honest language: Smoking and obesity are health problems. In fact, they are *widespread* health problems. But they are not public health problems.

Secretary Thompson should not require the taxpayers to pay for individual behavioral choices. But maybe if our taxes go up enough, we won't be able to afford to overeat.

Washington Times, July 21, 2004

The Selective "Right to Choose"

Today, President Bush signed into law a bill banning what opponents call "partial-birth abortion," and feminists are up in arms. After the Senate joined the House in passing the bill, Kate Michelman, president of NARAL

Pro-Choice America, announced that her group would challenge the law in court. "Today, women's right to privacy is being sacrificed to politics by the United States government," she said. "The Senate took its final step toward substituting politicians' judgment for that of a woman, her family, and her doctor."

The National Organization for Women and other feminist groups made similar charges. But only a week earlier, they played a different tune.

In between the House and Senate votes on what NOW called "anti-choice" legislation, the group took time out to condemn a Food and Drug Administration committee for recommending that silicone breast implants be made available again. NOW had no use for women's choices that day. Nor did other feminists.

Senator Barbara Boxer (D-Calif.) denounced the Senate's anti-abortion bill, saying, "I am not a doctor, and I am not God. I trust other human beings to make these decisions." But a few days earlier she had sent a letter to the FDA asking it not to allow women to get silicone implants. Diana Zuckerman, president of the National Center for Policy Research for Women and Families, had earlier complained, "The FDA has placed more emphasis on providing choices to patients, rather than the previous emphasis of keeping potentially unsafe products off the market."

Abortion always brings out the libertarian rhetoric in liberals. At a gala dinner for NARAL Pro-Choice America, Democratic presidential candidates fell over themselves to make the most ringing defense of abortion rights.

Howard Dean, former governor of Vermont, proclaimed, "This government is so impressed with itself in promoting individual freedom they can't wait to get into your bedroom and tell you how to behave." Sen. John F. Kerry (D-Mass.) promised to bring up the abortion issue if he finds himself debating President Bush next year: "I'll tell him, 'There's a fundamental difference between he and I: I trust women to make their own decisions. You don't.'" Former House Democratic leader Richard A. Gephardt acknowledged a change of heart on the abortion issue: "I came to realize that the question of choice is to be answered not by the state but by the individual." With language like that, Gephardt could run for the Libertarian Party nomination.

But the breast implant issue reminds us that too many people these days think "a woman's right to choose" only refers to abortion. After all, it looks like the *only* decision John Kerry trusts women to make is the decision to have an abortion. He doesn't trust a woman to make the decision to invest her Social Security taxes in private accounts that would provide her a more comfortable retirement. He doesn't trust a woman to own a gun. He doesn't trust a woman to make her own decision on where her children will go to school.

And what question of choice—other than abortion—does Gephardt think should be answered "not by the state but by the individual"? Like Kerry, he opposes Social Security choice, school choice, and the right of individuals to choose what drugs they will use, either for medical or recreational purposes. He voted to deny gays and lesbians the right to choose to marry.

And this month we've learned that the most vocal feminist advocates of "choice" don't believe a woman should have the right to choose silicone breast implants.

I'd like to hear a presidential candidate say, "I believe in a woman's right to choose. I believe in a woman's right to choose whether to have a child. I believe in a woman's right to choose any job someone will hire her for. I believe in a woman's right to choose to own a gun. I believe in a woman's right to choose the school she thinks is best for her child, public or private. I believe in a woman's right to choose to drive a cab, even if she doesn't have a taxi medallion. I believe in a woman's right to choose the employees she wants for her business, even if they don't fit some government quota. I believe in a woman's right to choose the drugs she prefers for recreation, whether she chooses Coors or cocaine. I believe in a woman's right to choose how to spend all of her hard-earned money, without giving half of it to the government."

Whatever one's decision on the right to choose abortion, surely that is a more difficult issue, involving more lives and more complexities, than the right to choose a breast implant, a school for your child, to use marijuana, or to own a gun. And yet many of the supporters of "a woman's right to choose" don't support a woman's right to make those choices.

It's great to hear feminists talk about freedom, trusting people to make their own decisions, and limiting the power of the state. It would be even better if they applied those noble principles to more than one issue.

Milwaukee Journal Sentinel, November 9, 2003

Where Have All the Smokers Gone?

Not to the pub, according to figures from Scotland, where anti-tobacco fascism is chipping away at freedom of choice.

Business is down 10 percent in Scottish pubs since the smoking ban went into effect in March, a poll of publicans says. About half of those responding said their regulars were visiting less often and spending less, while only 5 percent thought business was better.

Some people disagreed: JD Wetherspoon, which operates 40 pubs in Scotland and 650 in total, said sales were at normal levels. "It will hit profits for the first year and a half, but you have to think long-term," said its chief executive, John Hutson. "It's going to happen; you might as well make the best of it."

Of course, it may be easier for huge chains to weather a year and a half of reduced profits than it is for a local mom-and-pop operation.

Several years ago I was eating in a New York restaurant with my partner, an enthusiastic anti-smoking fascist. "This restaurant is *non-smoking*," he proudly proclaimed. (This was before Mayor Bloomberg's nanny state kicked into high gear and banned smoking in all restaurants and bars.) "Great," I replied. "I'm glad we're eating here. And people who like smoke can eat across the street."

But that kind of choice isn't good enough for the anti-smoking fascists. They don't want choice: they want virtue. Smoking is a sin, or at least the closest thing they can find to the concept of sin: it's unhealthy. The same people who sport bumper stickers reading "Don't Like Abortion? Don't Have One" never say "Don't Like Smoking? Avoid Bars with Smoking." No: their morality must be imposed on all.

I grew up in a smoking household, and I yield to no one—except maybe my brother and my sister—in my dislike for being around smoke. But I make choices about restaurants all the time, based on price, location, hours, parking, cuisine, quality, ambience, etc. Why shouldn't smoke be one of the many considerations I weigh in choosing a bar or restaurant? There are 925,000 restaurants in America. Surely we customers could choose among them.

For bars and pubs in particular, a big problem with smoking bans is that many drinkers like to smoke. Those of us who don't smoke are prone to saying that more people would go to bars if they didn't allow smoking. But the fact that very few bars voluntarily banned smoking suggests otherwise. Many restaurants did ban smoking, or created smoke-free areas, on their own, because lots of diners object to smoke. But apparently not many drinkers do. Furthermore, bartenders say drinkers who smoke linger longer and tip better.

Evidence about the effect of smoking bans in the United States is mixed. The blogger Dave Hitt presents evidence that the bans usually reduce business. Bar revenues declined in Seattle. Combined restaurant and bar revenues were up in Montgomery County, Maryland, a very wealthy suburb of Washington, D.C., but some long-established working-class bars went out of business.

That may be a common pattern: upscale restaurants and yuppie bars for the brie-and-chablis set do well, but working-class men and women still want to have a beer and a cigarette. That's what one Minnesota bar owner told the Associated Press.

> Dan O'Gara, owner of the St Paul bar and music venue O'Gara's
> Bar and Grill, said he's benefited from the Hennepin County ban
> because he allows smoking. But he worries he will lose customers
> if St Paul goes smoke-free. He said neighborhood bars would be
> devastated.
> "The blue-collar, working man's bar, which is a big thing in the
> Twin Cities, is probably going to be a thing of the past if this
> continues," O'Gara said.

And as Christopher Hitchens says, something is lost when you pick away at people's opportunities to relax, to have fun and to make their own decisions.

Comment Is Free, August 25, 2006

Thank You for Never Having Smoked

Cartoon editors are painstakingly working through more than 1,500 episodes of classic Tom and Jerry, Flintstones, and Scooby Doo cartoons to erase scenes of characters—gasp—smoking. Turner Broadcasting says it's a voluntary decision, but the move comes after a report from Ofcom, which has regulatory authority over British broadcasters. So in this case "censorship" seems a reasonable term.

It's not the first time. France's national library airbrushed a cigarette out of a poster of Jean-Paul Sartre to avoid falling a foul of an anti-tobacco law. The U.S. postal service has removed the cigarettes from photographs on stamps featuring Jackson Pollock, Edward R. Murrow, and Robert Johnson. And in the 20th-anniversary rerelease of *ET*, Steven Spielberg replaced the policemen's guns with walkie-talkies.

On one level, this is just a joke: they are redrawing cartoons to make them more kid-friendly. And just to make the rules completely PC, Turner is allowed to leave cigarettes in the hands of cartoon villains.

But there's something deeper here: an attempt to sanitize history, to rewrite it the way we wish it had happened. Smoking is a part of reality, and especially a part of history. Just look at any old movie. Everyone smokes: doctors, pregnant women, lovers. Real people smoked, too—people like Murrow and Pollock and Sartre. And some of them died of lung and throat cancer, which parents and teachers can point out. It's Orwellian to airbrush historical photos in order to remove evidence of that of which you disapprove.

Political correctness takes on a whole new dimension in American textbooks. No cigarettes, you can be sure of that. But big states and cities, who are big textbook purchasers in America's semi-decentralized school system, have forced "diversity" rules on the textbook publishers. Publishers say they are trying to avoid the old "white, suburban kids" textbook style. But they have instituted quotas that are just as far from reality.

McGraw-Hill's guidelines for elementary and high school textbooks say 40 percent of people depicted should be white, 30 percent Hispanic, 20 percent African-American, 7 percent Asian-American, and 3 percent Native American. The U.S. population is 67.4 percent non-Hispanic white. (And about 1 percent Native American.)

Harcourt demands somewhat fewer Hispanic faces but more African-Americans. The *Wall Street Journal* reports hilarious and depressing stories of publishers' attempts to avoid depicting Asian-Americans as intellectuals or mathematics students, or redesigning the cover of a first-grade reader because the picture of a pig might offend Muslims or Jews. As you might suspect, it's hard to find wheelchair-bound child models, so they have to depict able-bodied children as handicapped—all in the name of greater reality.

But the biggest problem is that the attempt to satisfy dozens of interest groups can sap the life out of literature and the history out of history, as Diane Ravitch discussed in her book *The Language Police*. Textbook editors are told to avoid words such as landlord, senior citizen, dogma, yacht or actress. One U.S. history textbook included a profile and photo of Bessie Coleman, the first African-American woman pilot, but no mention of Orville and Wilbur Wright.

All this activism has resulted in at least one correction of the historical record: Franklin D. Roosevelt spent decades trying to conceal the fact that he was confined to a wheelchair. Historians say that out of more than 10,000 photographs of FDR, only four show him using a wheelchair. Those are the ones that are now used in textbooks. One victory for historical accuracy. However, the FDR Memorial removed the ever-present cigarette from FDR's hands. Orwell's ministry of truth would be proud.

Comment Is Free, August 23, 2006

Traditional Values on Screen, and on Trial

Deploring the Sixties and the sexual revolution has become big business. Myron Magnet may have kicked it off with his book *The Dream and the Nightmare*, which focused on the poor. (The publisher bills this as "the book that made George W. Bush President," but honestly, I don't think you can blame Magnet for that.) He followed that with *Modern Sex: Liberation and Its Discontents*. For the younger generation, Wendy Shalit offered *A Return to Modesty*. Like a lot of conservative authors, she told us that the ladies of "Sex and the City" are a walking embodiment of "the failure of sexual liberation."

No doubt the new rules about sex, gender, courtship, and marriage have indeed brought much heartache. But there's a reason people threw over the old rules. We can point to some sociological explanations—the pill, for instance. Not to mention the pill appearing on the scene at the same time as the explosion in college attendance and the Vietnam war. See Brink Lindsey's book *The Age of Abundance: How Prosperity Transformed America's Politics and Culture* for some of that story.

But there's also a more personal reason that the old rules failed: they too caused a lot of pain. Friday night the TCM channel will broadcast a sweet and sad movie, *Cheers for Miss Bishop*, released in 1941 and set in the late 19th and early 20th centuries. Miss Bishop graduates from college and stays on to teach for 50 years. She never marries. And that means, given the strictures of the time, that she never experiences a full love affair. In her youth she is engaged to a young man, but he takes a tumble with her less-respectable cousin, so of course she can't marry him. Twenty years later, mirabile dictu, she gets another chance, with a cultured and educated visiting professor. But his wife won't give him a divorce, and she can't go off to Italy with a married-but-separated man. So it's back to spinsterhood for Miss Bishop.

I can never remember if this movie is called *Cheers for Miss Bishop* or *Tears for Miss Bishop*. It's presented as a touching story, with 50 years of students returning to celebrate the difference she made in their lives. And so she did. But she gave up two chances at real happiness because of the strictures of the old rules. The old rules certainly had their uses—there were fewer STDs and fewer fatherless babies (there's an irony, considering that it was *the pill* that helped to usher in the new world)—but they also condemned some people to lonely lives.

Watch *Tears*—I mean, *Cheers for Miss Bishop* Friday night and give two cheers for the sexual revolution.

Cato@Liberty, March 28, 2007

PART 11

Public Problems, Private Solutions

Seceding to Gated Communities

Private, gated communities are coming under intense media scrutiny, from the front page of the *New York Times* to prime-time magazine shows on television. An article in the *Washington Post* by architectural critic Roger K. Lewis recently deplored the trend this way: "Welcome to the new Middle Ages. We are building a kind of medieval landscape in which defensible, walled and gated towns dot the countryside."

As it happens, I read those words the morning after my car had been broken into—yet again—on a Friday evening, in the busy Dupont Circle area a mile or so from my home in Washington. Perhaps I will be forgiven if I have more sympathy for walled cities than critics from the ivory tower could muster.

Last fall, as it also happens, I visited some of the walled medieval cities of Spain and southern France. I said to my companion then, "Look at the width and strength of these walls. Imagine how dangerous the world outside must have been for people to spend so much effort building them." I added a speculation: "What do you think history will record as the period in which cities didn't need walls around them—about 1500 to 1995?"

People are flocking to gated communities for a very good reason: Cities are failing to provide the basic necessities for civilized life, notably physical safety.

In a sense, the rise of communities that increasingly rely on their own, private services is a peaceful but extreme response to the failure of big government. Like their federal counterpart, local governments today tax us more heavily than ever but offer deteriorating services in return. Not only do police seem unable to combat intolerable levels of crime, but the schools get worse, garbage and litter don't get picked up, potholes aren't fixed, panhandlers confront us on every corner.

Why pay taxes to a local government that can't provide basic services and physical safety?

Some fight city hall. Others just leave, as have 60,000 D.C. residents since the beginning of the 1980s, both black and white. Around the country, the trend is much the same: Residents are heading for the suburbs or for the safe confines of private communities. Experts estimate that 4 million Americans have chosen to live in some 30,000 private communities—28 million if you count privately guarded apartment houses, which are, after all, small gated communities.

In these communities, the homes, the streets, the sewers, the parks are all private—that is, independently owned and operated by the residents or a development company, not the local government. After buying a house or condominium there, residents pay a monthly fee that covers security, maintenance and management. Many of the communities are both gated and guarded, with entrance limited to residents and approved visitors. Guards patrol the area, with full authority to expel unauthorized persons.

Many have rules that would range from annoying to infuriating to unconstitutional if imposed by a government—regulations on house colors, shrubbery heights, on-street parking, even gun ownership. People choose such communities partly because they find the rules, even strict rules, congenial.

Private developments are often in the suburbs, on previously undeveloped land. But some are in the heart of major cities, such as Washington's Beekman Place off 16th Street across from Meridian Hill (Malcolm X) Park. In the article that caught my eye last October, *Washington Post* writer DeNeen L. Brown's description of the 216-unit complex sounds almost, well, medieval: "Beekman Place looks like a fortress overlooking the lights and sounds of the city below. The development of brick town houses is bordered by a century-old stone wall that once surrounded a castle that once sat on that hill. The stone wall remains as a barrier to the outside world."

Travel agent Bill Klass, who lives there, says Beekman Place "has a village atmosphere. All the neighbors know each other. . . . You don't have to lock your front door."

In some cities, neighborhoods are petitioning to privatize themselves or at least to erect gates on public streets. In Los Angeles, for instance, several dozen communities are closed off, and more are petitioning for barriers, a process that can take anywhere from two years to a decade.

Many social critics don't like these communities. They complain that fortressed enclaves are the essence of classism, a retreat from diversity. Los Angeles City Council member Rita Walters calls the demand for gates "Balkanization of the city." Writer Mike Davis says that gates will "Brazilianize Los Angeles," while a few miles south the nightmare analogy seems closer to home: San Diego resident Bill Dean says that gated communities reflect "the Los Angelization of San Diego."

The answer, according to many of these naysayers, is to tax people more, to put more money into the hands of government so that residents won't take it upon themselves to provide services they once considered the purview of government.

Listen again to the words of council member Walters: "If you're willing to pay the money it takes to wall off your community, to pay for private security, why not be willing to pay for an extra measure of tax that may not be as much, that will benefit the city as a whole and then you don't have to have these guards and walls?"

She continues, "It's like people who . . . won't vote for a bond issue for a public school but will pay to send their kids to private schools."

Indeed it is. But the fact that public officials are so willing to see more money as the solution is, in fact, exactly the problem. As the urban flight and rise of gated communities makes clear, people don't think they can improve city schools, for example, by giving them more money or by "getting involved" in a bloated system that operates hundreds of schools. The Los Angeles Unified School District has some 700 schools, the New York City system about 1,000. Even the D.C. school system operates 167 schools, and recent reports about problems ranging from textbooks to toilets demonstrate how unresponsive the bureaucracy is to such basic matters. Yet their problems clearly don't result from insufficient funds: As studies have shown, the District spends more per pupil than any large city in the country. So instead of paying more for less, people who can afford to move, or to send their children to private school, don't try to make the D.C. schools work, they simply get their kids out.

Nor do people believe that giving city governments more money will improve the quality of other basic services. Instead, many believe that smaller, more responsive private communities are better equipped to spend money in a way that will improve the residents' quality of life. The issue isn't frugality, it's practicality; often people pay association fees that are higher than the taxes in neighboring cities. The difference is that they see the tangible benefit of those payments.

Economists Donald J. Boudreaux and Randall G. Holcombe offer a theoretical explanation for the growing popularity of private communities, which they call "contractual governments." Having a set of rules drawn up by a single developer, who then offers the property and the regulations as a package to buyers, reduces the decision-making costs of developing appropriate rules and allows people to choose communities on the type of environment they offer. The desire to make money by attracting residents is a strong incentive for the developer to draw up rules that work.

Boudreaux and Holcombe write, "The establishment of a contractual government appears to be the closest thing to a real-world social contract that can be found because it is created behind something analogous to a veil [of ignorance], and because everyone unanimously agrees to move into the contractual government's jurisdiction."

Architecture critic Lewis, a University of Maryland professor, complains that residents of private communities are "abandoning the whole 'idea' of city," seeking a homogeneous community in which "their neighbors act and think much as they do."

Well, one might ask, what's wrong with that? Why shouldn't people live among people with whom they're comfortable? Even those of us who like the dynamism and diversity of the big city want some standards. When I dine at a sidewalk cafe, I revel in the vibrancy of the city even when it occasionally means enduring the rantings of a street person passing by. But when my car is broken into, when I feel unsafe sitting in the neighborhood park on a Sunday afternoon, I'm less tolerant.

Like most urban residents, I'm not trying to avoid people of a different color or socioeconomic status. I'm trying to avoid the culture of crime and social decay that I seem increasingly to find everywhere around me. Anybody who accepts basic social customs—don't rob, don't hit, don't urinate on the sidewalk—is welcome in my city. But when I pay high taxes to a city that can't pick up the garbage, maintain public civility, or keep my home, my car and my person safe from injury, living in a gated community starts looking mighty appealing.

Shortly after the *Post* warned about "the new Middle Ages," another *Post* story reported on the residents who are fleeing a "beautifully restored" apartment building in the heart of the city, with "a glorious view" of the Capitol and monuments, because of repeated muggings at the complex. Landlord Linda Look was asked how many of her tenants and friends had been mugged in the past year, and she ticked them off: "Well, there was Tracy and Shawn, and Sarah, and Jesse, and Todd and Kristin, and Jason and Jennifer, and then the other Tracy, and Graham, and Matthew— twice—and Reynolds, and Bill." Somehow she forgot Sarah's mother, mugged as she stepped out of the car that had brought her from National Airport for a visit.

"It's scary," mugging victim Kristin told the *Post*. "It's like we're entering the Dark Ages."

Exactly. And as long as city governments can't keep their citizens any safer than did medieval governments, we can expect Americans to respond just as the people of the Dark Ages did: by taking responsibility for our own safety by walling ourselves off from barbarian threats.

Washington Post, January 7, 1996

Privatize Air Traffic Control

The air traffic controllers' strike is just another example of the break-down of big government, albeit one that will have particularly serious consequences for users of the nation's airways. If OSHA agents went out on strike and President Reagan fired them, we'd all be better off. But an aviation system needs air traffic controllers.

One thing the strike clearly illustrates is how much more severe public sector strikes are than strikes by private sector workers. Because the air traffic control system is a monopoly, travelers cannot patronize a company whose workers are not striking. They are forced to suffer because of the government's monopoly over this service.

In addition, private companies have some degree of control over unions because they have to make a profit; inordinately excessive union demands may lead to bankruptcy for the company, and the union's awareness of this possibility holds their demands in check. We saw this recently in the case of the *Philadelphia Bulletin*, where management threatened to close the paper unless concessions from the union were forthcoming. In the wake of the *Washington Star's* demise, this threat was quite convincing, and the union was willing to bargain.

But governments can't go bankrupt; they just raise taxes or print more money. Businessmen face the test of the market; politicians face only the next election. Thus politicians have an incentive to give in to union demands. Failure to do so will generate hostility from a well-organized bloc of voters and possibly the general public if services are disrupted.

The impact of unions on government services and ultimately on the citizens who are forced to depend on those services is just another reason to transfer such services to the private sector. But how can we transfer air traffic control to private industry? Isn't air traffic something that has to be run by the government?

Not at all. Indeed, the recent record of the Federal Aviation Administration makes the FAA a prime candidate for dismantling. In 1962 the FAA announced a 10-year plan to automate the air traffic control system, but its plans—obsolete from the beginning—were a failure. In 1970 the editor of *Aviation Week*, Robert Hotz, accused the FAA of "technical incompetence and slothful leadership." The House Subcommittee on Government Activities pronounced the plan a failure.

In the 1970s the FAA tried again with its Radar Data Processing system—the one the controllers are complaining about today. A Senate study last fall concluded that management of the air traffic control system was so poor that the FAA had no way of knowing how long its present computer capacity would be adequate.

Air traffic control is too important to be left in the hands of a politically run bureaucracy. The safety of Americans demands a better system.

The Special Air Safety Advisory Group—six retired airline pilots appointed by the FAA in 1975 after a major crash that was blamed on FAA mistakes—suggested that the air traffic control system be operated as an independent public company along the lines of Comsat. A similar plan was endorsed in 1969 by the Professional Air Traffic Controllers Organization.

But such a public company would still be a monopoly, still be subject to political pressures and largely immune from the discipline of the market. Why not move to a strictly private system, either a profit-making company or perhaps a nonprofit corporation jointly owned by the airlines? There's ample precedent.

Aeronautical Radio Inc. (Arinc), a nonprofit corporation jointly owned by the airlines, was set up in 1929 to provide radio communications and navigation services between air and ground. Arinc set up the first air traffic control centers before the federal government preempted the field. After that, Arinc pioneered the development of airborne very high frequency radio, navigational beacons, and instrument landing systems. Today Arinc operates for the airlines the world's largest private-line intercity communications network and the computer system that links more than 40 airline reservations systems. Arinc's specifications for aviation electronics equipment are accepted worldwide. Arinc or a similar company could handle air traffic control.

In several foreign countries air traffic control is a private enterprise. Flights to Switzerland are under the control of Radio Suisse, a nonprofit corporation financed by user charges. Mexico's Radio Aeronautica de Mexico, S. A. (Ramsa), a joint air traffic control project of Mexican airlines, was privately operated until its nationalization in 1978. International Aeradio Ltd. provides user-financed air traffic control services in many parts of the former British Empire.

There's ample precedent for privately operated air traffic control systems. Such a system would operate more efficiently and keep pace with technology. Its rates and wages would be set by market forces, not by political pressures. It would provide American travelers with safe, efficient, technologically advanced services at a fair price.

Cato Policy Report, October 1981

Privatize Marriage

In the debate over whether to legalize gay marriage, both sides are missing the point. Why should the government be in the business of decreeing who can and cannot be married? Proponents of gay marriage see it as a civil-rights issue. Opponents see it as another example of minority "rights" being imposed on the majority culture. But why should *anyone* have—or need to have—state sanction for a private relationship?

As governments around the world contemplate the privatization of everything from electricity to Social Security, why not privatize that most personal and intimate of institutions, marriage?

"Privatizing" marriage can mean two slightly different things. One is to take the state completely out of it. If couples want to cement their relationship with a ceremony or ritual, they are free to do so. Religious institutions are free to sanction such relationships under any rules they choose. A second meaning of "privatizing" marriage is to treat it like any other contract: The state may be called upon to enforce it, but the parties define the terms. When children or large sums of money are involved, an enforceable contract spelling out the parties' respective rights and obligations is probably advisable. But the existence and details of such an agreement should be up to the parties.

And privatizing marriage would, incidentally, solve the gay-marriage problem. It would put gay relationships on the same footing as straight ones, without implying official government sanction. No one's private life would have official government sanction—which is how it should be.

Andrew Sullivan, one of the leading advocates of gay marriage, writes, "Marriage is a formal, public institution that only the government can grant." But the history of marriage and the state is more complicated than modern debaters imagine, as one of its scholars, Lawrence Stone, writes: "In the early Middle Ages all that marriage implied in the eyes of the laity seems to have been a private contract between two families. . . . For those without property, it was a private contract between two individuals, enforced by the community sense of what was right." By the 16th century the formally witnessed contract, called the "spousals," was usually followed by the proclamation of the banns three times in church, but the spousals itself was a legally binding contract.

Only with the Earl of Hardwicke's Marriage Act of 1754 did marriage in England come to be regulated by law. In the New England colonies, marriages were performed by justices of the peace or other magistrates from the beginning. But even then common-law unions were valid.

In the 20th century, however, government has intruded upon the marriage contract, among many others. Each state has tended to promulgate a standard, one-size-fits-all formula. Then, in the past generation, legislatures and courts have started unilaterally changing the terms of the marriage contract. Between 1969 and 1985 all the states provided for no-fault divorce. The new arrangements applied not just to couples embarking on matrimony but also to couples who had married under an earlier set of rules. Many people felt a sense of liberation; the changes allowed them to get out of unpleasant marriages without the often contrived allegations of fault previously required for divorce. But some people were hurt by the new rules, especially women who had understood marriage as a partnership in which one partner would earn money and the other would forsake a career in order to specialize in homemaking.

Privatization of religion—better known as the separation of church and state—was our founders' prescription for avoiding Europe's religious wars. Americans may think each other headed for hell, but we keep our religious views at the level of private proselytizing and don't fight to impose one religion by force of law. Other social conflicts can likewise be depoliticized and somewhat defused if we keep them out of the realm of government. If all arts funding were private (as 99 percent of it already is), for instance, we wouldn't have members of Congress debating Robert Mapplethorpe's photographs or the film *The Watermelon Woman*.

So why not privatize marriage? Make it a private contract between two individuals. If they wanted to contract for a traditional breadwinner/homemaker setup, with specified rules for property and alimony in the event of divorce, they could do so. Less traditional couples could keep their assets separate and agree to share specified expenses. Those with assets to protect could sign prenuptial agreements that courts would respect. Marriage contracts could be as individually tailored as other contracts are in our diverse capitalist world. For those who wanted a standard one-size-fits-all contract, that would still be easy to obtain. Wal-Mart could sell books of marriage forms next to the standard rental forms. Couples would then be spared the surprise discovery that outsiders had changed their contract without warning. Individual churches, synagogues, and temples could make their own rules about which marriages they would bless.

And what of gay marriage? Privatization of the institution would allow gay people to marry the way other people do: individually, privately, contractually, with whatever ceremony they might choose in the presence of family, friends, or God. Gay people are already holding such ceremonies, of course, but their contracts are not always recognized by the courts and do not qualify them for the 1049 federal laws that the General Accounting Office says recognize marital status. Under a privatized system of marriage, courts and government agencies would recognize any couple's contract—or, better yet, eliminate whatever government-created distinction turned on whether a person was married or not.

Marriage is an important institution. The modern mistake is to think that important things must be planned, sponsored, reviewed, or licensed by the government. The two sides in the debate over gay marriage share an assumption that is essentially collectivist. Instead of accepting either view, let's get the government out of marriage and allow individuals to make their own marriage contracts, as befits a secular, individualist republic at the dawn of the information age.

Slate, April 25, 1997

Privatize Social Security

Senator Daniel Patrick Moynihan recently identified the immediate problem with Social Security: excess revenues being used to fund unrelated Government spending. But that just obscures the more important point that the entire system is unfair, illogical and economically harmful.

Social Security (including disability and Medicare) will cost U.S. taxpayers $345 billion in fiscal year 1990. This is almost half of all federal spending, leaving aside the military and interest on the national debt.

The maximum payroll tax was $189 in 1958, $580 in 1967 and $1,931 as recently as 1977. But since then, with seven rate hikes during the tax-cutting 1980's, it has increased to about $7,850 a year. Most workers pay more in Social Security taxes than in federal income taxes.

Representative John Porter, Republican of Illinois, has suggested one way to stop the budgetary deceit that Senator Moynihan, Democrat of New York, pointed out: create an individual Social Security retirement account for every taxpayer, and refund to it the portion of payroll taxes not needed to pay for current benefits.

Other critics would simply let taxpayers invest the entire amount of their payroll taxes in a private super-individual retirement account. People taking this option would forgo Social Security benefits. For many, that's no great loss.

When Social Security began, participants often enjoyed liberal benefits. The famous first Social Security recipient, Ida M. Fuller, paid $44 in taxes and received $21,000 in benefits. But the best that today's young workers can expect ranges from a 1.5 percent return for low-income workers to an actual loss, in real terms, for upper-income participants.

In contrast, those who invested their retirement money in a private savings account could expect a long-term rate of return of 6 or 7 percent. Consider two minimum-wage workers investing during their working lives (from 18 to 67) in a conservative program yielding just 5.5 percent. They would accumulate $450,000 (in 1983 dollars) in their super I.R.A.

Social Security promises them $15,326 a year, but an annuity would give them a lifetime annual income of $49,509. Or they could receive an annual income of $24,878 and leave the entire $450,000 to their children— an important step toward breaking the poverty cycle.

A high-income couple could build a retirement fund of $1.5 million, assuming they contributed from age 24 to retirement. An average-income worker with a nonworking spouse could save enough to receive a yearly retirement income of $21,351 and leave $388,000 to their children.

If everyone opted for super I.R.A.'s, or if these I.R.A.'s were mandatory, they would inject about $200 billion in savings into the economy each year. Banks, brokerage firms and money-management companies could administer the funds, just as they do on a smaller scale with I.R.A.'s.

Not only would such a private system stimulate the productive economy, rather than government spending, it would offer better retirement security and create more widespread ownership of capital.

In any retirement plan, the savings have to be invested somewhere. Currently, Social Security revenues are invested in special Treasury debt instruments, which allows the government to spend money on other programs, from MX missiles to farm subsidies. But to call this "savings" is to fall victim to what economists call the money illusion. All that the "fund" provides is the likelihood of future tax hikes to buy back the bonds from the Social Security system.

Indeed, the former chief actuary for Social Security, A. Haeworth Robertson, has estimated that a payroll tax rate as high as 40 percent might ultimately be required to pay for the baby boomers' retirement. The Social Security Administration's own estimate is 26 percent—itself high enough to cause the economy to grind to a halt, if not cause intergenerational warfare.

An alternative to those phony investments in Treasury bonds is full funding—investing the Social Security Trust Fund in stocks and bonds. But the total capitalization of the companies listed on the New York Stock Exchange is about $3 trillion—precisely the value of the debt the Social Security system is scheduled to amass. If the revenues of a fully funded Social Security system were invested in the market, we would soon achieve full-fledged socialism.

Privatizing the retirement system would avoid the danger of both huge tax increases and trust-fund socialism. It would take retirement savings out of the hands of politicians, inject hundreds of billions of dollars into the productive economy and allow even low-income workers to leave their children enough money to buy homes, start businesses and send their children to decent schools.

If Senator Moynihan forces us to deal with these realities, he will have—perhaps inadvertently—done the nation a great service.

New York Times, March 21, 1990

End Taxpayer Funding of Public Broadcasting

Americans should not be taxed to fund a national broadcast network, and Congress should therefore terminate the funding for the Corporation for Public Broadcasting.

We wouldn't want the federal government to publish a national newspaper. Neither should we have a government television network and a government radio network. If anything should be kept separate from government and politics, it's the news and public affairs programming that informs Americans about government and its policies. When government brings us the news—with all the inevitable bias and spin—the government is putting its thumb on the scales of democracy. Journalists should not work for the government. Taxpayers should not be forced to subsidize news and public-affairs programming.

Much of the recent debate about tax-funded broadcasting has centered on whether there is a bias, specifically a liberal bias, at NPR and PBS. I would argue that bias is inevitable. Any reporter or editor has to choose what's important. It's impossible to make such decisions without a framework, a perspective, a view of how the world works.

As a libertarian, I have an outsider's perspective on both liberal and conservative bias. And I'm sympathetic to some of public broadcasting's biases, such as its tilt toward gay rights, freedom of expression, and social tolerance and its deep skepticism toward the religious right. And I share many of the cultural preferences of its programmers and audience, for theater, independent cinema, history, and the like. The problem is not so much a particular bias as the existence of any bias.

Many people have denied the existence of a liberal bias at NPR and PBS. Of course, the most effective bias is one that most listeners or viewers don't perceive. That can be the subtle use of adjectives or frameworks—for instance, a report that "Congress has failed to pass a health care bill" clearly leaves the impression that a health care bill is a good thing, and Congress has "failed" a test. Compare that to language like "Congress turned back a Republican effort to cut taxes for the wealthy." There the listener is clearly being told that something bad almost happened, but Congress "turned back" the threat.

A careful listener to NPR would notice a preponderance of reports on racism, sexism, and environmental destruction. David Fanning, executive producer of *Frontline* PBS's documentary series, responds to questions of bias by saying, "We ask hard questions to people in power. That's anathema to some people in Washington these days." But there has never been a *Frontline* documentary on the burden of taxes, or the number of people who have died because federal regulations keep drugs off the market, or the way that state governments have abused the law in their pursuit of tobacco companies, or the number of people who use guns to prevent crime. Those "hard questions" just don't occur to liberal journalists.

Anyone who got all his news from NPR would never know that Americans of all races live longer, healthier, and in more comfort than ever before in history, or that the environment has been getting steadily cleaner.

In Washington, I have the luxury of choosing from two NPR stations. On Wednesday evening, June 29, a Robert Reich commentary came on. I switched to the other station, which was broadcasting a Daniel Schorr commentary. That's not just liberal bias, it's a liberal roadblock.

In the past few weeks, as this issue has been debated, I've noted other examples. A common practice is labeling conservatives but not liberals in news stories—that is, listeners are warned that the conservative guests have a political agenda but are not told that the other guests are liberals. Take a story on the Supreme Court that identified legal scholar Bruce Fein correctly as a conservative but did not label liberal scholars Pamela Karlan and Akhil Amar. Or take the long and glowing reviews of two leftist agitprop plays, one written by Robert Reich and performed on Cape Cod and another written by David Hare and performed in Los Angeles. I think we can be confident that if a Reagan Cabinet official wrote a play about how stupid and evil liberals are—the mirror image of Reich's play—it would not be celebrated on NPR. And then there was the effusive report on Pete Seeger, the folksinger who was a member of the Communist Party, complete with a two-hour online concert, to launch the Fourth of July weekend.

And if there were any doubt about the political spin of NPR and PBS, it was surely ended when a congressional subcommittee voted to cut the funding for CPB. Who swung into action? Moveon.org, Common Cause, and various left-wing media pressure groups. They made "defending PBS" the top items on their websites, they sent out millions of emails, they appeared on radio and television shows in order to defend an effective delivery system for liberal ideas. Public broadcasters worked hand in glove with those groups, for instance linking from the NPR website to those groups' sites.

There are many complaints today about political interference in CPB, PBS, and NPR. I am sympathetic to those complaints. No journalist wants political appointees looking over his shoulder. But political interference is entirely a consequence of political funding. As long as the taxpayers fund something, their representatives have the authority to investigate how the taxpayers' money is being spent. Recall the criticism directed at PBS in 1994 for broadcasting *Tales of the City*, which has gay characters. Because of the political pressure, PBS decided not to produce the sequel, *More Tales of the City*. It appeared on Showtime and generated little political controversy because Showtime isn't funded with tax dollars. Remove the tax funding, and NPR and PBS would be free from political interference, free to be as daring and innovative and provocative as they like.

One dirty little secret that NPR and PBS don't like to acknowledge in public debate is the wealth of their listeners and viewers. But they're happy to tell their advertisers about the affluent audience they're reaching. In 1999 NPR commissioned Mediamark Research to study its listeners. NPR then enthusiastically told advertisers that its listeners are 66 percent wealthier than the average American, three times as likely to be college graduates, and 150 percent more likely to be professionals or managers.

But perhaps that was an unusual year? Mediamark's 2003 study found the same pattern. As NPR explained, based on the 2003 study:

> Public radio listeners are driven to learn more, to earn more, to spend more, and to be more involved in their communities. They are leaders and decision makers, both in the boardroom and in the town square. They are more likely to exert their influence on their communities in all types of ways—from voting to volunteering.
>
> Public radio listeners are dynamic—they do more. They are much more likely than the general public to travel to foreign nations, to attend concerts and arts events, and to exercise regularly. They are health conscious, and are less likely to have serious health problems. Their media usage patterns reflect their active lifestyles, they tend to favor portable media such as newspapers or radio.
>
> As consumers, they are more likely to have a taste for products that deliver on the promise of quality. Naturally, they tend to spend more on products and services.

Specifically, the report found, compared with the general public, NPR listeners are

- 55 percent less likely to have a household income below $30,000
- 117 percent more likely to have a household income above $150,000
- 152 percent more likely to have a home valued at $500,000 or more
- 194 percent more likely to travel to France
- 326 percent more likely to read the *New Yorker*
- 125 percent more likely to own bonds
- 125 percent more likely to own a Volvo.

PBS has similar demographics. PBS boasts that its prime-time viewers are

- 44 percent more likely than the average American to have a household income above $150,000
- 39 percent more likely to have a graduate degree
- 57 percent more likely to own a vacation home
- 177 percent likely to have investments valued at $150,000 or more.

Tax-funded broadcasting is a giant income transfer upward: the middle class is taxed to pay for news and entertainment for the upper middle class. It's no accident that you hear ads for Remy Martin and "private banking services" on NPR, not for Budweiser and free checking accounts.

Defenders of the tax-funded broadcast networks often point out that only about 15 percent of their funding comes from the federal government. Indeed, NPR and PBS have been quite successful at raising money from foundations, members, and business enterprises. Given that, they could certainly absorb a 15 percent revenue loss. Businesses and nonprofit organizations often deal with larger revenue fluctuations than that. It isn't fun, but it happens. In a time of $400 billion deficits, Congress should be looking for nonessential spending that could be cut. Tax-funded broadcasting is no longer an infant industry; it's a healthy $2.5 billion enterprise that might well discover it liked being free of political control for a paltry 15 percent cut.

Finally, I would note that the Constitution provides no authority for a federal broadcasting system. Members of Congress once took seriously the constraints imposed on them by the Constitution. In 1794 James Madison, the father of the Constitution, rose on the floor of the House and declared that he could not "undertake to lay his finger on that article of the Federal Constitution which granted a right to Congress of expending, on objects of benevolence, the money of their constituents." In 1887, exactly 100 years after the Constitution was drafted, President Grover Cleveland made a similar point when he vetoed a bill to buy seeds for Texas farmers suffering from a drought, saying he could "find no warrant for such an appropriation in the Constitution." Things had changed by 1935, when President Roosevelt wrote to Congress, "I hope your committee will not permit doubts as to constitutionality, however reasonable, to block the suggested legislation." I suggest that this committee take note of the fact that no article of the Constitution authorizes a national broadcast network.

Even if this committee comes to the conclusion that taxpayer funding for radio and television networks is imprudent and constitutionally unfounded, I recognize that you may hesitate to withdraw a funding stream that stations count on. In that regard, I would note again that federal funding is only about 15 percent of public broadcasting revenues. But you might also phase out the funding, perhaps on a five-year schedule. The total funding request for this year is about $500 million. Congress might decide to reduce it by $100 million a year, leaving the CPB entirely free of federal taxpayer funding at the end of five years.

But Congress's resolve in such matters is not trusted. Recall the 1996 Freedom to Farm Act, which likewise promised to phase out farm subsidies. Barely two years had passed when Congress began providing "emergency relief payments" to make up for the scheduled reductions. This time, if Congress pledges to phase out broadcasting subsidies, it needs to make sure that its decision sticks.

A healthy democracy needs a free and diverse press. Americans today have access to more sources of news and opinion than ever before. Deregulation has produced unprecedented diversity—more broadcast networks than before, cable networks, satellite television and radio, the Internet. If there was at some point a diversity argument for NPR and PBS, it is no longer valid. We do not need a government news and opinion network. More importantly, we should not require taxpayers to pay for broadcasting that will inevitably reflect a particular perspective on politics and culture. The marketplace of democracy should be a free market, in which the voices of citizens are heard, with no unfair advantage granted by government to one participant.

Testimony before Senate Appropriations Committee, July 11, 2005, reprinted in *Vital Speeches*, August 15, 2005

The Benefits of Private Regulation

The world is a complex place. Most of us seek more certainty in at least some aspects of our lives than might seem to occur naturally. Especially in modern market societies, many of us have tried to achieve certainty, security, or stability through regulation. What is often not understood, as John Blundell and Colin Robinson explain in *Regulation Without the State*, is that much of the "regulation" that improves our lives is not coercive or government-created but rather voluntary and the product of market decision-making. Indeed, the most important fact about private regulation is how pervasive it is in our lives, and how unaware of it we are most of the time.

Indeed, private systems that offer us some assurance of safety, quality, or other values take an amazing variety of forms: Better Business Bureaus, *Consumer Reports*, codes of professional responsibility, bond rating services, *Zagat Survey* of American restaurants, Underwriters Laboratories, kosher certifiers, brand names, franchises, private communities, and more.

In political discourse today, "regulation" is assumed to refer to government rules, the violation of which will result in legal penalties such as fines or even incarceration. But the original meaning of "regulate" was "to make regular." That is the sense in which the U.S. Constitution authorizes Congress to "regulate commerce . . . among the several states." Much of the political struggle in modern capitalist countries is over the extent of government regulation. But often the real issue at hand is not whether a particular activity will be regulated but whether it will be regulated coercively, by the state, or voluntarily, through private actions.

Charles Murray urges readers of his book *What It Means to Be a Libertarian* to imagine a law that would allow individual businesses to opt out of the entire system of state regulation. The only requirement would be that stores and manufacturers opting out of regulation would have to display large signs reading UNREGULATED. "Businesses that choose to remain within the regulatory system are free to display equally prominent signs reading something like, 'This business proudly complies with all government regulations.'" But of course, as Murray recognizes, it would be more fair and accurate for almost all the "unregulated" firms to be labeled "regulated by [various private entities and systems]" than "unregulated."

In her paper on the subject and in this volume, Yesim Yilmaz discusses some of the advantages of private regulation, notably its flexible, responsive, and dynamic character. Private regulation, driven by the needs of firms and customers, is much more able to change when it becomes either too permissive or too restrictive or when technological or other changes demand new rules.

In this comment I want to touch on some specific examples of private regulation.

Brand Names

Brand names are all around us, yet we often forget how useful they are in finding high-quality products. Economist Daniel Klein offers an example:

> Suppose the muffler drops off your car in the middle of Iowa. You pull off the interstate and find Joe's Auto Repair. The mechanics at Joe's see that you are from out of state. They know that, regardless of how fairly they treat you, you will not be returning and will not be speaking to other potential customers. Hence, caution is advised. Then you notice a Meineke shop down the road. You will never be returning to that Meineke shop either, but for some reason you have more trust in Meineke.

> Although you will never return to that particular Meineke shop, you might reach a judgment about Meineke shops in general on the basis of your experience at that shop. The franchisee at that shop doesn't care whether you ever go to another Meineke shop,

but the parent company does. The parent company wants that franchisee to treat you fairly, and it takes steps to make that happen. Meineke employs "mystery shoppers" who pose as ordinary consumers with broken cars. Also, the parent company receives and remedies customer complaints. Consumers might not be consciously aware of such trust building practices, but they rightly intuit that some kind of assurance lies in familiarity. The company name is a bit like a friend, and the serviceman wearing the company logo is like the friend of a friend. He is not your bridge to Meineke; Meineke is your bridge to him.

Kenneth D. Walker, president and CEO of Meineke, writes that Klein underestimates Meineke's efforts to ensure good service by each of its franchisees:

> Beyond the training, the resources, and the codified procedures we provide, the Meineke System provides numerous incentives for dealers to deliver quality to every Meineke customer. So in your hypothetical case where a Meineke dealer in the middle of Iowa spies your out-of-state license, he may not "care whether you ever go to another Meineke shop," but there are solid reasons why he should.
>
> Here are a couple of the primary reasons:
>
> 1. A fixed percentage of *every* Meineke sale goes into national advertising, which means that subsequent business conducted by a Meineke customer in New York City *does* substantially benefit the dealer in Iowa City. . . .
>
> 2. If the above math seems a bit abstract for the average Meineke dealer, our Intershop System is more down-to-earth. Linked to our nationwide warranty, our intershop system makes the original shop responsible for parts and service quality *no matter where* a customer might present his or her warranty. So if that replaced muffler drops off again between Cedar Rapids and the Bowery, our New York City shop calls up that Iowa City shop and requests repayment. . . .
>
> So throughout the Meineke chain, if our dealers wish to remain in good standing with the Home Office and their peers—or if they're blessed with enlightened self-interest—we do think our franchisees "care whether you ever go to another Meineke shop."

Meineke and other franchises care very much about their nationwide quality and create elaborate systems—which we could call regulation— to ensure that customers get uniformly good products and services. Retail stores have a similar investment in their reputations, so they also seek to guarantee high quality in the products they sell. Sears, Roebuck and Co., a pioneer in retail catalogue sales that now operates almost 3,000 stores, has been testing the products it sells since 1911. Its Sears Quality Evaluation Center in Chicago encompasses 33,000 square feet. "There's nothing we can't build here," says director Dave Macarus, "or break." Sears tests and sells all the products carrying its own labels (such as Craftsman and Weedwacker) and many of the products it sells under the manufacturer's name. A staff of more than 50 employees conducts about 400 evaluations a month. According to a *Washington Post* report,

> For many evaluations there is no precedent, government standard or easily measurable criteria such as pounds of pressure per square inch. That's when the technicians . . . have to be inventive.

They have to decide what the standard should be for a product and how to test to that standard. "At the Sears lab, experience and common sense bring at least as much to bear on product safety as dry, technical standards"—which might be one difference between flexible private systems and rigid, codified state systems.

Insurance

In a market society, insurance is one of the best regulators. Consumers carry insurance in case they get harmed. Firms carry insurance in case they get sued. In each case the insurance company has a strong incentive to know what liability it is assuming. Insurance companies sometimes deny liability coverage for products that lack the Underwriters Laboratories label. They impose requirements on homebuilders and other firms.

People have often thought that insurance is a valuable service for government to provide. Many of the largest federal programs are intended to insure Americans against economic and other risks: Social Security, Medicare and Medicaid, deposit insurance, flood insurance, and more. The general argument for insurance is that a loss that would be disastrous for a single individual can be absorbed by a large group of similarly situated individuals. We pool our money in an insurance plan to guard against the small possibility of a catastrophic event.

The argument for government insurance, as opposed to competitive private insurers, is that you can spread the risk over a larger number of people. But as George L. Priest of the Yale Law School points out, government insurance has had many unfortunate results. There's no economic advantage to creating an insurance pool larger than necessary, and there are definite disadvantages to large monopolies. Government is very bad at charging risk-appropriate premiums, so its insurance tends to be too expensive for risk-averse people and too cheap for those who engage in high-risk activities. And government dramatically compounds the "moral hazard" problem—that is, the tendency of people who have insurance to take more risks. Insurance companies try to control this by having deductibles and co-payments, so the insured will still face some loss beyond what insurance covers, and by excluding certain kinds of activities from coverage (like suicide or behavior that is more risky than the insurance pool is designed for). For both economic and political reasons, government usually doesn't employ such tools, so it actually encourages more risk.

Priest cites several specific examples:

- Federal savings-and-loan insurance increased the risk level of investments; the savings-and-loan companies would reap the profits from high-risk ventures, but the taxpayers would make up the losses, so why not go for the big return?
- Government-provided unemployment insurance increases both the extent and the duration of unemployment; people would find new jobs sooner if they didn't have unemployment insurance, or if their own insurance rates were affected by how much they used, as car insurance rates are.
- Priest writes, "I will not go so far as to claim that government-provided insurance increases the frequency of natural disasters. On the other hand, I have no doubt whatsoever that the government provision of insurance increases the magnitude of losses from natural disasters." Flood insurance, for instance, provided by the U.S. government at less than the market price, encourages more building on flood plains and on the fragile barrier islands off the East Coast.

The desire to reduce one's exposure to risk is natural, and markets provide people with means to that end. But when people sought to reduce risk through government insurance programs, the result was to channel resources toward more risky activities and thus to increase the level of risk and the level of losses suffered by the whole society.

Still, the market has provided many opportunities for people to choose the level of risk with which they are comfortable. Many kinds of insurance are available. Different investments—stocks, bonds, mutual funds, certificates of deposit—allow people to balance risk versus return in a way they prefer. Farmers can reduce their risks by selling their expected harvest before it comes in, locking in a price. They're protected against falling prices, though they lose the opportunity to make big profits from rising prices. Commodities futures markets give farmers and others the opportunity to hedge against price shifts. Many people don't understand commodities and futures markets, or even the simpler securities markets; in Tom Wolfe's novel *The Bonfire of the Vanities*, the bond trader Sherman McCoy thought of himself as a Master of the Universe but couldn't explain to his daughter the value of what he did. Politicians and popular writers rail against "paper entrepreneurs" or "money changers," but those mysterious markets not only guide capital to projects where it will best serve consumer demand, they also help millions of Americans to regulate their risks.

A new twist for farmers is the opportunity to contract with food processors to grow specific crops. More than 90 percent of vegetables are now grown under production contracts, along with smaller percentages of other crops. The contracts give farmers less independence but also less risk, which many of them prefer.

Meanwhile, major commodities markets like the Chicago Board of Trade, the Chicago Mercantile Exchange, and the New York Mercantile Exchange are looking for new investment options to offer to customers. In 1996 the Chicago Merc began offering milk price futures—allowing people to lock in milk prices, or bet on price shifts—in response to deregulation, which will likely mean lower but fluctuating prices. The Nymex established a market in electricity futures, which will come in handy as electric utilities are deregulated.

The Board of Trade is one of the players looking for new ways to protect insurance companies—and by extension everyone who buys insurance or invests in insurance companies—from the threat posed by mega-disasters. According to the *New York Times*, two of the most destructive natural disasters in American history have occurred in the past few years: Hurricane Andrew in 1992, which cost insurers $16 billion in South Florida, and the 1994 Los Angeles earthquake, which cost $11 billion. (Note that the reason these were the "most destructive" disasters ever is that Americans own more wealth than ever, so financial losses are greater.) Insurers fear a disaster of $50 billion magnitude, which could put insurance companies out of business and even be too much for the reinsurance business, which sells policies to protect insurers from large losses. They are looking for new ways to pool the risk, including catastrophe futures on the Board of Trade, with which insurers could hedge against the possibility of large losses. Investors would make money by, in effect, betting that there would be no such catastrophe.

Re-insurers are also offering "act of God" bonds that would pay very high interest but would require bondholders to forgo repayment in the event of disaster. Catastrophe futures and "act of God" bonds will help keep insurance coverage available and reasonably priced. They also raise the question: If the market can adequately deal with even the prospect of multibillion-dollar financial disasters, precisely what services can government supply better than the market?

Private Communities

One area where people seek safety and stability is in their residential environment. Some Americans move far from cities so they won't have to deal with externalities created by other people. Others have turned to zoning and other forms of state regulation to try to regulate their surroundings. Recently another approach has become widespread in the U.S.: some 4 million Americans have chosen to live in some 30,000 private, gated communities. Another 24 million live in locked condominiums, cooperatives, or apartment houses, which are small gated communities, and as many as 42 million live in community associations, some of which are not gated. Why do people choose to live in private communities? The first answer is, to protect themselves from crime and the dramatic deterioration of public services in many large cities. A college professor complains in the *Washington Post* about "the new Middle Ages . . . a kind of medieval landscape in which defensible, walled and gated towns dot the countryside." People built walls around their cities in the Middle Ages to protect themselves from bandits and marauders, and many Americans are making the same choice.

Private communities are a peaceful but comprehensive response to the failure of big government. Like their federal counterpart, local governments today tax us more heavily than ever but offer deteriorating services in return. Not only do police seem unable to combat rising crime, but the schools get worse and worse, garbage and litter don't get picked up, potholes aren't fixed, panhandlers confront us on every corner. Private communities can provide physical safety for their residents, partly by excluding from the community people who are neither residents nor guests.

But there's a broader reason for choosing to live in a private community. Local governments can't satisfy the needs and preferences of all their residents. People have different preferences in terms of population density, housing types, the presence of children, and so on. Rules that might cater to some citizens' preferences would be unconstitutional or offensive to the freewheeling spirit of other citizens.

Private communities can solve some of these public goods problems. In the larger developments, the homes, the streets, the sewers, the parklands are all private. After buying a house or condominium there, residents pay a monthly fee that covers security, maintenance, and management. Many of the communities are both gated and guarded.

Many have rules that would range from annoying to infuriating to unconstitutional if imposed by a government—regulations on house colors, shrubbery heights, on-street parking, even gun ownership. People choose such communities partly because they find the rules, even strict rules, congenial.

Economists Donald J. Boudreaux and Randall G. Holcombe offer a theoretical explanation for the growing popularity of private communities, which they call contractual governments. Having constitutional rules drawn up by a single developer, who then offers the property and the rules as a package to buyers, reduces the decision-making costs of developing appropriate rules and allows people to choose communities on the basis of the kind of rules they offer. The desire to make money is a strong incentive for the developer to draw up good rules.

Boudreaux and Holcombe write,

> The establishment of a contractual government appears to be the closest thing to a real-world social contract that can be found because it is created behind something analogous to a veil [of ignorance], and because everyone unanimously agrees to move into the contractual government's jurisdiction.

Fred Foldvary points out that most "public goods" exist within a particular space, so the goods can be provided only to people who rent or purchase access to the space. That allows entrepreneurs to overcome the problem of people trying to "free-ride" off others' payments for public goods. Entrepreneurs try to make their space attractive to customers by supplying the best possible combination of characteristics, which will vary from space to space. Foldvary points out that private communities, shopping centers, industrial parks, theme parks, and hotel interiors are all private spaces created by entrepreneurs, who have a much better incentive than governments to discover and respond to consumer demand. And many private entrepreneurs competing for business can supply a much wider array of choices than governments will.

Private communities—including condominiums and apartment buildings—come in virtually unlimited variety. Prices vary widely, as does the general level of amenities. Some have policies banning children, pets, guns, garish colors, rentals or whatever else might be perceived to reduce residents' enjoyment of the space. The growing "co-housing" movement responds to the need many people feel for a closer sense of community by offering living spaces centered around a common house for group meals and activities. Some people create co-housing arrangements based on a shared religious commitment.

Shopping malls might also be considered both private communities and private regulatory systems. Malls try to provide shoppers with a more pleasant experience than traditional on-street stores can offer. Their advantages include the proximity of many stores, protection from the weather, cleanliness and protection from crime and disruptive behavior. As governments become less able to supply clean, peaceful, pleasant city streets, people increasingly choose private malls that offer what customers seek. Because they are private, malls are more responsive to consumer demand. They can require that stores contribute to general maintenance, decoration and security; and stores are happy to do so because they find

---

Rules of Etiquette

WELCOME TO THE SHOPS AT NATIONAL PLACE

In order to provide a safe, secure and pleasant shopping experience, we ask for your cooperation in complying with the rules of etiquette to be followed by all patrons. These activities are prohibited at The Shops at National Place:

1. Loitering
2. Smoking
3. Solicitation in The Shops
4. Presence in The Shops without shoes or shirt
5. Any act which could result in physical harm to persons or property
6. Use of loud or obscene language or gestures
7. Blocking store fronts, fire exits or stairways
8. Standing or walking in large groups which cause an inconvenience to others
9. Running, shouting, horseplay, throwing any type of object or debris, disorderly or disruptive conduct of any nature
10. The playing of radios or musical instruments unless part of an activity approved in advance by The Shops Management
11. Use of skateboards, roller skates or bicycles on The Shops property
12. Literature distribution without the written permission of The Shops Management
13. Possession of alcoholic beverages or illegal substances
14. Any criminal act under any federal, state or local statute or ordinance
15. Use of public restroom facility for any purpose other than intended (e.g., sinks for washing of face and hands only)

A violation of these rules may result in expulsion from The Shops or other legal action as deemed necessary.

---

that their money is spent efficiently on services that benefit them. Also because they are private, malls can exclude from their premises people who don't abide by bourgeois standards of behavior. Mall security officers rarely have to eject anyone; the mere knowledge that they could do so is usually enough to encourage proper behavior by visitors. Suburban malls seem to assume that standards of behavior are within the implicit knowledge of their customers. An urban mall near my office in Washington, D.C., makes the rules explicit (see box).

Private communities are a vital part of civil society. They give more people an opportunity to find the kinds of living (or working, or shopping, or entertainment) arrangements they want. They reflect the understanding of a free society as not one large community but a community of communities. And like most forms of private regulation, they offer several advantages over state regulation: flexibility, small scale, voluntariness and a wide array of choices.

Conclusion

Regulation without the state is all around us. I'll mention just a few examples in closing. Companies such as Microsoft, Novell and Cisco

Systems offer certification for people who pass examinations proving their skills in handling complex engineering tasks. These certification programs are not only an important form of private regulation, they may well be the leading edge of an educational revolution in which businesses will look to such examinations and certificates rather than to diplomas and degrees of dubious quality when judging job applicants. Another part of the education revolution is the growing number of government, non-profit, and for-profit entities publishing data on schools to help parents make informed decisions. I have on my desk the fourth edition of *Codes of Professional Responsibility*, a book of 1,149 pages that includes codes of ethics for hundreds of business, medical, and legal associations. The website www.getnetwise.org offers parents advice on regulating their children's use of the internet and links to more than 100 software tools for monitoring and regulating internet use. Instead of a one-size-fits-all government censor, such competing forms of regulation allow individuals, families, and businesses to select the level and type of regulation that they prefer. The American Society for Testing and Materials coordinates 132 standards-writing committees and publishes standard test methods, specifications, practices, guides, classifications, and terminology. More than 10,000 ASTM standards are published each year in the 72 volumes of the *Annual Book of ASTM Standards*, used throughout the world.

Although private regulation surrounds us, there are many opportunities for expanding it. Yilmaz offers some suggestions, as does *Regulation Without the State*. Other authors have suggested that the U.S. government replace Food and Drug Administration regulation on medical devices with third-party certification or that market arrangements replace subsidized crop insurance for American farmers. Regulation without the state warrants both further research and wider use.

Regulation Without the State . . . The Debate Continues, ed. John Blundell and Colin Robinson (London: Institute for Economic Affairs, 2000)

PART **12**

A Drug-Free America?

Let's Quit the Drug War

An antiwar song that helped get the Smothers Brothers thrown off network television in the 60's went this way: "We're waist deep in the Big Muddy, and the big fool says to push on." Today we're waist-deep in another unwinnable war, and many political leaders want to push on. This time it's a war on drugs. About 23 million Americans use illicit drugs every month, despite annual federal outlays of $3.9 billion. Even the arrests of 824,000 Americans a year don't seem to be having much effect.

As in the case of Vietnam—and Prohibition, another unwinnable war—many politicians can't stand losing a war. Instead of acknowledging failure, they want to escalate.

Mayor Edward I. Koch of New York suggests that we strip search every person entering the United States from Mexico or Southeast Asia. The White House drug adviser, Donald I. Macdonald, calls for arresting even small-time users—lawyers with a quarter-gram of cocaine, high school kids with a couple of joints—and bringing them before a judge.

Where will we put those two-bit "criminals"? The Justice Department recommends doubling our prison capacity, even though President Reagan's former drug adviser Carlton E. Turner already brags about the role of drug laws in bringing about a 60 percent increase in our prison population in the last six years. Bob Dole calls for the death penalty for drug sellers.

Like their counterparts in Los Angeles and Chicago, the Washington, D.C., police are to be issued semiautomatic pistols so they can engage in ever bloodier shootouts with drug dealers. Members of the District of Columbia Council call for the National Guard to occupy the city. We've already pressed other governments to destroy drug crops and to help us interdict the flow of drugs into the United States. Because those measures have largely failed, the Customs Service asks authorization to "use appropriate force" to compel places suspected of carrying drugs to land, including the authority to shoot them down.

It's time to ask ourselves: What kind of society would condone strip searches, large-scale arrests, military occupation of its capital city and the shooting of possibly innocent people in order to stop some of its citizens from using substances that others don't like?

Prohibition of alcohol in the 1920's failed because it proved impossible to stop people from drinking. Our 70-year effort at prohibition of marijuana, cocaine, and heroin has also failed. Tens of millions of Americans, including senators, presidential candidates, a Supreme Court nominee and conservative journalists, have broken the laws against such drugs. Preserving laws that are so widely flouted undermines respect for all laws.

The most dangerous drugs in the United States are alcohol, which is responsible for about 100,000 deaths a year, and tobacco, which is responsible for about 350,000. Heroin, cocaine and marijuana account for a total of 3,600 deaths a year—even though one in five people ages 20 to 40 use drugs regularly.

Our efforts to crack down on illegal drug use have created new problems. A Justice Department survey reports that 70 percent of those arrested for serious crimes are drug users, which may mean that "drugs cause crime." A more sophisticated analysis suggests that the high cost of drugs, a result of their prohibition, forces drug users to turn to crime to support an unnecessarily expensive habit.

Drug prohibition, by giving young people the thrill of breaking the law and giving pushers a strong incentive to find new customers, may actually increase the number of drug users. Moreover, our policy of pressuring friendly governments to wipe out drug cultivation has undermined many of those regimes and provoked resentment against us among their citizens and government officials.

We can either escalate the war on drugs, which would have dire implications for civil liberties and the right to privacy, or find a way to gracefully withdraw. Withdrawal should not be viewed as an endorsement of drug use; it would simply be an acknowledgment that the cost of this war—billions of dollars, runaway crime rates and restrictions on our personal freedom—is too high.

New York Times, March 17, 1988

Czar Bennett's War on Drugs

The argument that drug prohibition is doomed to failure seems to have set off a slow but steady increase in support for the legalization of drugs, and that trend has drug czar William Bennett sputtering in outrage and frustration. One is reminded of some tongue-in-cheek advice offered to young lawyers: "When the law is against you, argue the facts. When the facts are against you, argue the law. When the law and the facts are against you, pound on the table."

My article, "Let's Quit the Drug War," in the *New York Times* in March 1988 was followed in short order by Baltimore mayor Kurt Schmoke's call for a national debate on legalization, Rep. Pete Stark's request that his colleagues in Congress consider legalizing drugs, and discussions of legalization on *Nightline, This Week with David Brinkley*, and the *CBS Evening News*. In 1989 James Ostrowski's Cato Policy Analysis, "Thinking about Drug Legalization," along with Ethan Nadelmann's work one of the most comprehensive critiques of prohibition published recently, set off a new round of debate.

Those critics and others have argued that prohibition is just as futile in the '80s and '90s as it was in the '20s and '30s. Moreover, they have pointed out that prohibition causes crime, by leading addicts to commit crimes to pay for a habit that would be easily affordable if it were legal and by creating huge enterprises with no means of settling their differences except gunfire; spreads AIDS, by outlawing the purchase of needles; corrupts law enforcement officials; and destroys inner-city communities.

Bennett has responded not with logical rebuttals of that argument but with denunciations and sneers. When a Cato Sponsor wrote to him to ask whether he had read the Ostrowski paper, he replied, "This office is currently conducting a broad review of possible options in our national drive against illegal drugs. We are reasonably open-minded about our project; most questions at issue are very much open to consideration. One that is not, however, is the proposal you advocate. . . . Under no circumstances will this office endorse legalization of drugs." Publicly, he has denounced legalization as "morally scandalous" and "dopey," as "surrender" and "capitulation." He declared in the *Wall Street Journal* that he found it "difficult to respect" Nobel laureate Milton Friedman's case for legalization.

It may be that Bennett simply doesn't understand the effects of prohibition and the argument for legalization. When he was asked after a recent Harvard speech how his addiction to nicotine differed from a drug addiction, he responded, "I didn't do any drive-by shootings." Does he actually believe that cocaine use causes drive-by shootings? Does he truly not understand why illegal drug markets are marked by violence?

A more likely explanation is that Bennett's near-hysterical invective is just part of an effort to generate a war mentality to sustain his "war on drugs." War, as Randolph Bourne wrote in 1918, "is the health of the state," the only way to create a herd instinct in a free people and the best way to extend the powers of government. In fact, Thomas Paine wrote, the British government didn't raise taxes in order to wage war; it waged war in order to raise taxes. In our own history, wartime has occasioned such extensions of state power as conscription, the income tax, tax withholding, wage and price controls, rent control, and Prohibition, which really began with the Lever Act of 1917.

Bennett is particularly frustrated when the media give coverage to legalization advocates because he knows how important the media are in rallying the citizenry. As Paul Fussell wrote of World War II in his new book, *Wartime*, "Because in wartime the various outlets of popular culture behaved almost entirely as if they were the creatures of their governments, it is hardly surprising to find that they spoke with one voice. Together with skepticism, irony, and doubt, an early casualty was a wide variety of views about current events."

Bennett is hardly alone in his reluctance to engage in a rational debate about drugs. When reporters questioned President Bush about his claim on national television that drugs could be bought in Lafayette Park, across the street from the White House—having learned how difficult it had been for drug agents to lure a dealer to such an unlikely location—Bush's response was, "I don't understand. Has somebody got some advocates here for this drug guy?" And Rep. Charles Rangel, who heads the House Select Committee on Narcotics Abuse and Control, maintained that former secretary of state George Shultz's call for drug legalization would be a "declaration of defeat" and "does not belong in any true forum for national policy making."

As more and more respected Americans argue that drugs should be legalized—to reduce the crime, corruption, and chaos of prohibition—Czar Bennett gets more and more frenzied in his denunciations, but there is some evidence that the media are slowly coming to recognize the validity of the argument. *Newsweek*, which now openly includes opinions in its news stories (as does *Time*), stated in May 1988 that legalization would be "simply a nightmare" and would create millions of new drug addicts. By December 1989 *Newsweek* had retreated to the position that "legalization *could* become the national disaster Bennett predicts" (emphasis added). It took Western journalists about 75 years to discover that the Soviet economy wasn't outpacing ours; drug prohibition is now 75 years old, so maybe the truth about it is dawning on them.

Cato Policy Report, January/February 1990

America after Prohibition: The Corner Drugstore

Defenders of drug prohibition have two basic tactics. One is to repeat over and over, "Drugs are dangerous. Therefore, they should be illegal"— a syllogism that would earn a failing grade in Logic 101. The other is to challenge their opponents to describe exactly how drugs would be legalized.

That is apparently supposed to be a devastating question, but it doesn't strike me as particularly difficult. Our society has had a lot of experience with legal dangerous drugs, particularly alcohol and tobacco, and we can draw on that experience when we legalize marijuana, cocaine, and heroin—as we will, fairly soon, when more Americans come to understand the costs of prohibiting them.

Some critics of prohibition would legalize only "soft" drugs—just marijuana in many cases. That policy would not eliminate the tremendous problems that prohibition has created. As long as drugs that people very much want remain illegal, a black market will exist. If our goal is to rid our cities of crime and corruption, it would make more sense to legalize cocaine and heroin, while leaving marijuana illegal, than vice versa. The lesson of alcohol prohibition in the 1920s and the prohibition of other drugs today is that prohibition creates more problems than it solves. We should legalize all recreational drugs.

Then what? When we legalize drugs, we will likely apply the alcohol model. Drinking laws, of course, differ from state to state, and *Reason* readers don't have to be told how ludicrous some of those laws are. Even with decidedly little research, I have run across a variety of asinine policies: In New Hampshire, food must be purchased with a drink—$1.50 worth, to be exact, so every bar has a nice array of desserts and cheese plates that sell for $1.50—and a small pitcher of beer can't be served to one person. In Virginia, establishments that serve alcohol must earn a majority of their revenue from the sale of meals, and it's illegal to serve drinks to "known homosexuals." In some states, only private clubs— which may be joined on the spot for a token fee—can serve drinks. In other states, liquor is sold only in state stores. It is illegal to sell alcohol in Bourbon County, Kentucky.

But notwithstanding those absurdities (mostly the result of political logrolling between moralizers and profit-maximizing interest groups), there are a few essential features of U.S. alcohol policies that would surely be applied to marijuana, cocaine, and heroin. Those drugs would be sold only in specially licensed stores—perhaps in liquor stores, perhaps in a new kind of drugstore. Warning labels would be posted in the stores and on the packages. It would be illegal to sell drugs to minors, now defined as anyone under 21. It would be illegal to advertise drugs on television and possibly even in print. Committing a crime or driving under the influence of drugs would be illegal, as with alcohol.

It is quite possible that such a system would be less effective in attracting young people to drug use than the current system of schoolyard pushers offering free samples. Teenagers today can get liquor if they try, and we shouldn't assume that a minimum purchasing age would keep other drugs out of their hands. But we don't see liquor pushers peddling their wares on playgrounds. Getting the drug business out of our schoolyards and streets is an important benefit of legalization.

It is likely that drug use would initially increase. Prices would be much lower, and drugs would be more readily available to adults who prefer not to break the law. But those drugs would be safer—when's the last time you heard of a liquor store selling gin cut with formaldehyde?—and people would be able to regulate their intake more carefully.

In the long run, however, I foresee declining drug use and weaker drugs. Consider the divergent trends in legal and illegal drugs today. Illegal drugs keep getting stronger—crack, PCP, ecstasy and other designer drugs—as a result of what Richard Cowan, writing in *National Review*, has called the Iron Law of Prohibition: the more intense the law enforcement, the more potent the drugs, because there is more profit in producing and selling powerful, highly concentrated drugs. Such drugs as crack probably would not exist if we had had a legal drug market for the past decade.

In contrast, *legal* drugs are getting weaker—for example, low-tar cigarettes and wine coolers. About 40 million Americans have quit smoking since the Surgeon General's report in 1964, and sales of spirits are declining; beer and wine keep the alcohol industry stable. As Americans become more health-conscious, they are turning away from drugs. Drug education could do more to encourage this trend if it was separated from law enforcement.

At least half of the violent crime in major U.S. cities is a result of drug prohibition. Legalization would save Americans tens of billions of dollars, but more important, it would greatly increase the sense of safety in our most dangerous neighborhoods. It would take the astronomical profits out of the drug trade, and the Colombian cartel would collapse like a punctured balloon. Drugs would be sold by Fortune 500 companies and friendly corner merchants, not by Mafiosi and 16-year-olds with BMWs and Uzis. Legalization would put an end to the corruption that has engulfed so many Latin American countries and tainted the Miami police and U.S. soldiers in Central America. Legalization would not solve all of America's drug problems, but it would make our cities safer, make drug use healthier, eliminate a major source of revenue for corruption here and abroad, and make honest work more attractive to inner-city youth—pretty good results for any reform.

Reason, October 1988

Journalists and the Drug War

"War is the health of the state," wrote Randolph Bourne in 1918, explaining why wars, destructive as they are, are often popular with those who run the state. War has always been, for instance, an ideal reason to raise taxes on an otherwise recalcitrant citizenry. Indeed, Thomas Paine said in *The Rights of Man* that the British government didn't raise taxes to fight wars, it fought wars to raise taxes.

Throughout American history governments have used the exigencies of war as an excuse to constrict the constitutional liberties of American citizens. Among the extensions of federal authority conducted under cover of wartime are conscription, standby censorship authority, the Trading with the Enemy Act, the income tax, tax withholding, wage and price controls, rent control, and Prohibition, which really began with the Lever Act of 1917. Not to mention the imperial presidency.

Advocates of extensive government recognize the truth of Bourne's insight. When the British scholar Michael Foot was leader of the Labor Party, he was asked for an example of the kind of socialism he favored. He replied, "The best example that I've seen of democratic socialism operating in this country was during the second world war. Then we ran Britain highly efficiently, got everybody a job. . . . The conscription of labor was only a very small element of it. It was a democratic society with a common aim." Here Foot has put his finger on it, to mix a metaphor: Outside of wartime it is very difficult, indeed impossible, to rally millions of free citizens around a common aim.

The American socialist Michael Harrington also hailed the efficient planning and social justice practiced by the American government during World Wars I and II. Unlike some more bloodthirsty rulers and court intellectuals, collectivists such as Foot and Harrington don't relish the killing involved in war, but they love its domestic effects: the centralization and extension of government power.

The connection between war and overweening government was also noted by conservative William F. Buckley, Jr., who wrote at the dawn of the Cold War that "we have to accept Big Government for the duration— for neither an offensive nor a defensive war can be waged . . . except through the instrument of a totalitarian bureaucracy within our shores."

The media, of course, play an important role in the modern state's warmaking abilities. It is through the media that the citizenry must be rallied, and so it is essential that the media not confuse the issue through debate and dissension. As Paul Fussell writes of World War II in his recent book *Wartime*, "Because in wartime the various outlets of popular culture behaved almost entirely as if they were the creatures of their governments, it is hardly surprising to find that they spoke with one voice. Together with skepticism, irony, and doubt, an early casualty was a wide variety of views about current events."

But wars are dangerous in the nuclear age, and ever since Vietnam we're not even sure we'll win. So today—or at least until the election of President George "Old Death and Taxes" Bush—the government looks for crusades that may be designated metaphorically as wars, or as the moral equivalent of war, a term originated by William James, who wanted to conscript American youth into a vast social-work army to "get the childishness knocked out of them." Now this isn't all bad; better metaphorical wars than real wars. But metaphorical wars do have a lot of the unfortunate consequences of shooting wars.

The modern era of metaphorical wars probably originated with the War on Poverty, which began about the same time as the Vietnam War and ended about as successfully. There was great media acclaim for the War on Poverty and little real debate. It was a war, after all, and America could do anything if she just put her mind to it.

Later we got President Jimmy Carter's Moral Equivalent of War— the energy crisis, with its Jamesian emphasis on government direction, sacrifice, and reduced living standards. This too was warmly embraced by the national media. Establishment liberal columnist Joseph Kraft wrote that President Carter must "generate a sense of urgency" about the crisis, while establishment conservative George Will headlined his column, "Hit Us Hard, Please, Mr. Carter."

Time gushed over Energy Secretary James Schlesinger, who "views the energy crisis as a blessing in disguise, a beneficial testing of the nation's spirit and ability to cope. In his estimation, the crisis, if handled properly, will provide the opportunity for the American people to recapture the old virtues of sacrifice and a sense of shared destiny." Schlesinger no doubt would have considered it defeatism to point out that a simple lifting of price controls would end the energy crisis, as indeed it did just four years later.

And then we got the war on drugs. Much more than Carter's Moral Equivalent of War, this one has it all—a well-defined enemy, threats to children, gun battles, bodies in the street. Like shooting wars, it brings with it a lot of deaths and a lot of civil liberties abuses. War fever and the need to rally 'round the general may explain why there was no media criticism of Bennett's statement on *Meet the Press* that we need to move beyond beheading drug dealers to start executing bankers who "trade in drug cash"—virtually every banker in today's world.

Who would have thought that a generation of journalists who laughed at *Reefer Madness* in college would have enlisted so readily in the War on Drugs? Yet every television network and major newspaper enthusiastically became part of the propaganda machine. *Newsweek* runs cover stories on "The War in America's Cities" and promises to cover it "as aggressively and . . . as regularly as we did . . . the war in Vietnam." And it did: eight cover stories in 1988–89, articles on the drug war in 29 issues during 1989 alone. Drugs are an epidemic, *Newsweek* says, "as pervasive and dangerous in its way as the plagues of medieval times." *U.S. News and World Report* calls drugs "the nation's No. 1 menace." CBS News has a running segment called "One Nation, Under Siege," and the *Washington Post* reports on Washingtonians who are "on the front lines."

When Drug Czar—and what a warlike term that is—William Bennett unveiled his battle plan at the National Press Club, the club's president, Peter Holmes of the *Washington Times*, who presided over the event, selected only softball questions from those submitted by the audience (including two tables full of oppositionists). There were tough questions submitted about the efficacy of Bennett's strategy, the past failures of alcohol and drug prohibition, and so on, but the hardest-hitting one put to him by the National Press Club was, "Do you think bureaucratic turf wars will interfere with your strategy?"

(Bennett, of course, has been replaced by ousted Florida governor Bob Martinez, who has little to recommend him for the position except, apparently, President Bush's feeling that Republican chief executives who violated their campaign promises not to raise taxes should stick together. But in keeping with our theme, it's interesting to note Bush's stated reason for his choice: He praised Martinez for having "signed more than 130 death warrants" and thus having earned a "battlefield promotion.")

Concern over drugs rose from 10 percent to 60 percent in national polls in less than a year—while reported drug use was falling. Why? It might have something to do with the constant media hype about drugs—*Time* and *Newsweek* covers, nightly network coverage, whole shows devoted to drugs. The media's stance in the drug war, so reminiscent of Paul Fussell's recollections about World War II, was summed up by Associated Press senior columnist Walter Mears: "In President Bush's renewed war on drugs, there's no political argument about the enemy, the objective or even the weapons." Not much for journalists to do but get the word out, then.

Journalists always have a weakness for terrifying statistics—Paul Ehrlich's population projections, Mitch Snyder's homelessness numbers—and the drug war provides plenty of them. Crack-addicted babies have become a genuinely frightening media story, with columnist Jack Anderson and former *New York Times* editor A. M. Rosenthal leading the pack, warning that 375,000 crack-addicted babies were born last year. What's the truth? It's hard to say. But considering that the 1988 Household Survey on Drug Abuse reported that some 484,000 people used crack on a monthly basis, it would seem unlikely that 79 percent of them had babies. Bennett's official strategy document claimed "as many as 200,000 babies are born each year to mothers who use drugs" as well as "100,000 cocaine babies are born each year." Bennett told Ann Landers' 90 million readers that 100,000 babies each year are born to mothers who use crack—upping the ante from simple cocaine.

The only hard number is a report of 8,974 "crack baby cases" in eight cities. Drug researcher Dale Gieringer suggests that that makes Bennett's 100,000 figure plausible, though it seems likely that New York, Los Angeles, Chicago, Miami and four smaller cities would have a lot more than 9 percent of all the crack babies in the United States. *Newsweek* quotes a researcher as saying, "It's as if the part of the brain that makes us human beings capable of discussion or reflection is wiped out." But in fact two out of three crack-exposed babies show no obvious problems at birth, and Dr. Ira Chasnoff, director of the National Association for Perinatal Addiction Research and Education, says that crack babies develop "within the normal range for cognitive development and are not, as some people have stated, brain damaged."

It's also unlikely that anyone would have figured out from the media coverage of crack babies that women have four times as much risk of delivering low-birth weight babies if they use cocaine throughout pregnancy, compared to three times as much risk if they use tobacco regularly. Occasional cocaine use creates a risk factor of 1.8, about the same risk created by having three drinks a day.

Journalists and politicians have swallowed whole the most alarming allegations about the danger and addictiveness of crack. Peter Jennings said on the *ABC Evening News* that using crack "even once can make a person crave cocaine for as long as they live." Pat Buchanan declared on CNN's *Crossfire* that "I've talked to people in the drug war, and they say . . . crack—if some kid gets involved in that and gets hooked on that, in a couple of weeks you can finish off a human being." Rep. Patricia Schroeder (D-Colo.) asserted on PBS's *Firing Line* that crack has a 70 percent addiction rate. Yet the government's own figures report that about 2.4 million people have tried crack while only 484,000 have used it in the past month—an addiction rate of 20 percent at most.

The media have also credulously reported assertions by Bennett and other drug warriors about the effects of drugs on worker productivity: drug abuse costs the United States $34 billion—or maybe $60 billion—a year, drug users are 3.6 times as likely to injure themselves or another worker in the workplace. "Drugs: Silent Killer of Profits," headlines the

Boston Globe. These figures seem to stem from two "studies," both of which have been thoroughly discredited by John P. Morgan of City University of New York Medical School. A Firestone Tire and Rubber Company study was never published, just discussed in an in-house newsletter, and in any case drew its conclusions from interviews with workers who had sought or been referred for treatment—hardly a random sample. A Research Triangle Institute study found that households containing someone who had ever been a regular marijuana user had lower incomes than other households—thus the lost-productivity claim. But it showed nothing about current marijuana use, and it failed to account for the possibility that marijuana use might be more prevalent among those with lower economic opportunities. (And as drug policy researcher James Ostrowski has pointed out in a major study for the Cato Institute, 80 percent of the RTI study's estimated social costs of drug abuse are more properly described as the costs of drug *prohibition*.)

For journalists the silver lining in the unprecedented flow of drugs into the United States is the opportunity for great photographs of Drug Enforcement Administration agents or local law-enforcement personnel with huge quantities of captured cocaine. It seems that not a week goes by without a report of "New Hampshire's biggest drug bust," "the biggest drug bust in middle Georgia history," "the largest drug bust ever in the United States outside of Florida," "the second-largest drug bust ever by European law enforcement," and—drum roll, please—"the largest drug bust in history." Dollar figures are always provided by helpful police flacks—cocaine with a street value of $3.3 million, $20 million, $73 million, $2 billion. By going to Arkansas personally to lead a nationwide series of raids on marijuana fields, former attorney general Edwin Meese III got his picture in every paper in the country—ironically wearing his Adam Smith tie as he raided small businesses. Perhaps the high point of media hype for the DEA was NBC's three-night miniseries "Drug Wars: The Camarena Story," featuring Tom Brokaw as himself.

These days the media seem willing to blame everything on drugs. The bombs mailed to federal judges were immediately blamed on drug defendants—until a civil rights lawyer received one. KPIX-TV in San Francisco produced a segment, also broadcast on KING-TV in Seattle, saying that marijuana caused cancer. Other than the California doctor who made the charge, no one has offered any evidence of such effects by a drug that was described by administrative law judge Francis L Young of the Drug Enforcement Administration as "one of the safest therapeutically active substances known to man." Journalists at first even fell for President Bush's televised claim that drugs are sold in Lafayette Park, across the street from the White House. (Though considering more recent reports of journalists being offered drugs in Justice Department corridors, that one may not seem so unlikely.) One might even point out the frequent use of the term "drug-related murders" when every cop on the beat knows that such murders are a result of drug prohibition, not drug use.

One of the biggest distortions of the media war on drugs is the emphasis on illicit drugs rather than alcohol and tobacco. *Newsweek*'s 29 stories on drugs in 1989—many of them multi-parters—compared with 5 stories on alcohol. Nobody covers alcohol or tobacco regularly as "a plague upon the land." Yet tobacco kills about 390,000 Americans a year, alcohol about 150,000, while total deaths from illegal drugs are about 5,000 a year. According to Ostrowski, "for every death caused by the intrinsic effects of cocaine, heroin kills 20, alcohol kills 37, and tobacco kills 162" (assuming the same number of users). There are apparently no deaths traceable to marijuana. Alcohol is clearly the drug with the most social costs in terms of accidents, violence, lost productivity, and effect on babies. But you wouldn't know it from watching the evening news.

Media credulity about drugs didn't begin with the Bush years, of course. Why did *Washington Post* editors and Pulitzer jurors believe Janet Cooke's pharmacomythological tale in 1980 about an eight-year-old heroin addict? Because they knew almost nothing and believed almost anything about drugs. That same year the media were up in arms about an invasion of heroin from Iran; "Mideast Heroin Flooding Europe," the *New York Times* warned, while the *Los Angeles Times* chimed in with "Iran Heroin Flooding U.S., Agents Report," explaining that "more than 10 times the amount available in the late 60s may end up in the United States." A year later a Drug Enforcement Administration agent acknowledged to *Inquiry* magazine that the flood never arrived.

Drug legalization, the moral equivalent of the anti-war movement, has been relegated to fringe television time and occasional op-ed articles. Politicians and their handmaidens in the media have scared people so much that they're ready to jettison the Bill of Rights—perhaps, for some officials, the real point of the drug war.

Rep. Charles Rangel, the Harlem Democrat who heads the House Select Committee on Narcotics Abuse and Control, illustrated the wartime mentality in his response to former secretary of state George Shultz's call for legalization. Such a policy, Rangel said, would be a "declaration of defeat," and even discussions of it "do not belong in any true forum for national policy making." Jesse Jackson makes the wartime analogy explicit: "If someone is caught transmitting the death agent to Americans, that person should face wartime consequences." President Reagan's assistant secretary of state for narcotics, Ann B. Wrobleski, declared Eli Lilly & Co. "AWOL" in the war on drugs when it declined to sell the government a herbicide to be sprayed on coca crops in Peru and Bolivia.

The drug war serves several related purposes right now. One is to provide a new national enemy as the Cold War winds down—a reason to keep the military budget up. The movie *Lethal Weapon 2* jumped on two bandwagons by making its villains South African drug dealers. But South Africa, abhorrent as its political system is, is not really very threatening to Americans, so drug dealers will have more staying power—though Japanese businessmen, "invading" our shores with cars and VCRs, may yet edge out the drug dealers. And most recently, of course, we have discovered another Hitler in the Persian Gulf, and the outbreak of a shooting war has made even a War on Drugs seem uninspiring.

Another purpose of the drug war is to give liberals a chance to demonstrate their toughness. Liberals who were never very keen on fighting communism have been gung-ho about invading Colombia, assassinating Panama's tinpot dictator Manuel Noriega, and using the military to keep out drugs.

Finally, like everything in Washington these days, the drug war feeds the tax lust of the establishment, including both the permanent government and the media. Lesley Stahl of CBS News couldn't wait for Bennett to finish explaining his drug program so she could ask him breathlessly, "Doesn't this mean we'll need a tax increase?" Democrats and network journalists joined in the chorus for a tax hike to fight the drug war. After Budget Director Richard Darman conceded to a congressional committee that yes, the Bush administration would support a tax increase in case of war, conservative economist Herbert Stein rejoiced; well, then, he said, how about the war on poverty, the war on illiteracy, the war on drugs, whatever, let's get on with it.

Politicians have only to say the magic word *war* to get journalists enlisted in their latest crusade. Maybe if the word were banned from political discourse we could rediscover the tradition of adversary journalism that was awakened during the Vietnam War, the tradition by which journalists hold governments accountable for their actions. Journalists gathering at the National Press Club to debate changing the name of the H. L. Mencken Library, while people die a few blocks away in an unwinnable war, would do well to recall Mencken's words: "The function of a newspaper in a democracy is to stand as a sort of chronic opposition to the reigning quacks."

Liberty, May 1991

The Hydra-Headed Drug Business

At last we've turned the corner in the war on drugs. Attorney General Janet Reno and Treasury Secretary Robert E. Rubin announced more than 100 indictments and the seizure of some $150 million from Mexican banks, surely a successful conclusion to "the largest, most comprehensive drug money laundering case in history." The druglords must really be on the ropes now.

But careful news watchers have heard those words before. It seems that not a week goes by without a report of "New Hampshire's biggest drug bust," "the biggest drug bust in middle Georgia history," "the largest drug bust ever in the United States outside of Florida," or—drum roll, please—"the largest drug bust in history."

Law enforcement agents and journalists both love those stories—they publicize the "success" of the war on drugs, and they offer the journalists great visuals and great numbers. Helpful police flacks always provide some sexy dollar figures—cocaine with a street value of $3.3 million, $20 million, $73 million, $2 billion.

In a 1991 San Francisco case, billed as the biggest heroin bust ever, television cameras panned over 59 boxes containing 1,080 pounds of heroin—enough to supply each of the country's estimated 500,000 heroin addicts for a month. Drug war officials said the street value of the heroin was $2.7 billion to $4 billion.

It's true that the drug warriors are interdicting more drugs at our borders all the time. Seizures of cocaine rose from 20,000 pounds in 1983 to 179,000 pounds in 1989 to 239,000 pounds in 1997. But does that indicate success? More likely, it means that more drugs are crossing our borders and officials are interdicting about the same percentage as before.

As Mark A. R. Kleiman, a specialist on drug policy at Harvard University, said about the California raid, "For any shipment like this that you catch, you can assume that many more get through."

When Americans read about ever-larger drug busts, or when we watch television shows about drug enforcement, we get the impression that drug enforcement agents are clever and innovative, always staying one step ahead of the sinister pushers. But in reality the drug distributors are the innovative ones—because they have a financial incentive to be.

The Drug Enforcement Administration and other law enforcement agencies are bureaucracies, and like all bureaucracies they tend to be inefficient. Police officers and drug agents get paid whether they slow drug traffic or not. In fact, they may receive more funding if the drug problem gets worse. Drug dealers, on the other hand, are entrepreneurs. If they outwit the officers, they make big money. That economic incentive spurs creativity, innovation, and efficiency.

Every week brings reports of innovations in drug smuggling: people who swallow heroin and carry it into the United States in their stomachs, drugs placed in the luggage of unaccompanied children on international flights, cocaine implanted in a passenger's thighs—and those are just the methods police have discovered.

Recently, partly because the Supreme Court approved surveillance flights over private property to search for marijuana fields, marijuana growers have been moving indoors and underground. In November 1990 five subterranean marijuana farms were found by law enforcement officials in Southern California and Arizona; imagine how many were not found. One near Lancaster, California, cost about $1 million to build, police said, and had the potential to produce an annual profit of $75 million from 8,500 plants harvested four times a year.

Around the world, drug enforcers face what Ethan Nadelmann of the Lindesmith Center calls the "push-down/pop-up factor": push down drug production in one country, and it will pop up in another. Marijuana and opium can be grown almost anywhere, and coca is being grown in places previously considered unsuitable.

As long as Americans want to use drugs, and are willing to defy the law and pay high prices to do so, drug busts are futile. Other profit-seeking smugglers and dealers will always be ready to step in and take the place of those arrested.

"We've cut off the head of the dragon," said Robert Bender, head of the DEA's San Francisco office, in announcing the 1991 heroin bust.

But in the years that followed, the DEA discovered that it had cut off the head, not of a dragon, but of a Hydra—the nine-headed monster in Greek mythology that couldn't be killed because whenever one of its heads was cut off, two more grew to replace it. Now, we've cut off 100 heads of the drug-smuggling cartels. Will 200 more grow back to replace them?

National Review, May 16, 2001

The War on Drugs

Ours is a federal republic. The federal government has only the powers granted to it in the Constitution. And the United States has a tradition of individual liberty, vigorous civil society, and limited government. Identification of a problem does not mean that the government ought to undertake to solve it, and the fact that a problem occurs in more than one state does not mean that it is a proper subject for federal policy.

Perhaps no area more clearly demonstrates the bad consequences of not following such rules than drug prohibition. The long federal experiment in prohibition of marijuana, cocaine, heroin, and other drugs has given us unprecedented crime and corruption combined with a manifest failure to stop the use of drugs or reduce their availability to children.

In the 1920s Congress experimented with the prohibition of alcohol. On February 20, 1933, a new Congress acknowledged the failure of alcohol prohibition and sent the Twenty-First Amendment to the states. Congress recognized that Prohibition had failed to stop drinking and had increased prison populations and violent crime. By the end of 1933, national Prohibition was history, though many states continued to outlaw or severely restrict the sale of liquor.

Today Congress confronts a similarly failed prohibition policy. Futile efforts to enforce prohibition have been pursued even more vigorously in the 1980s and 1990s than they were in the 1920s. Total federal expenditures for the first 10 years of Prohibition amounted to $88 million—about $733 million in 1993 dollars. Drug enforcement, which cost about $22 billion in the Reagan years and another $45 billion in the four years of the Bush administration, costs about $17 billion a year now in federal spending alone.

Those mind-boggling amounts have had some effect. Total drug arrests are now more than 1.5 million a year. Since 1989 more people have been incarcerated for drug offenses than for all violent crimes combined. There are about 400,000 drug offenders in jails and prison now, and over 80 percent of the increase in the federal prison population from 1985 to 1995 was due to drug convictions.

Yet, as was the case during Prohibition, all the arrests and incarcerations haven't stopped the use and abuse of drugs, or the drug trade, or the crime associated with black-market transactions. Cocaine and heroin supplies are up; the more our Customs agents interdict, the more smugglers import. And most tragically, the crime rate has soared. Despite the good news about crime in the past few years, crime rates remain at unprecedented levels.

As for discouraging young people from using drugs, the massive federal effort has largely been a dud. Despite the soaring expenditures on anti-drug efforts, about half the students in the United States in 1995 tried an illegal drug before they graduated from high school. Every year from 1975 to 1995, at least 82 percent of high school seniors said they found marijuana "fairly easy" or "very easy" to obtain. During that same period, according to federal statistics of dubious reliability, teenage marijuana use fell dramatically and then rose significantly, suggesting that cultural factors have more effect than the "war on drugs."

The manifest failure of drug prohibition explains why more and more people—from Baltimore mayor Kurt Schmoke to Nobel laureate Milton Friedman, conservative columnist William F. Buckley Jr., and former secretary of state George Shultz—have argued that drug prohibition actually causes more crime and other harms than it prevents.

Repeal the Controlled Substances Act

The United States is a federal republic, and Congress should deal with drug prohibition the way it dealt with alcohol prohibition. The Twenty-First Amendment did not actually legalize the sale of alcohol; it simply repealed the federal prohibition and returned to the several states the authority to set alcohol policy. States took the opportunity to design diverse liquor policies that were in tune with the preferences of their citizens. After 1933 three states and hundreds of counties continued to practice prohibition. Other states chose various forms of alcohol legalization.

The single most important law that Congress must repeal is the Controlled Substances Act of 1970. That law is probably the most far-reaching federal statute in American history, since it asserts federal jurisdiction over every drug offense in the United States, no matter how small or local in scope. Once that law is removed from the statute books, Congress should move to abolish the Drug Enforcement Administration and repeal all of the other federal drug laws.

There are a number of reasons why Congress should end the federal government's war on drugs. First and foremost, the federal drug laws are constitutionally dubious. As previously noted, the federal government can exercise only the powers that have been delegated to it. The Tenth Amendment reserves all other powers to the states or to the people. However misguided the alcohol prohibitionists turned out to have been, they deserve credit for honoring our constitutional system by seeking a constitutional amendment that would explicitly authorize a national policy on the sale of alcohol. Congress never asked the American people for additional constitutional powers to declare a war on drug consumers. That usurpation of power is something that few politicians or their court intellectuals wish to discuss.

Second, drug prohibition creates high levels of crime. Addicts are forced to commit crimes to pay for a habit that would be easily affordable if it were legal. Police sources have estimated that as much as half the property crime in some major cities is committed by drug users. More dramatically, because drugs are illegal, participants in the drug trade cannot go to court to settle disputes, whether between buyer and seller or between rival sellers. When black-market contracts are breached, the result is often some form of violent sanction, which usually leads to retaliation and then open warfare in the streets.

Our capital city, Washington, D.C., has become known as the "murder capital" even though it is the most heavily policed city in the United States. Make no mistake about it, the annual carnage that stands behind America's still shockingly high murder rates has nothing to do with the mind-altering effects of a marijuana cigarette or a crack pipe. It is instead one of the grim and bitter consequences of an ideological crusade whose proponents will not yet admit defeat.

Third, drug prohibition channels over $40 billion a year into the criminal underworld. Alcohol prohibition drove reputable companies into other industries or out of business altogether, which paved the way for mobsters to make millions through the black market. If drugs were legal, organized crime would stand to lose billions of dollars, and drugs would be sold by legitimate businesses in an open marketplace.

Fourth, drug prohibition is a classic example of throwing money at a problem. The federal government spends some $16 billion to enforce the drug laws every year—all to no avail. For years drug war bureaucrats have been tailoring their budget requests to the latest news reports. When drug use goes up, taxpayers are told the government needs more money so that it can redouble its efforts against a rising drug scourge. When drug use goes down, taxpayers are told that it would be a big mistake to curtail spending just when progress is being made. Good news or bad, spending levels must be maintained or increased.

Fifth, the drug laws are responsible for widespread social upheaval. "Law and order" politicians too often fail to recognize that some laws can actually cause societal disorder. A simple example will illustrate that phenomenon. Right now our college campuses are relatively calm and peaceful, but imagine what would happen if Congress were to institute military conscription in order to wage a war in Bosnia or fight a dictator in the Middle East. Campuses across the country would likely erupt in protest—even though Congress did not desire that result. The drug laws happen to have different "disordering" effects. Perhaps the most obvious has been turning our cities into battlefields and upending the normal social order.

Drug prohibition has created a criminal subculture in our inner cities. The immense profits to be had from a black-market business make drug dealing the most lucrative endeavor for many people, especially those who care least about getting on the wrong side of the law.

Drug dealers become the most visibly successful people in inner-city communities, the ones with money, and clothes, and cars. Social order is turned upside down when the most successful people in a community are criminals. The drug war makes peace and prosperity virtually impossible in inner cities.

Students of American history will someday ponder the question of how today's elected officials could readily admit to the mistaken policy of alcohol prohibition in the 1920s but recklessly pursue a policy of drug prohibition. Indeed, the only historical lesson that recent presidents and Congresses seem to have drawn from Prohibition is that government should not try to outlaw the sale of booze. One of the broader lessons that they should have learned is this: prohibition laws should be judged according to their real-world effects, not their promised benefits. If the 106th Congress will subject the federal drug laws to that standard, it will recognize that the drug war is not the answer to problems associated with drug use.

Respect State Initiatives

The failures of drug prohibition are becoming obvious to more and more Americans. A particularly tragic consequence of the stepped-up war on drugs is the refusal to allow sick people to use marijuana as medicine. Prohibitionists insist that marijuana is not good medicine, or at least that there are legal alternatives to marijuana that are equally good. Those who believe that individuals should make their own decisions, not have their decisions made for them by Washington bureaucracies, would simply say that that's a decision for patients and their doctors to make. But in fact there is good medical evidence of the therapeutic value of marijuana— despite the difficulty of doing adequate research on an illegal drug. A recent National Institutes of Health panel concluded that smoking marijuana may help treat a number of conditions, including nausea and pain. It can be particularly effective in improving the appetite of AIDS and cancer patients. The drug could also assist people who fail to respond to traditional remedies.

More than 70 percent of U.S. cancer specialists in one survey said they would prescribe marijuana if it was legal; nearly half said they had urged their patients to break the law to acquire the drug. The British Medical

Association reports that nearly 70 percent of its members believe marijuana should be available for therapeutic use. Even President George Bush's Office of National Drug Control Policy criticized the Department of Health and Human Services for closing its special medical marijuana program.

Whatever the actual value of medical marijuana, the relevant fact for federal policymakers is that in 1996 the voters of California and Arizona authorized physicians licensed in those states to recommend the use of medical marijuana to seriously ill and terminally ill patients residing in the state without being subject to civil and criminal penalties.

In response to those referenda, however, the Clinton administration announced, without any intervening authorization from Congress, that any physician recommending or prescribing medicinal marijuana under state law would be prosecuted. In the February 11, 1997, *Federal Register*, the Office of National Drug Control Policy announced that federal policy would be as follows: (1) physicians who recommend and prescribe medicinal marijuana to patients in conformity with state law and patients who use such marijuana will be prosecuted; (2) physicians who recommend and prescribe medicinal marijuana to patients in conformity with state law will be excluded from Medicare and Medicaid; and (3) physicians who recommend and prescribe medicinal marijuana to patients in conformity with state law will have their scheduled-drug DEA registrations revoked.

The announced federal policy also encourages state and local enforcement officials to arrest and prosecute physicians suspected of prescribing or recommending medicinal marijuana and to arrest and prosecute patients who use such marijuana. And adding insult to injury, the policy also encourages the Internal Revenue Service to issue a revenue ruling disallowing any medical deduction for medical marijuana lawfully obtained under state law.

Clearly, this is a blatant effort by the federal government to impose a national policy on the people in the states in question, people who have already voted for a contrary policy. Federal officials do not agree with the policy the people have chosen; they mean to override it, local rule notwithstanding—just as the Clinton administration has tried to do in other cases, such as the California initiatives dealing with racial preferences and state benefits for immigrants.

Congress and the administration should respect the decisions of the voters in Arizona and California, and in the other states where such initiatives passed in 1998. One of the benefits of a federal republic is that different policies may be tried in different states. One of the benefits of our Constitution is that it limits the power of the federal government to impose one policy on the several states.

Repeal Mandatory Minimums

The common law in England and America has always relied on judges and juries to decide cases and set punishments. Under our modern system, of course, many crimes are defined by the legislature, and appropriate penalties are defined by statute. However, mandatory minimum sentences and rigid sentencing guidelines shift too much power to legislators and regulators who are not involved in particular cases. They turn judges into clerks and prevent judges from weighing all the facts and circumstances in setting appropriate sentences. In addition, mandatory minimums for nonviolent first-time drug offenders result in sentences grotesquely disproportionate to the gravity of the offenses. Absurdly, Congress has mandated minimums for drug offenses but not for murder and other violent crimes, so that a judge has more discretion in sentencing a murder than a first-time drug offender.

Rather than extend mandatory minimum sentences to further crimes, Congress should repeal mandatory minimums and let judges perform their traditional function of weighing the facts and setting appropriate sentences.

Conclusion

Drug abuse is a problem, for those involved in it and for their family and friends. But it is better dealt with as a moral and medical than as a criminal problem—"a problem for the surgeon general, not the attorney general," as Mayor Schmoke puts it.

The United States is a federal republic, and Congress should deal with drug prohibition the way it dealt with alcohol prohibition. The Twenty-First Amendment did not actually legalize the sale of alcohol; it simply repealed the federal prohibition and returned to the several states the authority to set alcohol policy. States took the opportunity to design diverse liquor policies that were in tune with the preferences of their citizens. After 1933 three states and hundreds of counties continued to practice prohibition. Other states chose various forms of alcohol legalization.

Congress should repeal the Controlled Substances Act of 1970, shut down the Drug Enforcement Administration, and let the states set their own policies with regard to currently illegal drugs. They would do well to treat marijuana, cocaine, and heroin the way most states now treat alcohol: It should be legal for licensed stores to sell such drugs to adults. Drug sales to children, like alcohol sales to children, should remain illegal. Driving under the influence of drugs should be illegal.

With such a policy, Congress would acknowledge that our current drug policies have failed. It would restore authority to the states, as the Founders envisioned. It would save taxpayers' money. And it would give the states the power to experiment with drug policies and perhaps devise more successful rules.

Repeal of prohibition would take the astronomical profits out of the drug business and destroy the drug kingpins who terrorize parts of our cities. It would reduce crime even more dramatically than did the repeal of alcohol prohibition. Not only would there be less crime; reform would also free police to concentrate on robbery, burglary, and violent crime.

The war on drugs has lasted longer than Prohibition, longer than the Vietnam War. But there is no light at the end of this tunnel. Prohibition has failed, again, and should be repealed, again.

Cato Handbook for Congress, 1999

PART **13**

America and the World

Hating Freedom

The monstrous attacks of Sept. 11 have brought Americans together like nothing since Pearl Harbor. Flags fly from homes and offices, Hollywood stars sing patriotic songs, and Republicans and Democrats in Congress praise each other. The attack on America was so shocking that it even caused Bill and Hillary Clinton to join Lee Greenwood in singing "God Bless the U.S.A.," a song usually heard only on country radio and at Republican conventions.

Most Americans have rallied around President Bush's eloquent defense of American values: "This is civilization's fight. This is the fight of all who believe in progress and pluralism, tolerance and freedom."

But not quite everyone. There are a few people who don't "believe in progress and pluralism, tolerance and freedom." Jerry Falwell and Pat Robertson got the most attention for arguing on national television that God had given the United States "probably what we deserve" because of "the feminists, and the gays and the lesbians," and the ACLU. Leftist filmmaker Michael Moore matched them in vitriol with this ugly statement on his website: "They did not deserve to die. If someone did this to get back at Bush, then they did so by killing thousands of people who DID NOT VOTE for him! Boston, New York, D.C. and the planes' destination of California—these were places that voted AGAINST Bush!"

Even more disturbing are the comments of presumably more sophisticated thinkers. Katha Pollitt writes in the *Nation* that she won't fly the American flag because "the flag stands for jingoism and vengeance and war." Even when terrorists kill thousands of American citizens, she sees nothing but evil in the symbol of America.

Nobel Prize-winning playwright Dario Fo wrote in a widely circulated e-mail: "The great speculators wallow in an economy that every year kills tens of millions of people with poverty, so what is 20,000 dead in New York? Regardless of who carried out the massacre, this violence is the legitimate daughter of the culture of violence, hunger and inhumane exploitation."

That sums up the criticism of America that unites the Islamic terrorists, the anti-globalization street protesters, the resentful right, and the literary left: They hate the culture of markets and liberalism. They hate the Enlightenment and modernity.

They hate reason, science, technology, individualism, pluralism, tolerance, progress and freedom. To be more specific, they hate Wall Street,

Hollywood, McDonald's, Starbucks, Microsoft, and the casual joy of American freedom. These people share H. L. Mencken's definition of Puritanism: "The haunting fear that someone, somewhere, may be happy."

Most of these people wouldn't blow up a building. But when someone does blow one up—especially the tallest, most arrogant buildings on Wall Street—they can't bring themselves to say killing innocent people is evil. (And if some would object that Wall Street greed is hardly innocent, they should consider Samuel Johnson's observation: "there are few ways in which a man can be more innocently employed than in getting money.")

Indeed, some of the people whose job is to warn us against evil can't bring themselves to see it. Seattle Presbyterian pastor John Worster complained to National Public Radio about President Bush's use of religious language—good vs. evil—to discuss a political conflict. "When, from the highest office in our government that kind of language is used, it seems to me it's just an attempt to stir up a kind of blind patriotism that says, 'We can do no wrong, and anybody who doesn't follow our style of life must be evil.'"

But Bush didn't say that other lifestyles are evil. He said that terrorism is evil. That should be an easy distinction to understand.

One consequence of the evil acts of Sept. 11 was to help us all remember what is good about America. And another was to give a few people an opening to reveal to us what they really think about America—they don't like our freedom, our openness, our tolerance, our prosperity, our exuberance.

Chicago Sun-Times, October 2, 2001

Prosecuting the War

Many of us at the Cato Institute find ourselves in an unusual position these days. In the first place, starting early last year, we found ourselves harboring generally positive thoughts about the incumbent president, a feeling we had rarely known. Despite his unfortunate initiatives on education centralization, energy subsidies, and some other areas, President Bush strongly advocated tax reduction, rejected the costly and unnecessary Kyoto agreement on global warming, and stuck to his guns on Social Security reform.

And then came September 11. Now we find ourselves not just supporting a president but supporting an American war against the terrorists who attacked us and their Taliban protectors. We have, of course, long criticized the United States' interventionist foreign policy. We warned that military intervention around the world was dangerous. We even warned that it could lead to terrorist attacks on the United States. We pointed out that our recent wars did not involve the vital interests of the United States. But we always said that the United States would have to respond, and respond vigorously, to an attack.

Now we have been attacked. Cato scholars immediately called for a military response. On September 11, Ted Galen Carpenter wrote: "The first order of business must be to determine who is responsible for these terrible acts and to order appropriate retaliation. Terrorist assaults of this magnitude should be treated as an act of war against the United States, not merely as a criminal justice matter. The president should immediately seek the full authorization of Congress to use whatever military force is necessary against the guilty parties. If the perpetrator is a government, the objective of the United States should be nothing less than the removal of that government. If the perpetrator is a terrorist organization without government sponsorship, the objective of the United States should be to track down and eliminate the members of that organization."

We also sought to define the nature of the conflict. As Ed Crane wrote in the last issue of *Cato Policy Report:* "Those attacks were attacks on the essence of America. They were not attacks on the 'mixed economy' or on the 'Third Way.' They were attacks on true liberalism—the idea that individual human life is important and that social institutions should reflect that fact. America is a great nation because it was created with a Declaration of Independence and a Constitution designed to acknowledge and enhance the importance and dignity of human beings."

President Bush and his team have made a good start in eliminating those who attacked us. The president offered a vigorous but measured response, carefully planned and focused on the perpetrators of the September 11 atrocities and those who harbored them.

Cato scholars will be offering several recommendations as we continue the war against the terrorists who attacked America, including:

Improve civil defense. Administration officials tell us that "there is a clear, present danger" of worse attacks than we have experienced, a point that government reports have made over the past decade. Yet, as a November 2000 Cato study warned, the federal government has done little to educate Americans about how to respond to nuclear, biological, or chemical attacks, or to stockpile antidotes and anti-viruses. It's time to do so.

Round up al Qaeda operatives in the United States. Our leaders are right to warn us against hate crimes directed at Muslims and at people who "look like Arabs." We must not forget the kind of country we are. But when we find people living in this country who are involved in a terror network, we need to move forcefully.

If we know of noncitizens involved with terrorists, we should round them up. If the evidence isn't there to prosecute them for a crime, we can still deport them—not because of their ethnicity but because the FBI has identified them as agents of a terror network. No one has the right to come to this country for the purpose of mayhem and murder.

Build a new bomber. In conflicts such as the one we're entering, the United States may find air bases close to the fighting unavailable or vulnerable to enemy attack—especially by ballistic missiles. Yet the U.S. Air Force is investing billions of dollars in two new types of tactical fighter aircraft that require access to such bases. In contrast, the Air Force will not begin research and development on a new long-range bomber until 2013 and will not begin producing the aircraft until 2034. Heavy bombers can carry heavier payloads over much longer ranges than can fighters and can operate from less-vulnerable bases in theaters that are farther away from the fighting or even from bases in the United States. No matter what type of foreign policy the United States adopts in the future, it will need the ability to project power abroad. It's time to start developing a new bomber.

Spend our defense dollars wisely. Advocates of increased military spending have seized on the atrocities of September 11 as an excuse to spend "hundreds of billions more" on the military. But we don't need another million men, or more tanks and cruise missiles, to fight this war. Instead of throwing money at the problem, we should take a close look at the Pentagon's budget: eliminate what we don't need and reallocate resources to real needs like civil defense, missile defense, and human intelligence. We should close obsolete military bases, terminate wasteful and unnecessary weapons programs, and withdraw our troops from Korea.

Reorient drug war resources to the war on terrorism. Some officials have compared the new war on terrorists with the war on drugs. That's a depressing thought: We've been fighting the drug war for 87 years, and drug use is as high as ever. A better tack is to take the $40 billion we spend annually on the futile drug war and reallocate it to the war on terrorism. Use the Drug Enforcement Administration's agents to search for pipe bombs, not marijuana pipes.

Protect civil liberties. Cato scholars Robert Levy and Timothy Lynch have been among the most forceful critics of President Bush's executive order empowering himself to order military trials of non-U.S. citizens—even if they are arrested here, are tried here, and reside here legally. Bush need only assert that he has "reason to believe" the noncitizen is involved in international terrorism. Combatants encountered on the battlefields of Afghanistan may be dealt with militarily, but people legally residing in the United States have rights that must be protected. We should also be very concerned about the expansion of federal search and surveillance powers—involving bank accounts, e-mail, business records, and so on—in the name of fighting terrorism.

Protect the taxpayers. It's understandable that the federal government will need to increase spending in some areas to fight terrorism. But since September 11 we have seen everything from airline bailouts to peanut subsidies to steel protectionism justified in the name of national security. A more sensible approach would be to cut low-priority spending in order to fund higher-priority needs.

Usually, libertarians enter public debates to call for restrictions on government activity. In the wake of September 11, we have all been reminded of the proper purpose of government: to protect our lives, liberties, and property from violence. Now would be a good time for the federal government to do its job with vigor and determination.

Cato Policy Report, January/February 2002

Word Associations

Let me start by saying that I was not and am not a supporter of the Iraq war, and I'm almost equally skeptical of all religions. But I was appalled to hear Seyyed Hossein Nasr, a leading Islamic scholar, declare on an NPR interview show on Tuesday that the Pope's statements criticizing Islam "themselves are acts of violence."

Interviewer Diane Rehm wanted to make sure what she'd heard. She asked him, "You're saying that the language itself is an act of violence?" "Of course it is," Nasr replied. Discussing the violent reaction to the Pope's quotation, he declared, "He who uses the sword shall perish by the sword."

Later in the show, Rehm read a quotation from a column by Anne Applebaum, who wrote that westerners of all political stripes "can all unite in our support for freedom of speech—surely the Pope is allowed to quote from medieval texts—and of the press. And we can also unite, loudly, in our condemnation of violent, unprovoked attacks on churches, embassies and elderly nuns."

Asked for his reaction, Nasr said that the attacks were not unprovoked. "Because words are violence?" asked Rehm. "Of course," replied Nasr, "of course."

I want to be careful not to pick out obscure members or adherents of any philosophy and draw large conclusions from them. But Nasr is not so obscure. He's a distinguished professor at a leading American university. He holds a PhD in the history of science and philosophy from Harvard and is the author of more than 20 books, from publishers including Oxford University Press. His university held a conference honoring him, titled Beacon of Knowledge. The website of the Seyyed Hossein Nasr Foundation declares him "one of the most important and foremost scholars of Islamic, religious and comparative studies in the world today." So it seems fair to say that Nasr is not an oddity; he's a recognized Islamic scholar.

And that's why it's so shocking to hear the claim that words "are acts of violence" from such a distinguished scholar. A scholar, we might note, who teaches at George Washington University, named in honor of the great Enlightenment statesman. I don't want to believe that we are faced with a clash of civilizations, much less the third world war. But if Islamic scholars who teach at great American universities believe that violent attacks "on churches, embassies and elderly nuns" are "provoked" by the words of a religious leader in a university speech a thousand miles away, then we certainly have a clash of world views.

The West went through the wars of religion and emerged with a modern understanding of toleration. We have learned through bitter experience that we can worship God without forcing everyone else to worship in the same way. We allow our neighbors to practice their religion, we practice our own or none at all, we criticize views we deem unsound, and we accept that our own views and faith will also be subject to criticism.

What we forswear is violence in response to words. In the present crisis we should seek peaceful dialogue between Muslims and Christians, not to mention Jews and freethinkers and all the others who share our world. But we who live in Enlightenment societies should not apologize for the fact that freedom of thought and freedom of speech sometimes lead to hurtful words.

Instead, we should reaffirm our own commitment to free speech—"hate speech" laws, anyone?—and urge Muslims to appreciate the benefits of liberal values, such as liberty and prosperity and social harmony. And we should hold Muslim leaders to the same standards we expect of western leaders, both civil and religious: we expect them to condemn, yes, "unprovoked" violence.

Comment Is Free, September 20, 2006

Promoting Democratic Capitalism

Libertarians spend quite a bit of effort criticizing the government of the United States and recommending major policy changes. This is obviously appropriate to our role as an American public policy institute. But as we look at the world in a broader sense, it is clear that the sins of the United States government, great as they are, pale in comparison with those of the rest of the world. We Americans are richer and in many ways freer than any other people on earth now or ever in history.

Caught up in our important battles to preserve and expand freedom in the United States, we sometimes forget that much of the rest of the world remains in misery. The contrast between the relative freedom and prosperity of the capitalist democracies and the poverty and oppression of the Second and Third Worlds is so stark as to be hardly imaginable. Every American, of course, has been touched by the pictures of famine victims in Ethiopia, but the temptation is to set that aside as an occurrence more extraordinary than it really is.

Two other recent depictions of Third World poverty brought this lesson home to me. Jonathan Kwitny's descriptions in his book *Endless Enemies* of the bleakness of life in Africa and Afghanistan are heartbreaking. And the Cambodia portrayed in the movie *The Killing Fields*, even before the victory of the murderous Khmer Rouge, is a place where life seems hardly human to an American.

Another way to comprehend the gap between the capitalist democracies and the Third World is to look closely at the complaints about life in the United States. A recent country song features a lament by a "working man" who has "four bald tires on my pickup truck and no credit left on my credit card." Imagine trying to explain his sad plight to a Nicaraguan or a Zairian.

Clearly we would do far more for the cause of global freedom and justice by bringing the Third World into the democratic capitalist world than by moving the United States closer to the ideal of freedom. (Of course, the latter may well be the best way to accomplish the former.)

Military intervention seems to have failed. Even when the United States was successful in installing or maintaining friendly rulers in Third World nations, its chosen representatives hardly advanced our stated values of democracy and free enterprise: consider the Shah of Iran, Somoza in Nicaragua, Marcos in the Philippines, Mobutu in Zaire. When the United States backs autocrats like the Shah and Somoza, is it any wonder that intellectuals and others in society are driven into the arms of Marxism or radical Islam? Besides the risk of war for the United States, military intervention is an ultimately futile way to promote our values in the Third World.

More recently, many Americans have endorsed a government effort to "foster the infrastructure of democracy" overseas, in President Reagan's words. The chosen instrument for this effort is the National Endowment for Democracy. It has given money, for instance, to the Nicaraguan newspaper *La Prensa* and to Polish emigré journals. Now, because we yield to no one in our enthusiasm for such publications, we must ask, do we really want *La Prensa* to become known as a CIA front? That will be the result of U.S. government support for it, and there will then be no respected independent voice in Nicaragua.

Ideas garner more respect in the Third World when they do not appear to be put forward by a government that has a long history of unwarranted meddling around the world. Advocates of capitalism and democracy should work to spread their ideas through as many non-governmental means as possible. The Cato Institute has endeavored to spread its ideas beyond the United States, notably with its 1982 book *Solidarity with Liberty* distributed widely in Poland. At our last two Summer Seminars in Political Economy, we have had participants from more than a dozen foreign countries, including not just Canada and Western European nations, but Nigeria, South Africa, Ecuador, Brazil, and Guatemala, as well as American citizens born and educated in Korea and Iran. These efforts are important and should be expanded.

As usual, the words of Thomas Jefferson are a good guide for us: "Peace, commerce, and honest friendship with all nations—entangling alliances with none." Cultural and economic relationships with the nations of the world will help us spread our ideas and our values; military and political entanglements have tragically failed to do so. If we care about peace, prosperity, and freedom around the world, we must live up to our values, not try to export them by force.

Cato Policy Report, July/August 1985

Flood South Africa with American Culture

A popular bumper sticker in Washington reads, "Boycott South Africa, Not Nicaragua." This seems to sum up the level of debate in town: we've decided to boycott somebody; now we're just arguing about who it should be.

In neither case is it clear exactly why we're boycotting. Presumably we want to punish someone. But the advocates of sanctions rarely stop to consider just who will be hurt by our sanctions. Sometimes they're proud of this lack of interest in results. *Washington Post* columnist Richard Cohen wrote recently, "Maybe in the short run [sanctions] will hurt poor blacks more than rich whites. But the idea, first and foremost, is to make a moral statement: to answer the question: 'Which side are you on?'"

Cohen offers a parody—or perhaps just the quintessence—of modern American liberalism, which often seems to feel that striking a moral pose is more important than achieving positive results. Welfare probably hurts the poor, but upper-middle-class Americans feel good about paying taxes for welfare. We've done something about the poor, they can tell themselves. Never mind whether the poor are better off.

Similarly, sanctions against the racist government of South Africa will make Americans feel better. Never mind whether they help the oppressed majority in South Africa.

In fact, if we really want to move South Africa into the modern world, we shouldn't boycott it—instead, we should swamp South Africa with American culture. Our culture portrays a way of life that is tremendously appealing to people in many countries, including South Africa. And one of the key aspects of the American way of life is racial integration.

Why should we want to deny South Africans, black and white, the opportunity to see a free, prosperous, and racially diverse society that works so well? Let South Africans watch "The Cosby Show," listen to Bruce Springsteen records, go to Diana Ross concerts, read American books, laugh at "Doonesbury." The message of this great mélange of cultural variety is that America is what a country should be. South Africa needs more American influence, not less.

Another problem with sanctions is that they will weaken the business community, the most progressive part of South African society. The English in South Africa, who dominate the economy, are far more liberal than the Afrikaners, a rather primitive tribe suited mainly for such simple tasks as farming and government. English-speaking businessmen have pushed the limits of apartheid, admitting blacks to white restaurants before it was legal to do so, training blacks for skilled-worker jobs, and so on. By cutting off South African trade with Americans, we would weaken the position of business and tip the balance of power in society further toward the Afrikaners and the government.

And, of course, pulling American companies out of South Africa is not likely to result in a more liberal economy or society. (However, it is entirely appropriate for American companies to refuse to do business with the South African *government*, as when General Motors announced recently that it will continue to sell cars in South Africa but will stop its sales to the South African police and military. Such actions will have the beneficial effect of continuing American interaction with South African society but not strengthening the government.)

Ironically, many of the people who understand the problems with sanctions against South Africa support President Reagan's embargo against Nicaragua. Again, some of them defended it despite their understanding of those problems. Sen. Nancy Kassebaum (R-Kans.) said, "I never believed sanctions will make a lot of difference. I just felt it was important to take an action that could be legally done and would show we're not going to carry on business as usual with the Sandinistas."

Of course, the same considerations noted above apply in this case as well. The embargo, if it has any effect at all, will weaken Nicaragua's already staggering private sector. It will cut off Nicaraguans' ties with the democratic capitalist world and probably strengthen the position of the Sandinistas in Nicaraguan society. As with South Africa, surely the last thing we want to do in Nicaragua is tilt the balance of power further toward the government.

Will economic sanctions improve the lives of either South African blacks or Nicaraguan campesinos? Almost certainly not. Do the advocates of sanctions care, or are they just engaging in moral posturing?

Cato Policy Report, July/August 1986

Free Trade, Limited Government, and Secession

Multinational states and empire-states are tottering around the world. The Soviet colonies have suddenly seized their independence, and now the internal empire is coming apart. Lithuania has declared its independence, Estonia and Latvia are on the verge of doing so, the Central Asian republics are restive, and even Russia itself may be finding imperialism a burden rather than a benefit. Meanwhile, North American newspapers are full of dire predictions that the Quebecois really mean it this time and are going to secede from Canada, and the countries of Central Europe, out from under the boot of Stalinist oppression, are beginning to wonder just *how* they got their present boundaries.

Perhaps the centuries-long era of the nation-state is coming to an end. In separate studies, Richard McKenzie and George Gilder have recently pointed out that governments are losing their ability to tax and regulate. Because value is increasingly found inside the human mind rather than in natural resources or huge factories, capital can more easily flee repressive regimes.

One of the most important lessons of America's economic success is the value of broadening the geographic area in which trade is free. Smaller countries such as Hong Kong and Switzerland have prospered by keeping their borders open to trade, and Europe is struggling toward that goal with its 1992 process.

If national borders are not used for the mercantilist purpose of regulating trade, how important are they? We live increasingly in a world of international culture, united more and more by a global language. Border guards and strong central governments are fighting a rear-guard action, trying to maintain their control over land and people.

Another lesson of the American experience is the value of federalism and a strictly limited central government. Switzerland may be an even better example. Although it has only about 7 million people, Switzerland has three major language groups and people with distinctly different cultures. It has solved the problem of cultural conflict with a very decentralized political system—20 cantons and 6 half-cantons, responsible for most public affairs, and a weak central government that handles foreign affairs, money creation, and enforcement of a bill of rights.

In their book *After Apartheid: The Solution for South Africa*, Frances Kendall and Leon Louw propose a similar model for South Africa: 150 or so virtually autonomous cantons and a federal government whose activities would be restricted to foreign affairs, national defense, currency issue, major infrastructure, and the enforcement of a bill of rights. They argue that such a system would be the best way to guarantee individual rights for all South Africans and that competition among the cantons would help to limit economically destructive legislation. It might also be a good solution for the rest of Africa, which is still suffering much ethnic strife because of the absurd "national" borders left behind by the colonial powers.

One of the key insights offered by the Swiss system is that cultural conflicts can be minimized when they don't become political conflicts. Thus the more of life that is kept in the private sphere or at the local level, the less need there is for cultural groups to go to war over religion, education, language, and so on. The American Founders were the first to recognize the value of separation of church and state; since the state didn't impose one religion on everyone, it wasn't important for religious groups to fight for control of the state. A free market serves the same function: by limiting the number of decisions made in the public sector, it reduces the need for groups to vie for political control.

Separation of education and state could be just as beneficial as separation of church and state. Ethnic Hungarians in Romania, for instance, could choose to send their children to Hungarian-language schools. Much Catholic resentment in Northern Ireland stems from having to send children to state schools in which they must say Anglican prayers.

Similar constitutional arrangements might reduce other cultural and social conflicts. The *intifada* might never have arisen on the West Bank if the Palestinians living there had had self-government, their own schools, and the right to engage freely in commerce. And certainly religious freedom, privatization of schools, and an absence of economic regulation would help to avoid the potential ethnic conflicts in Central Europe.

People around the world are coming to understand the benefits of limited government and devolution of power. Even in faraway Azerbaijan, a young liberal recently reported, "My friends and I have been thinking, couldn't we solve the conflict between Armenians and Azerbaijanis not by moving the borders but by making them unimportant—by abolishing internal passports and allowing property ownership and the right to work on both sides of the border?"

Classical liberals need not fear the breakup of nation-states, large or small. Large political units should be given no automatic preference. Secession should be favored where a clear popular consensus exists in the seceding territory and the newly independent country will respect minority rights. And most important, limited constitutional government, free trade, free markets, protection of individual rights, and devolution of power reduce social conflict and make questions of national borders and secession much less urgent.

Cato Policy Report, July/August 1990

The Return of Woodrow Wilson

In July 1990 the Cato Institute invited journalists and others to an August 7 luncheon at which we would release "America's Peace Dividend," a 64-page study of reducing military spending in the post-cold-war era. On August 2 Iraq invaded Kuwait.

Many of our friends expressed their sympathy, suggesting that our study was no longer relevant. Our timing *was* bad in the sense that journalists mesmerized by the prospect of war were no longer very eager to cover analyses of the new strategic realities that point to a reduced U.S. military presence around the world. But in another sense, our study was perfectly timed—if we are going to withdraw American troops from the far corners of the world and reduce military spending, the Persian Gulf crisis is just the sort of conflict we are going to have to stay out of.

By the time this is printed, the United States may be at war in the Persian Gulf. If things go very smoothly—for either side—the war may even be over. But win, lose, or continue the stand-off, it is probably safe to predict that American troops will be in the Middle East for some time. The 400,000 troops in the gulf or headed there in December constitute the largest concentration of American forces outside the United States since the Vietnam War.

A number of arguments for U.S. intervention have been offered; the most popular seems to be "We just can't let Saddam get away with it." But what is the "it" we can't tolerate? Unprovoked aggression? Condemnable as unprovoked aggression surely is, we tolerate it all the time. In recent years, we have tolerated China's occupation of Tibet, Vietnam's invasion of Cambodia, Russia's occupation of the Baltic nations, Indonesia's invasion and annexation of East Timor, and—in just the past few weeks—the conquest of Lebanon by our new ally Syria. And we didn't complain about Iraq's unprovoked attack on Iran a few years ago.

Though sophisticated defenders of our intervention insist that the issue is not access to oil, it's clear that if the major export from the Arabian Peninsula were coffee we wouldn't have 400,000 troops there. Oil is what President Bush had in mind when he said that we have "to protect our way of life" and what Secretary of State James A. Baker III meant by "in a word, jobs." But oil is not sufficient reason for war.

The most likely motivation for Bush, Baker, and the rest of the foreign policy establishment is not to punish aggression or to secure access to oil. It is to preserve the military-industrial complex, an inspiration perhaps best explained by scholars of public choice. The United States has recently been spending $300 billion a year on its military and some $20 billion more on the State Department, foreign aid, international lending agencies, and the like. The collapse of the Soviet threat called that spending into question. The Bush administration agreed to reduce the armed forces by 25 percent, and Congress was threatening even greater cuts. Outside experts were questioning the rationale for keeping 320,000 troops in Europe—to defend whom from whom?—and 110,000 in East Asia.

Then Saddam Hussein invaded Kuwait, and the military-industrial complex breathed a sign of relief. The long twilight struggle against communism would be succeeded by an even longer struggle for a "new world order" characterized by "international stability." Of course, the new crusade is supposed to spread freedom and democracy, an awkward point when the immediate beneficiaries are hereditary monarchies, but stability will suffice for the moment.

The ghost of Woodrow Wilson stalks Washington, as policy analysts in the State Department and in think tanks churn out papers calling for a new global strategy of "nation building" and "low-intensity conflict."

The quest for a new world order is a prescription for perpetual conflict. Not only does it provide a pretext for keeping 2.1 million troops under arms, it offers full employment till kingdom come for the State Department, the Agency for International Development, the National Endowment for Democracy, the World Bank, the International Monetary Fund, and all the other members of the military-diplomatic-foreign aid complex.

But there are increasing signs that Americans are growing tired of playing world policeman. As the crisis in the Persian Gulf stretches into a long-term expedition, support for the president's policies is dropping in the polls. Despite the tax rate cuts of 1981, the federal tax burden is now unprecedentedly high, and another tax revolt is brewing. Americans have paid for the cold war for 40 years, and they are ready to collect the peace dividend that should be theirs at the end of that struggle.

To reduce military spending and give that much-deserved relief to American taxpayers, we need to rethink our strategy of global alliances and interventionism. We must accept that the world is full of unfortunate and even outrageous acts that are simply not the business of the U.S. government and recognize that U.S. intervention frequently causes more problems than it cures. If the era of John Foster Dulles is over, we must look again not to the messianic crusading of Woodrow Wilson but to the vision of John Quincy Adams: "America goes not abroad in search of monsters to destroy. She is the well-wisher to the freedom and independence of all. She is the champion and vindicator only of her own."

Cato Policy Report, January/February 1991

Private Property from Soweto to Shanghai

A trip around the world provides evidence of just how wrong Harvard economist John Kenneth Galbraith was in his influential book *The Affluent Society*. (Granted, one need not go nearly so far to find such evidence.)

Galbraith observed that everywhere one looked, privately provided goods and services—homes, automobiles, factories, "handsomely packaged products"—were clean, shiny, and of high quality. Yet publicly provided services—schools, parks, streets—were old, overcrowded, and poorly maintained. Galbraith called it "an atmosphere of private opulence and public squalor."

From those accurate if unremarkable observations, Galbraith drew the remarkably misguided conclusion that the problem was too little spending on the public sector. It seems astonishing today that a brilliant man could have gone so far astray; after all, the economic theory of private property was well known 30 years ago—but maybe not at Harvard. His book, published in 1958, had a great deal of influence on the explosion in government spending over the next decade. We are still paying a heavy price—in high taxes and poor public services—for Galbraith's error.

It may already have occurred to the reader that we are now spending much more on the public sector than we were 30 years ago—real government spending has increased from $528 billion in 1958 to $1,640 billion in 1988—yet government services are still shoddy, overcrowded, and poorly maintained.

The reason—which Galbraith missed completely—is that shoddiness is inherent in government ownership because of a lack of incentives. Homeowners generally take good care of their property—they paint the house regularly, fix the roof, plant grass and trees, and call a plumber promptly when they discover a leak. Why? Because they are the sole claimants to the property's value. If they try to sell their property, they will reap the benefits of the house's good condition or pay a price for its disrepair. Tenants tend to take less care of their homes, though landlords generally check on the condition of the property regularly. Tenants in government housing show the least concern for the condition of their homes—and because there's no owner who would pay a price for the declining value of the property, no one else has much incentive to improve it. And public housing is always in disrepair, to say the least.

Most privately owned stores are clean and well lit with friendly, helpful clerks—at least compared with, say, the post office. The Postal Service doesn't seek out rude and indifferent employees; it's just that neither its clerks nor their supervisors have anything to gain by treating customers well. On a recent trip around the world, I found shop clerks in Shanghai just as indifferent to customers as U.S. postal workers.

It is economic analysis and, more important, such observations that have created a worldwide trend toward privatization. The Thatcher government has sold public housing units to their tenants, sold Great Britain's largest trucking company to its employees, and sold the telephone company to private shareholders. Japan recently sold off its telephone company as well. New Zealand privatized its national oil company. Nigeria plans to privatize 160 state-owned companies, and Togo intends to sell all of its public-sector enterprises.

Even behind the Iron Curtain, privatization is making inroads. China has in effect privatized agricultural land, and Mikhail Gorbachev has proposed to do the same in the Soviet Union. Cuba has begun allowing tenants to purchase government housing.

On my trip, which took me from South Africa to China (with a few stops in between), I saw some dramatic examples of the differences between private and public ownership, between private opulence and public squalor.

In many ways apartheid (particularly in South Africa's black townships) was the purest form of communism the world had ever seen. The government built the townships, where urban blacks are forced to live. It built thousands of small, identical brick houses and assigned people to them with no regard to tribal origin, family relationships, income, or personal preferences. Unlike the residents of a normal town, they could not choose to live near their friends or relatives or people of similar educational or occupational background, nor, of course, did they have property rights. Not only could a tenant not sell his house, the government could and did take it away from him at will. Naturally, the unfortunate residents of Soweto did not see much point in taking good care of the houses.

Recently, however, the government quietly began to allow Sowetans to purchase their homes. The results have been just what one should expect: people are cleaning, painting, and fixing up their houses. The first thing they do is make the house look different from the government issue. They buy a wooden door to replace the standard metal one. They cover the brick with stucco—a design choice that I found strange until I was told that the brick symbolizes government housing. They buy decorative windows, put a fence around the yard, and even add a room or an upper floor.

Buyers must generally continue living in the houses they already occupy, which leads to the strange phenomenon of a well-kept, newly enlarged house sitting between two ill-kept government hovels. In a freer market, an affluent homeowner would probably move to a better neighborhood—or someone would buy the houses next door and fix them up—but in Soweto he takes advantage of the few options he has and improves his own lot.

There is a section of expensive new homes in Soweto. (Yes, there are rich people in Soweto; South African blacks have at least some opportunity to become rich, but their money won't free them from the requirement to live in the townships.) A visitor can stand in the middle of this impressive new development and look across the road at the government-provided barracks where single men live under truly appalling conditions. It's a striking example of private vs. public property.

At the other end of the scale from the impressive new houses are the shanties, built by blacks who migrated to the Johannesburg area because there was work there and were denied access to government housing. At first the government bulldozed the shanties, saying that the occupants were illegal squatters. More moderate voices finally persuaded the government that because it was not providing those blacks with housing (or allowing them to live outside the townships), it should at least leave the shanties alone. So now the shanties are tolerated, but they have no legal right to exist. The residents of the shanties don't bother to improve them—the government retains the right to expel the occupants or bulldoze the buildings at any time—but inside are appliances and televisions for which electricity is supplied by enterprising neighbors. In other words, Galbraith could find private opulence and public squalor within one small shack; people spend their money on the things they can own.

Obviously, a civilized South African government would repeal the Group Areas Act and let people live wherever they want to live. But the incentives of privatization and property rights can work even in the interstices of freedom overlooked by a repressive government.

In many ways, China is one big Soweto. Housing is owned and allocated by the government. Not surprisingly, the housing stock is old, over-crowded, dirty, and in disrepair. One gets the impression that little has been built and nothing has been washed since the Communist takeover in 1949.

Once again, the market works at the edges. Because of the de facto privatization of agricultural land, rural Chinese are more prosperous than city dwellers. I was told that two million people come into Shanghai every day to shop, and the tourist on Nanjing Road or in No. 1 Department Store wouldn't doubt it. For obvious reasons, people spend little money on the upkeep of their homes, but many are well dressed, and a Shanghai college student spoke disparagingly of the unfashionable clothes that "we won't buy" in a state department store. Old habits die hard, though; he explained to me that privately run stores are not allowed on Nanjing Road "because this is the main shopping center."

Appropriately enough, while I was in China for a conference on eco-nomic reform, the government announced plans to begin selling houses to the tenants. The professed reason was to dampen demand for appliances, which consumers were spending too much on; I hope that was just a cover story to obscure the fact that the largest Communist government in the world was legalizing private property. Presumably the Chinese government has noticed the success of privatization and property rights in the West; on its doorstep in Hong Kong, Taiwan, and South Korea; and finally in its own rural areas.

If China does in fact privatize a significant amount of its housing, I fully expect that when I return I will see not only housing that has been built since 1949 but older housing that has been repaired and even washed.

From the United States to Soweto to Shanghai, economic forces are the same. Owners have an incentive to take care of their property, but government property is owned by everyone and therefore by no one. It is no mystery that China's housing is rundown or that America's infrastructure is falling apart while shiny new office buildings are going up in every U.S. city.

Experience shows that the relationship between private opulence and public squalor is the reverse of what John Kenneth Galbraith concluded. The public sector will always tend to be squalid, which is why leaders around the world—from Margaret Thatcher to Deng Xiaoping—are moving essential services into the private sector. A little more of that, and the whole world could become the affluent society.

The Freeman: Ideas on Liberty, November 1989

From Russia, with Surprise

Gavriil Popov, the stooped, mustachioed economist turned mayor of Moscow, shuffles up to the podium. He tells the Soviet and Western participants in the Cato Institute's conference, "Transition to Freedom: The New Soviet Challenge," that prime Minister Nicolai Ryzhkov has betrayed the radicals by going back on his promise to submit to parliament a plan for rapid transition to the free market. Thus, Popov says, the radicals will take to the streets on Sunday to demand far-reaching privatization and the resignation of the Ryzhkov government. The next night, at an open forum attended by about 800 Muscovites, Popov delivers the most libertarian speech I've ever heard from a politician; he discusses the individualism and free markets of the 19th century, the unfortunate turn to Marxism and Keynesianism in the 20th century, and the bright prospect of a return to liberalism and capitalism by the beginning of the 21st.

What a delight to be in a country where "radical," "liberal," and "left" all carry the traditional meaning of support for democracy, free markets, and civil liberties. "Conservatives" defend the *ancien régime* of statism and privilege, as they did when the word was coined, and liberals call for progress toward private property and limited, decentralized government. Cato chairman William Niskanen reads in *The Economist* that the most popular words in the Soviet Union are, in ascending order, "radical, liberal, expert, economist." He's in heaven.

Outside the conference hall, it is easy to see why there is so much agitation for markets. Communism seems to do two things well: preserve old buildings—no creative destruction here—and build really big new buildings, row after row, block after block of ugly apartment buildings unsurprisingly reminiscent of American public housing. Our conference hotel, owned by the prestigious Academy of Sciences of the USSR, reminds us of a dormitory at a mediocre college after, say, 30 years of hard use. (Even that is too flattering; there are, for instance, no showers, and dish-cloths suffice for towels.) We are stunned to learn that it was built a year and a half ago. The windows don't quite close (who would have anticipated mosquitos in Moscow in September?), the floors have buckled, the bricks on the front gate are held together with wire. Mysteriously, the elevator offers buttons for floors 1 through 10, though the building is only three stories high. In one elevator, the buttons have been installed wrong and the proper numbers are penciled in.

Earlier on this trip, I had discovered the same huge, ugly buildings in East Berlin. All my life I have anticipated the fear and titillation I would get from crossing to the other side of the legendary Berlin Wall. But now, as Sidney Blumenthal reported in a recent *New Republic*, the Wall is mostly gone, and traffic moves freely between East and West Berlin. Now East Berlin is just sad, ugly, and boring. Maybe the ex-Communist countries should keep small areas of traditional police-state communism around behind a wall, to attract tourists—the way the British keep the monarchy around.

Comfort and convenience are not hallmarks of communism. All the stories you've heard about communist toilet paper are true. Fortunately, we've all brought our own, along with bottled water. We leave the water in our rooms for toothbrushing and so on, and we get desperately thirsty through long, salty meals with nothing but Russian champagne and warm Pepsi to drink. As for meals, we're covered. Mayor Popov has generously arranged sufficient stocks for us, which are brought to the hotel by armed guard. Twice a day, every day, in the hotel or at restaurants, we have the same meal. Variety is one of the spices of life missing in the Soviet Union. Meals on our own are much more difficult. One day several of us decide to spend the afternoon in downtown Moscow, eat dinner, and visit Red Square at night. Don't be ridiculous, our Russian host tells us, you can't expect to just walk into a restaurant and be served; there are restaurants, but you have to make reservations well in advance. We begin to wonder just who planned this system.

And speaking of planning: In all of Moscow there is one really beautiful building, the colorful onion-domed St. Basil's Cathedral in Red Square. When you buy the official pack of 18 Moscow postcards, there's no picture of St. Basil's.

It's not easy to say what the dollar-ruble exchange rate is. In the hard-currency stores, prices are marked in "rubles," which turn out to be worth $1.60 each. But at a bank you get 6 rubles (which cannot be used in the hard-currency stores) for a dollar, and the rate is anywhere from 10 to 20 for a dollar on the black market. But I never change any money on the black market because there is almost nothing I want in Moscow or Leningrad that can't be obtained for dollars. In Moscow, we have to go to the Arbat shopping street to find people selling the famous Russian matryushka dolls, black lacquer boxes, chess sets, and thousands of pins commemorating the triumphs of the Communist Party and the Soviet state. Walk down the street speaking English, and you will be offered other items, notably Gorby dolls—a set of matryushka dolls featuring a large doll painted to look like Gorbachev, with smaller dolls depicting Brezhnev, Khrushchev, Stalin, and Lenin inside. Sometimes the inside dolls are displayed, but never the Gorbachev doll—presumably because of the law making it a crime to insult the president. Most purchases are made in dollars, but the sellers always look both ways for policemen and sometimes tell us to hand the money to their associates a block away. Things are more open in Leningrad—as soon as we step off a tour bus, we are besieged with opportunities to buy military uniforms, fur hats, and caviar, and no one seems concerned about taking dollars. Gorby dolls are displayed openly.

So far there seems to have been lots of *glasnost* but very little *perestroika*. The people at our conference talk freely about radical political and economic changes, the newspapers publish Solzhenitsyn and other former dissidents, our Leningrad tour guides boast of the support for changing the city's name back to St. Petersburg. During our three days in Leningrad, the words "Marxism-Leninism" come down from a prominent building formerly adorned with the slogan "Long Live Marxism-Leninism." But there are long lines for cigarettes and gasoline—not to mention Baskin-Robbins and McDonald's—and shortages of bread are reported. With no private property, no one has an incentive to produce more, to invest, to offer better service, or even to wash anything. The beautiful old buildings of Leningrad could keep a sand-blasting company busy for decades.

The participants in our conference are mostly liberal intellectuals; they include journalists, scholars, activists, and elected officials. They're much more pro-capitalist than intellectuals and politicians in the West, but many are very pessimistic about the prospects for privatization. Three of them, one a member of the Moscow City Council, corner me at a reception. (And I do mean corner; they stand much closer than Americans like, and I keep backing up until I'm flat against the wall, unable to move my feet.) We know that Russia needs private property and free markets, they say, so tell us how to get there. I offer a plan for privatization, then another and another, and they tell me that "the people" will reject each of them. The people are afraid of inequality, resentful that some of their neighbors may become wealthy. Finally, I tell them that there is no magic path to capitalism and prosperity, that if the Soviet people are genuinely opposed to private property, then Russia will remain poor and backward and will fade into the sidelines of history. They continue to press me for some sort of answer that will allow them to bring about a modern capitalist system, and I retreat, feeling guilty and depressed at having no answer for them.

When one of our party complains about something at the hotel, the desk clerk responds, "It's not my fault; it's the housekeeper's fault." Fred Smith, president of Washington's Competitive Enterprise Institute, launches into an explanation of hotel management: "The customer doesn't care whose fault it is. When you're sitting at this desk, you are the hotel. He just wants you to fix his problem." The desk clerk has never heard of such a notion.

Travelling from Moscow to Leningrad, we take the overnight train, which turns out to be similar to Japan's love hotels. Young couples, married or not, forced to share a three-room flat with parents and siblings, spend the night on the way back, visit Leningrad for a day, then spend another night of conjugal bliss on the train. Over a bottle of champagne, three of us make bets on the Soviet Union's future. I say that bad as things in Moscow look, we Westerners are exaggerating the notion of crisis and collapse and that the system is going to muddle along at subsistence level with no real reform for the foreseeable future. A Wall Street whiz kid predicts bloodshed. But a libertarian economist, not given to optimism about what governments will do, is the only one of us who has attended the conference's final session on the 500-day plan drawn up by Stanislav Shatalin. It's a very radical plan, he says, it's already been passed by the Russian parliament (though not the Soviet Union's parliament), and Russia will be as capitalist as Western Europe in five years.

Liberty, January 1991

PART 14

The Nature of Government

The Who and Why of Big-Bucks Politics

Special-interest contributions to Congress are up sevenfold in the last nine years, but the new giving has just raised the price of influence.

Prominent lobbyist J. D. Williams laments, "The edge you get from raising money has been diluted. A few years ago, when fund raising as we now know it was in its infancy, it was vitally important.... Now ... there is such an availability of funds that it's not as important as it used to be." But fund raising goes on.

Pity the poor lobbyists. Every time they learn a new technique—PAC contributions, direct mail, grass-roots campaigns, junkets to Las Vegas—everyone else learns it, too, and soon there's no profit in it. But they can't stop doing it as long as their competitors are doing it.

Should any of this surprise us? Business people know that you have to invest to make money. Businesses invest in factories, labor, research and development, marketing, and all the other processes that bring goods to consumers and, they hope, lead to profits. They also invest in political processes that may yield profits.

If more money can be made by investing in Washington than by drilling another oil well, money will be spent there.

Nobel laureate F.A. Hayek explained the process 40 years ago in his prophetic book *The Road to Serfdom*: "As the coercive power of the state will alone decide who is to have what, the only power worth having will be a share in the exercise of this directing power."

As the size and power of government increase, we can expect more of society's resources to be directed toward influencing government. And indeed that is just what we have seen: Federal spending has risen from $200 billion in 1970 to more than $800 billion today. The staff size of regulatory agencies (a very rough estimate of the impact of regulation on society) has risen two-thirds in a decade.

Recognizing this increasing opportunity for political profits, interest groups have responded as we would expect. In 1971, New York had twice as many national trade associations as Washington. Today, Washington has 3,136 associations—500 more than New York—with 80,000 employees. Within the past decade, the number of Washington offices of out-of-town law firms has tripled. In 1970, five state governments had Washington offices; today the figure is 34. Total campaign spending rose from $425 million in 1972 to $1.2 billion in 1980. Now, 65 percent of the chief executive officers of Fortune 200 companies come to Washington at least once every two weeks, up from less than 15 percent a decade earlier.

What do all these people want in Washington? Money, of course, first of all. Every dollar spent by the federal government ends up in someone's pocket as a salary, a transfer payment, a subsidy, a purchase or a loan. But there are other valuable services available, too: regulations that eliminate or hamstring your competitors, for instance, or a tax provision that induces consumers to purchase your product.

In its successful effort to obtain a $1.1 billion loan guarantee for a shale-oil project, Tosco Corp. hired the Republican firm Black, Manafort, & Stone and former Reagan adviser Peter Hannaford, along with Democratic lobbyist Marcus Sisk, former Democratic Rep. William Moorhead and former Carter White House official Anne Wexler. Charlie Black explained candidly, "By using Moorhead and Sisk and Wexler on the Democratic side and us and Hannaford on the Republican side, they got better quality and better access for less money."

Efforts to restrain this growing special-interest influence on government have predictably failed. After the Watergate scandal, Congress placed severe limits on individual contributions to federal candidates. What happened? PAC spending soared. When the government taxes or regulates private economic activity, people find ways to get around the restrictions and continue supplying goods and services to others at a profit. And as long as there is a profit to be made by influencing government, people will find a way around those restrictions as well.

Despite our attempted restrictions, Mr. Hayek's dictum seems to remain true: When government decides "who is to have what," political power becomes "the only power worth having." Before the special-interest bidding for control of a powerful government gets completely out of hand, can we find a way to treat causes rather than symptoms?

Wall Street Journal, November 15, 1983

The Tentacles of Federal Funding

The government forbids arts agencies funded by the National Endowment for the Arts to present any "obscene" art.

Under pressure from the federal drug czar, Stanford University has fired an instructor who said he carried drugs in his backpack on campus.

And now the Supreme Court has ruled that the federal government may prohibit federally funded family-planning clinics from giving their clients advice about abortion.

The chickens are coming home to roost.

For decades opponents of big government have warned that government funding would mean government control. That insight, of course, is part of our folk wisdom: "He who pays the piper calls the tune." "Who takes the king's shilling sings the king's song." As each new program was created, opponents warned that government money always comes with strings attached.

But as long as liberals were in charge of both the funding and the control, they ignored the warnings. Government funding of everything under the sun was not only a way of redistributing wealth, it was a way of bringing everyone's actions under the control of progressive, fair-minded bureaucrats in Washington.

The laws sounded reasonable enough: Any college, or business, or hospital, or nonprofit agency that is a recipient of federal funds must abide by certain federal regulations. After all, it was reasoned, the federal government has a responsibility to monitor how taxpayers' money is being spent. So firms that did business with the government became subject to affirmative-action regulations, and health and safety regulations, and medical cost-containment rules, and drug-free workplace requirements.

Colleges that eagerly took the carrot of federal funding soon felt the stick of federal regulations. They faced myriad reporting requirements, especially to document compliance with anti-discrimination rules. Every member of Congress who had a good idea about how colleges should be run added an amendment to an appropriations bill: Any college receiving federal funds shall do thus and so.

But soon it came to pass that almost every company in America was doing some business with the feds and every college was receiving federal aid. It became almost impossible to escape the tentacles of Leviathan. And still the liberals in Washington were not worried, because they were writing the regulations.

But then came the 1980 election, and suddenly there were conservatives staffing the all-powerful federal government and imposing their values on the recipients of federal aid. Addicted to the narcotic of taxpayers' money, most recipients felt they had no choice but to comply.

Conservatives had once opposed most of the grant-making programs—federal aid to education, and health care, and the arts, and family-planning clinics, and so on. They had said that taxpayers were already overburdened, that such programs belonged at the state or local level if anywhere, and that the freedom and diversity of our society would be threatened by the spread of federal aid and control. But now, finding themselves in control of the federal purse strings, they decided it would be easier to make the programs reflect conservative values than to abolish the agencies and programs.

And so they did: using the Education Department to support a traditional curriculum, giving money to conservative scholars and foundations rather than liberal ones, putting anti-abortion restrictions on family-planning clinics, restricting the National Endowment for the Arts' ability to fund gay and avant-garde artists, proposing to forbid anti-racist speech codes on campus.

And suddenly liberals discovered the danger of big government. They wailed that the federal government was censoring, stifling, restricting—as indeed it was, and had been for decades. Only now it was conservatives doing the censoring and restricting.

Duke University law professor Walter Dellinger warned that such rules are "especially alarming in light of the growing role of government as subsidizer, landlord, employer and patron of the arts."

Dellinger is right. But the only way to solve the problem he raises is to reduce the government's role in society. Surely we can't expect taxpayers just to hand over $1.5 trillion a year to various agencies and interests without regulating how the money is spent. Their representatives in Congress and the administration think that those who are paying for the education, or the art, or the medical care have a right to say just what they will and will not pay for.

Fund recipients could thwart the government's intrusiveness by refusing to accept taxpayer funds, and a few are doing just that. Hillsdale College in Michigan is raising an endowment sufficient to ensure that none of its students will have to take federal loans, thus freeing itself from the heavy hand of the Education Department. A Fund for Gay Artists is raising private support for those who can't get federal funding. Some family planning clinics have announced that they will give up federal money in order to go on giving their clients the advice they think best, even about abortion.

But can we really imagine Stanford University turning down $260 million a year in federal funding just to protect its academic freedom? Will doctors refuse Medicare payments to avoid paperwork and red tape? Will the arts community turn down even the 7 percent of its total funding that it gets from government?

No, the reality is that as long as the government is handing out $1.5 trillion a year, most of us will be willing takers, and we will accept the controls that go with subsidies. If we want to preserve academic, artistic, economic, professional and speech freedoms, our only hope is to take away the federal government's role as the biggest subsidizer, landlord, employer and patron of the arts in our society.

Chicago Tribune, June 20, 1991

The Distended Public Sector

The United States has the highest quality health care in the world. At no previous time in history, and in no other country in the world, have we been able to cure as many people of as many injuries and diseases.

Our medical triumphs have had many side effects, one of the most obvious of which is rising costs. Medical costs have increased for a variety of reasons, including new technology and our ability to keep very sick people alive much longer.

Another reason for rising health care costs was identified in 1966 by economists William J. Baumol and William G. Bowen. They called it "the cost disease of the personal services," but most economists call it Baumol's disease. The thesis that productivity in personal services does not improve has recently been forcefully advanced in the health care debate by Sen. Daniel Patrick Moynihan, who argues, "Productivity in most sectors has improved dramatically in the past 200 years, but not in jobs such as the arts, teaching, law and health care, which require a high level of personal input."

He offers a persuasive example of how personal services resist productivity improvement: "In 1793 to 'produce' a Mozart quartet required four persons, four stringed instruments, and, say, 35 minutes. To produce a Mozart quartet today requires—four persons, four stringed instruments, 35 minutes."

Yet many more of us can hear a Mozart quartet today than in 1793. Why? In 1793 perhaps a few hundred people could hear each performance, and it was difficult and expensive for the players to move on to the next town where several hundred more people might gather. Today, however, the musicians can travel by bus, train, or airplane and reach many more audiences. Even more dramatically, the performance can be broadcast over radio and television to reach millions of listeners at once. Or it can be recorded and distributed worldwide on records, tapes, or compact discs. Thus, despite the apparent lack of any change in musical productivity, people today have the output of dozens of musical groups at their fingertips.

Moynihan identifies a number of services afflicted with Baumol's disease: "The services in question, which I call The Stagnant Services, included, most notably, health care, education, legal services, welfare programs for the poor, postal service, police protection, sanitation services, repair services . . . and others." He points out that many of those are

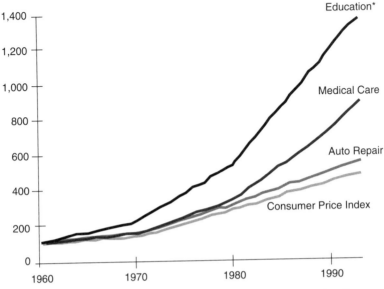

Price Trends: Health Care and Other Services vs the CPI
(1960 = 100)

*per-pupil education spending

provided by government and posits that "activities with cost disease migrate to the public sector."

But maybe he has it backwards. Maybe activities that migrate to the public sector become afflicted with cost disease. The conservative magazine *National Review*, which, surprisingly, seems to accept Moynihan's thesis, has inadvertently supplied us with some evidence on this point.

Ed Rubinstein, *National Review's* economic analyst, writes, "For more than three decades health-care spending has grown faster than national income. . . . The trend in health-care costs is no different from that of other services." He cites education and auto repair as examples. However, the numbers Rubinstein provides don't support his—or Moynihan's—point. Look at the accompanying figure.

The cost of auto repair, a service provided almost entirely in the private sector, has barely outpaced inflation. The cost of medical care increased twice as fast as inflation. Government's share of medical spending increased from 33 percent in 1960, when the chart begins, to 53 percent in 1990. Meanwhile, the cost of education, almost entirely provided by government, increased three times as fast as inflation—despite the constant complaints about underfunded schools.

The lesson is clear: Services provided by government are afflicted with Baumol's disease in spades. Services provided in the private sector, where people spend their own money, are much less likely to soar in cost.

Medical care is a good area in which to test this theory because over the past 30 years it has been paid for in three different ways: out-of-pocket spending by consumers; insurance payments, mostly provided by employers; and government payments. As out-of-pocket spending declines in importance, medical inflation heats up. And private-sector spending on medical care rose only 1.3 percent a year between 1960 and 1990, while government spending rose more than three times as fast—4.3 percent a year.

When services are provided privately, and consumers can decide whether to purchase them, or choose another provider, or do without, there's a powerful incentive to improve productivity and keep costs down. Stagnant productivity in government-run services reflects not so much Baumol's disease as what we might call Clinton's disease, the notion—even now, in 1994—that government can provide services more efficiently and cost-effectively than can the marketplace.

Senator Moynihan says the lesson of all this is that health care costs will keep rising as a percentage of our national income no matter how we pay for medical care. But the evidence points to a different lesson: people spend their own money more carefully than any senator or bureaucrat. To keep costs down, keep health care in the competitive marketplace.

Liberty, November 1994

The Big Government Building Boom

Remember when President Bill Clinton said, "The era of big government is over"? You couldn't tell it by my neighborhood.

I work in a less developed part of downtown Washington, D.C., which is now booming.

Construction cranes dot the sky. To walk two blocks to lunch, I keep having to cross the street to avoid sidewalks blocked by new construction. The big, solid, modern office building next door has been torn down—to be replaced by a larger and more luxurious building.

Yes, in the fifth year of Republican control of Washington, Washington is booming.

Republicans took control of Congress in 1994 by promising "the end of government that is too big, too intrusive, and too easy with the public's money." A look out my window says that isn't happening.

A review of the federal budget confirms it. Federal spending was up 33 percent in President Bush's first four years, making Bush the fastest spender of taxpayer dollars since President Lyndon Johnson. Between the pork-filled highway bill, the emergency spending bills for the war in Iraq and now the blank-check plans for Hurricane Katrina, he's breaking that record now.

When Katrina spending is factored in, Bush will likely be the fastest-spending president since Franklin D. Roosevelt during World War II.

Predictably, as resources are pulled from around the country to the capital, Washington is thriving. In the past four years, the Washington area gained more jobs than any other U.S. metro area. Real-estate prices have risen 89 percent in five years.

Three of the four richest counties in America are Washington suburbs. Only two states had faster income growth last year than D.C.

That's good news for those of us who own homes in Washington and enjoy the finer restaurants that serve a larger and wealthier population. But it's not good news for the rest of the country.

Money spent in Washington is taken from the people who produced it all over America. Washington produces little real value on its own. National defense and courts are essential to our freedom and prosperity, but that's a small part of what the federal government does these days. Most federal activity involves taking money from some people, giving it to others and keeping a big chunk as a transaction fee.

Every business and interest group in society has an office in Washington devoted to getting some of the $2.5 trillion federal budget for itself: senior citizens, farmers, veterans, teachers, social workers, oil companies, labor unions—you name it.

Walk down K Street, the heart of Washington's lobbying industry, and look at the directory in any office building. They're full of lobbyists and associations that are in Washington for one reason: because, as Willie Sutton said about why he robbed banks, "That's where the money is."

It's not just money that's being sucked into Washington. It's human talent, the most valuable productive asset of all. Too much of the talent at America's most dynamic companies is now diverted from productive activity to either getting corporate welfare from Congress or protecting the company from political predation.

Slow economic growth can be blamed in large measure on just this process—the expansion of the parasite economy into the productive economy. The number of corporations with Washington offices increased 10-fold between 1961 and 1982. The number of people lobbying in Washington doubled in the late 1970s—and it has doubled again just since 2000. The number of lawyers per million Americans stayed the same from 1870 to 1970, then more than doubled in just 20 years. The Federal Register, where new regulations are printed, now prints a record 75,000 pages a year.

As the parasite economy grows, taxing some people and doling out favors to others, everybody gets sucked in. Even if you don't want a government subsidy, you need a lobbyist to protect you from being taxed and regulated by the other groups and their lobbyists.

No wonder so many corporations have opened Washington offices, and so many luxury condominiums are being built in the blocks around my office.

New York Post, October 3, 2005

PART **15**

Life and Liberty

What to Be Thankful For

Not long ago a journalist asked me what freedoms we take for granted in America. Now, I spend most of my time sounding the alarm about the freedoms we're losing. But this was a good opportunity to step back and consider how America is different from much of world history—and why immigrants still flock here.

If we ask how life in the United States is different from life in most of the history of the world—and still in 2004 different from much of the world—a few key elements come to mind.

Rule of law. Perhaps the greatest achievement in history is the subordination of power to law. That is, in modern America we have created structures that limit and control the arbitrary power of government. No longer can one man—a king, a priest, a communist party boss—take another person's life or property at the ruler's whim. Citizens can go about their business, generally confident that they won't be dragged off the streets to disappear forever, and confident that their hard-earned property won't be confiscated without warning. We may take the rule of law for granted, but immigrants from China, Haiti, Syria, and other parts of the world know how rare it is.

Equality. For most of history people were firmly assigned to a particular status—clergy, nobility, and peasants. Kings and lords and serfs. Brahmans, other castes, and untouchables in India. If your father was a noble or a peasant, so would you be. The American Revolution swept away such distinctions. In America all men were created equal. Thomas Jefferson declared "that the mass of mankind has not been born with saddles on their backs, nor a favored few booted and spurred, ready to ride them legitimately, by the grace of God." In America some people may be smarter, richer, stronger, or more beautiful than others, but "I'm as good as you" is our national creed. We are all citizens, equal before the law, free to rise as far as our talents will take us.

Equality for women. Throughout much of history women were the property of their fathers or their husbands. They were often barred from owning property, testifying in court, signing contracts, or participating in government. Equality for women took longer than equality for men, but today in America and other civilized parts of the world women have the same legal rights as men.

Self-government. The Declaration of Independence proclaims that "governments are instituted" to secure the rights of "life, liberty, and the pursuit of happiness," and that those governments "derive their just powers from the consent of the governed." Early governments were often formed in the conquest of one people by another, and the right of the rulers to rule was attributed to God's will and passed along from father to son. In a few places—Athens, Rome, medieval Germany—there were fitful attempts to create a democratic government. Now, after America's example, we take it for granted in civilized countries that governments stand or fall on popular consent.

Freedom of speech. In a world of Michael Moore, Ann Coulter, and cable pornography, it's hard to imagine just how new and how rare free speech is. Lots of people died for the right to say what they believed. In China and Africa and the Arab world, they still do. Fortunately, we've realized that while free speech may irritate each of us at some point, we're all better off for it.

Freedom of religion. Church and state have been bound together since time immemorial. The state claimed divine sanction, the church got money and power, the combination left little room for freedom. As late as the 17th century, Europe was wracked by religious wars. England, Sweden, and other countries still have an established church, though their citizens are free to worship elsewhere. Many people used to think that a country could only survive if everyone worshipped the one true God in the one true way. The American Founders established religious freedom.

Property and contract. We owe our unprecedented standard of living to the capitalist freedoms of private property and free markets. When people are able to own property and make contracts, they create wealth. Free markets and the legal institutions to enforce contracts make possible vast economic undertakings—from the design and construction of airplanes to worldwide computer networks and ATM systems. But to appreciate the benefits of free markets, we don't have to marvel at skyscrapers while listening to MP3 players. We can just give thanks for enough food to live on, and central heating, and the medical care that has lowered the infant mortality rate from about 20 percent to less than 1 percent.

A Kenyan boy who managed to get to the United States told a reporter for *Woman's World* magazine that America is "heaven." Compared to countries that lack the rule of law, equality, property rights, free markets, and freedom of speech and worship, it certainly is. A good point to keep in mind this Thanksgiving Day.

Washington Times, November 25, 2004

Liberty at the Movies

Today's topic is libertarian movies from Hollywood—and there have been more than you might think.

Shenandoah, a 1965 film starring Jimmy Stewart, is often regarded as the best libertarian film Hollywood ever made. Stewart is a Virginia farmer who wants to stay out of the Civil War. Not our fight, he tells his sons. He refuses to let the state take his sons, or his horses, for war. Inevitably, though, his family is drawn into the war raging around them, and the movie becomes very sad. I cried when I was 11 years old, and I teared up again when I saw it recently. This is a powerful movie about independence, self-reliance, individualism, and the horrors of war.

War may be the most awful thing men do, but slavery is also a contender for that title. Steven Spielberg's *Amistad* (1997) tells a fascinating story about a ship full of Africans who turned up in New England in 1839. The question: Under American law, are they slaves? A long legal battle ensues, going up to the Supreme Court. Libertarians like to joke about lawyers. Sometimes we even quote the Shakespeare line, "The first thing we do, let's kill all the lawyers"—not realizing that that line was said by a killer who understood that the law stands in the way of would-be tyrants. *Amistad* gives us a picture of a society governed by law; even the vile institution of slavery was subject to the rule of law. And when the former president, John Quincy Adams, makes his argument before the Supreme Court, it should inspire us all to appreciate the law that protects our freedom.

Lawyers play an important role in two other fine libertarian films. *The Castle* was produced in Australia in 1997 but reached the United States in 1999. It's a very funny film about a character who thinks that living near the airport is just great. He even likes looking up at the massive power lines near his house because they remind him of what man can accomplish. Shades of Ayn Rand! Anyway, a man's home is his castle, and the protagonist is shocked when the airport decides to seize his property to extend its runway. He fights the system to no avail until a smooth, well-dressed lawyer—way out of the lead character's league— shows up and offers to take his case. Again we see powerful interests forced to defend themselves in a law-governed society. A nice defense of private property, and very funny to boot.

That same season in 1999 I also enjoyed *The Winslow Boy*, a David Mamet remake of a Terrence Rattigan play/movie from 1948. Despite a very different atmosphere—a stuffy, bourgeois family in Victorian England vs. a comic contemporary Australian family—it has two things in common with *The Castle*: a proud father who will do anything to defend his home and family, and a distinguished British lawyer who comes to the family's aid. Mr. Winslow's teenage son is expelled from the Naval Academy. Convinced his son is innocent, Winslow challenges the expulsion. When the Academy refuses any sort of due process, Winslow exhausts his life savings in a fight through the courts. The theme is the right of every person in a decent society to justice.

So Big (1953) stars Jane Wyman as a wealthy young woman suddenly delivered into poverty. She becomes a teacher, marries a farmer, has a son, loses her husband, and must run the farm on her own, at a time when women didn't do that. It's an inspiring story of self-reliance, and the disappointment she feels when her son chooses money and society over the architecture he loves. Based on a novel by Edna Ferber, the screenplay sounds almost Randian at times. Don't see the 1932 version starring Barbara Stanwyck; it's flat and boring. The difference is unbelievable.

The Palermo Connection (1990) is an odd Italian-made movie (but in English) cowritten by Gore Vidal. New York city councilman Jim Belushi runs for mayor on a platform to legalize drugs and take the profits out of the drug trade. The Mafia isn't happy. His life is threatened. So he decides to go on a honeymoon, in the middle of his campaign—to Sicily. I said it was odd. But interesting, and very pointed.

Pacific Heights (1990) is a thriller that is almost a documentary on the horrors of landlord-tenant law. A young couple buys a big house in San Francisco and rents an apartment to a young man. He never pays them, and they can't get him out, and then things get really scary. The lawyer lectures the couple—and the audience—on how "of course you're right, but you'll never win." I just knew this happened to someone—maybe the screenwriter or someone he knew. Sure enough, when Cato published William Tucker's book *Rent Control, Zoning, and Affordable Housing*, and I asked *Pacific Heights* director John Schlesinger for a jacket blurb, he readily agreed to say "If you thought *Pacific Heights* was fiction, you need to read this book"; and he told me that the screenwriter had a relative who had gone through a tenant nightmare.

Finally, I'll mention *My Beautiful Laundrette*, made for British television in 1985. What's interesting about this film is that novelist/screenwriter Hanif Kureishi thought he was making a savage indictment of Thatcherite capitalism. But to me, the good characters in the movie—white and Pakistani, gay and straight—are the ones who work for a living, and the bad characters are clearly the whining socialist immigrant intellectual, who doesn't like his son opening a small business, and the British thugs who try to intimidate the young Pakistani businessman. My favorite line: The enterprising brother of the layabout intellectual takes a young working-class Briton with him to evict some deadbeat tenants. The young Brit suggests that it's surprising the Pakistani businessman would be evicting people of color. And the businessman says, "I'm a professional business-man, not a professional Pakistani. There is no question of race in the new enterprise culture." I think Kureishi thinks that's a bad attitude. The joke's on him.

Cato.org, June 20, 2005

Where Are the Anti-Communist Movies?

The new movie *The Wind That Shakes the Barley*, about the Irish struggle for independence in the early 1920s, has beautiful Irish cinematography and effectively shows us the poverty of Ireland, the commitment of the rebels, the conflicts inevitable in any political movement, and the brutality of the British occupiers. Critics complain it goes overboard on that last point. Michael Gove protested in the *Times* of London that it portrays the British Black and Tans as "sub-human mercenaries burning thatched cottages, torturing by using pliers to rip out toenails [actually fingernails] and committing extreme violence against women." It's not the first movie to be criticized for making the British out to be more brutal than they actually were. Mel Gibson's *The Patriot* depicted the British army herding all the residents of a town into a church and then setting it on fire. Never happened, historians say.

But hey, the British Empire committed plenty of crimes over the centu-ries, so I'm not so upset that the Australian right-winger Mel Gibson and the English left-winger Ken Loach may have overreached on the details. What I'm wondering about is, Where are the films depicting Commu-nist atrocities?

Anti-Nazi movies keep coming out, from *Confessions of a Nazi Spy* and *Hitler, Beast of Berlin* in 1939 and on through *The Great Dictator*, *The Mortal Storm*, *The Diary of Anne Frank*, *Sophie's Choice*, *Schindler's List*, right up to the current *Black Book*. And many of these have included searing depictions of Nazi brutality, both physical and psychological.

But where are the anti-communist movies? Oh, sure, there have been some, from early Cold War propaganda films to such artistic achievements as *The Red Danube*, *Ninotchka*, *One Day in the Life of Ivan Denisovich*, *The Killing Fields*, *East-West*, and *Before Night Falls*. But considering that

National Socialism lasted only 12 years in one country (and those it occupied), and Communism spanned half the globe for 75 years, you'd think there'd be lots more stories to tell about Communist rule.

No atrocities, maybe? Nazis and Brits were vicious, but Communists were just intellectually misguided? Well, that seems implausible. They murdered several times as many people. If screenwriters don't know the stories, they could start with the *Black Book of Communism*. It could introduce them to such episodes as Stalin's terror-famine in Ukraine, the Gulag, the deportation of the Kulaks, the Katyn Forest massacre, Mao's Cultural Revolution, the Hungarian revolution, Che Guevara's executions in Havana, the flight of the boat people from Vietnam, Pol Pot's mass slaughter—material enough for dozens of movies.

Some might say that the Soviet Union is no more, this is ancient history, and we should let bygones be bygones. But Ken Loach's new movie depicts events of the 1920s, and the Nazi regime fell in 1945. The Soviet Union continued until 1991, and Communism continues in Cuba, China, and Vietnam. Besides, as the great historian Lord Acton knew, the historian must be a moral judge. The muse of the historian, he thought (in the words of his colleague John Neville Figgis), is not Clio, but Rhadamanthus, the avenger of innocent blood. The victims of Communism, and its heroic resisters, deserve to have their stories remembered.

TCSdaily.com, May 2, 2007

Fine Words

Can you be fined for expressing a political opinion in the District? Definitely. It happened to me. Last June I was driving along U Street NW about 5:15 p.m. when a motorcycle policeman pulled me over. I asked him what the problem was, and he said I was driving without a seat belt.

Now, I don't like laws intended to protect me from the consequences of my decisions. I think adults should make their own decisions about what to read, what to eat, what to smoke and whether to wear a seat belt. Further, research shows that drivers who feel safer often drive more recklessly, so when seat belts are mandated, some drivers become a greater danger to themselves and others.

But I didn't mention any of this to the officer because I didn't think it would do me any good in the circumstances.

After going through the standard checks, the officer asked me to sign what I thought was a ticket, although I was to find out a few minutes later that it really was only a warning. As I signed, he said, "It's $50 and two points." With that, I assumed that our interaction was over, and I said, "Well, I feel much safer now. There are 300 murders a year in the District, but at least you got me."

The officer told me to hand back the ticket, and he returned to his motorcycle, where I could see him writing some more. Then he returned with a different ticket for me to sign.

"What's this?" I asked.

"It's a $50 ticket, not a warning," he said. "Sometimes it's better to keep your mouth shut."

"So I'm getting a ticket for what I said?" I asked.

"Yes," he answered and walked away.

What I had said was, of course, provocative, but I never raised my voice. Yet because I said something the officer didn't like, he changed a warning into a ticket.

I appealed the ticket and was given a hearing date eight months later. At that hearing the officer and I related the facts in similar terms. The officer said he had discretion about issuing a ticket or a warning and that he changed his decision after I made my comment. The hearing officer in the D.C. Department of Motor Vehicles said that I had violated the law, that the police officer had acted within his discretion and that I was required to pay the $50 fine.

I understand that the D.C. Council requires drivers to wear seat belts and has authorized a fine for violation of that requirement. It seems odd to stop someone for this infraction when that person is violating no other law, but I accept that the police officer had the legal authority to do so. However, the officer made it clear that I was being fined not for violating the seat-belt law but for expressing an opinion about the law and the enforcement decisions of the D.C. police.

It is illegal and unconstitutional for any government to penalize a citizen for the expression of a political opinion. Indeed, this is a classic case of the arbitrary use of government power in such a way as to have a "chilling effect" on political expression.

Does anyone doubt that if I had said, "Thank you, officer for doing such a professional job in a difficult occupation," I would have gotten off with a warning? Indeed, the officer himself confirmed that I was being penalized for the content of my remarks—"Sometimes it's better to keep your mouth shut."

That's not a healthy attitude for a government official in a constitutional democracy. And it's even more disturbing that an administrative officer would uphold the police officer's action.

Fined for a political opinion? The D.C. Council should tell the police department that the First Amendment applies in the District.

Washington Post, April 15, 2001

The Separation of Art and State

The American Founders declared, "All men are endowed by their creator with certain unalienable rights, that among these are life, liberty, and the pursuit of happiness," and they wrote a Constitution that granted the federal government only a few enumerated and limited powers.

Things had changed by 1935, when President Roosevelt wrote to Congress, "I hope your committee will not permit doubts as to constitutionality, however reasonable, to block the suggested legislation."

Since then it's been open season on taxpayers' wallets. Congress has ignored the Constitution and assumed that it had the power to ban, require, regulate, or spend money on, anything under the sun.

And that's how we ended up here, discussing threats to artistic freedom from the 104th Congress. There would have been little fear of such threats from, say, the 54th Congress a century ago. The First Amendment prevented Congress from abridging freedom of speech, and the doctrine of enumerated powers meant that Congress couldn't involve itself in the arts at all. Emily Dickinson and Winslow Homer, Sinclair Lewis and Aaron Copland plied their trade blithely unaware of Congress.

Today, however, the federal Leviathan concerns itself with every nook and cranny of our lives, and the arts have not escaped its tender, stifling embrace.

I don't have to tell this audience about the importance of the arts, whether we're talking about literature, drama, painting, music, sculpture, or, lest I forget, dance. President Kennedy—or one of his talented speechwriters—put it this way: "Art establishes the basic human truths which must serve as the touchstones of our judgment. The artist, however faithful to his personal vision of reality, becomes the last champion of the individual mind and sensibility against an intrusive society and an officious state."

More recently, the managing director of Center Stage in Baltimore told the *Baltimore Sun*, "Art has power. It has the power to sustain, to heal, to humanize . . . to change something in you. It's a frightening power, and also a beautiful power. . . . And it's essential to a civilized society."

It is precisely because art has power, because it deals with basic human truths, that it must be kept separate from government. Government, as I noted earlier, involves the organization of coercion. In a free society coercion should be reserved only for such essential functions of government as protecting rights and punishing criminals. People should not be

forced to contribute money to artistic endeavors that they may not approve, nor should artists be forced to trim their sails to meet government standards.

Government funding of anything involves government control. That insight, of course, is part of our folk wisdom: "He who pays the piper calls the tune."

Defenders of arts funding seem blithely unaware of this danger when they praise the role of the national endowments as an imprimatur or seal of approval on artists and arts groups. NEA chairman Jane Alexander says, "The Federal role is small but very vital. We are a stimulus for leveraging state, local and private money. We are a linchpin for the puzzle of arts funding, a remarkably efficient way of stimulating private money."

Drama critic Robert Brustein asks, "How could the NEA be 'privatized' and still retain its purpose as a funding agency functioning as a stamp of approval for deserving art?"

In 1981, as conservative factions battled for control of the National Endowment for the Humanities, Richard Goldstein of the *Village Voice* explained the consequences this way:

> The NEH has a ripple effect on university hiring and tenure, and on the kinds of research undertaken by scholars seeking support. Its chairman shapes the bounds of that support. In a broad sense, he sets standards that affect the tenor of textbooks and the content of curricula. . . . Though no chairman of the NEH can single-hand-edly direct the course of American education, he can nurture the nascent trends and take advantage of informal opportunities to signal department heads and deans. He can "persuade" with the cudgel of federal funding out of sight but hardly out of mind.

I suggest that that is just the kind of power no government in a free society should have.

It is often said that other governments have long subsidized the arts. True, but as Jonathan Yardley, book critic for the *Washington Post*, points out, the examples usually cited are of autocratic, even tyrannical governments. Do we really want our government to emulate the Roman Empire, or the Medicis, or Louis XIV?

Now it's also true that the social democracies of Western Europe subsidize the arts more extensively than we do. But those countries too are different in important ways from the United States. First, as Yardley says, "They are accustomed to state influences (in religion as in the arts) that our ancestors crossed the ocean to escape." As we should not want an established church, so we should not want established art.

Second, the European countries are small and homogeneous compared with the United States. Thus they can "reach consensus on certain matters that we, precisely because we cannot agree on them, prefer to keep out of the hands of government." No European country was founded on the principles of the Declaration of Independence, nor does any European country have such a limited government.

Let me take just a moment to note that the amount of arts funding in the federal budget is quite small. That might be taken as a defense of the funding, were it not for the important reasons to avoid any government funding of something as intimate yet powerful as artistic expression. I bring up the dollar amount for another reason—to point out how small it is as a percentage of the total arts budget in this country. The National Endowment for the Arts has a budget of $167 million—less than 2 percent of the over $9 billion in private contributions to the arts from corporations, foundations, and individuals in 1993. According to the chair of the American Arts Alliance, the arts are a $37 billion industry. Surely they will survive without whatever portion of the NEA's budget gets out of the Washington bureaucracy and into the hands of actual artists or arts institutions.

So far I've looked at arts funding from the perspective of art and political philosophy. Let me take just a moment to consider the taxpayer's perspective. In that marvelous British television show, "Yes, Minister," Sir Humphrey Appleby once said, "Subsidy is for art, for culture. It is not to be given to what the people want. It is for what the people don't want but ought to have. If they want something, they'll pay for it themselves."

Take a typical American taxpayer. She's on her feet eight hours a day selling blue jeans at Wal-Mart. She serves spaghetti twice a week because meat is expensive, and when she can scrape together a little extra she likes to hear Randy Travis or take her daughter to see Mariah Carey. Now what gives us the right to tax her so that lawyers and lobbyists can save a few bucks on Kennedy Center tickets?

Thus the case against government funding of the arts. But the question posed tonight is not, "Should the government fund the arts?" but "How will the 104th Congress affect artistic freedom?" If Congress takes my advice and eliminates the endowments, artistic freedom will be better protected than ever before. But alas, Congress frequently ignores my advice, and as long as government funding remains, there is a real threat of government meddling in the arts.

The latest newsletter from People for the American Way identifies a lot of threats to free expression. Some involve an actual assault on private actions—such as censorship of the Internet, a ban on flag-burning, a denial of tax exemption to groups that support ideas some congressman doesn't like—and fortunately the First Amendment will protect us from most of these. But most of them involve restrictions on the way government funds can be used. Duke University law professor Walter Dellinger, now a member of the Clinton White House, warned recently that such rules are "especially alarming in light of the growing role of government as subsidizer, landlord, employer and patron of the arts."

Dellinger is right. But the only way to solve the problem he raises is to reduce the government's role in society. Surely we can't expect taxpayers just to hand over $1.5 trillion a year to various agencies and interests without regulating how the money is spent. Their representatives in Congress and the administration think that those who are paying for the education, or the art, or the medical care have a right to say just what they will and will not pay for.

Thus the Georgia legislature punishes Georgia Public Television for the PBS broadcast of *Tales of the City*. Thus Congress bars the arts endowment from funding obscene work. Thus public schools are pressured not to teach *Huckleberry Finn*. Thus the director of the National Air and Space Museum is forced to resign after criticism of an exhibit on the bombing of Japan.

Whether the pressure comes from Jesse Helms or Jesse Jackson, the Rainbow Coalition or the Christian Coalition, taxpayers' money is subject to political control. On NPR this morning, an activist complained about the forced resignation of the museum director, saying, "My ancestors didn't fight for the concept of official history in official museums." But when you have official museums, or a National Endowment for the Arts serving as a "seal of approval" for artists, you get official history and official art—and citizens will fight over just which history and which art should have that imprimatur.

We fought these battles before, in the Wars of Religion. The American Founders knew that the solution was the separation of church and state. Because art is just as spiritual, just as meaningful, just as powerful as religion, it is time to grant art the same independence and respect that religion has. It is time to establish the separation of art and state.

Vital Speeches, July 15, 1995

PART **16**

Characters

The Heart and Soul of Ronald Reagan

Ronald Reagan was the most eloquent spokesman for limited government of our time. Through 25 years of tirelessly "raising a banner of no pale pastels, but bold colors" of political principle, he succeeded in changing the climate of opinion in the United States and around the world.

From his first appearance on the national political scene in 1964, he spoke for the values he set forth in his nationally televised speech just before that election:

> You and I are told we must choose between a left or right, but I suggest there is no such thing as a left or right. There is only an up or down. Up to man's age-old dream—the maximum of individual freedom consistent with order—or down to the ant heap of totalitarianism.

As a liberal who moved to the right, he might have been called the first neoconservative. Except that he had been a liberal anticommunist, not a communist like the original neoconservatives. And his conservatism involved making government smaller, not using big government for conservative goals. We miss that kind of conservatism in Washington today.

In his first inaugural address, he proclaimed:

> In this present crisis, government is not the solution to our problem; government is the problem.
> It is my intention to curb the size and influence of the Federal establishment and to demand recognition of the distinction between the powers granted to the Federal Government and those reserved to the States or to the people.

His actions in office did not always fulfill those promises. Government spending continued to grow, there was little devolution of power to the states, and the cost of federal regulation continued to increase. Instead of abolishing two Cabinet departments, as he had promised (Education and Energy), he created one (Veterans Affairs). We owe to him the presidencies of George H. W. Bush and George W. Bush, neither of whom shared his commitment to liberty and limited government.

Nevertheless, after he succeeded a president who gave us good reason to believe that our nation was in a malaise, he revived our spirits and our faith in free enterprise. He slashed marginal tax rates and revived the sagging economy. Along with Margaret Thatcher, he both symbolized and galvanized a renewed enthusiasm for entrepreneurship and free markets. In his second inaugural, he echoed his words from 20 years earlier:

> By 1980, we knew it was time to renew our faith, to strive with all our strength toward the ultimate in individual freedom consistent with an orderly society. We believed then and now there are no limits to growth and human progress when men and women are free to follow their dreams.

Reagan was regarded as a social conservative, and he often spoke of "our values of faith, family, work, and neighborhood." But he rarely sought to use government to impose those values. In 1978 he spoke out against an antigay initiative in California. Robert Kaiser of the *Washington Post*, noting that the Reagans were the first White House occupants to have hosted a gay couple overnight, dubbed him in 1984 a "closet tolerant."

Much of Reagan's presidency, of course, was dominated by the Cold War and the long struggle with communism. In a 1983 speech he shocked the chattering classes by telling the truth about the Soviet Union:

> I believe that communism is another sad, bizarre chapter in human history whose last pages even now are being written. . . .
> I urge you to beware the temptation of pride—the temptation of blithely declaring yourselves above it all and label both sides equally at fault, to ignore the facts of history and the aggressive impulses of an evil empire.

One could debate the advisability of particular foreign policy initiatives, but it was surely a good thing to be honest about the nature of totalitarian communism. His words declared an end to "moral equivalence" and a determination to seize the moral high ground in the struggle with communism, and they inspired people behind the Iron Curtain to believe that they might indeed be able to put an end to the "sad, bizarre chapter of human history" they were forced to live through.

As the last pages of that chapter did indeed begin to unfold, Reagan went to Berlin and in perhaps his most famous words ever, issued a challenge to Soviet leader Mikhail Gorbachev:

> Mr. Gorbachev, open this gate. Mr. Gorbachev, tear down this wall!

A year later, in 1988, Reagan visited Gorbachev in Moscow. Allowed to speak to students at Moscow State University, he gave them a brilliant discussion of the nature of a free society:

> Freedom is the right to question, and change the established way of doing things. It is the continuing revolution of the marketplace. It is the understanding that allows us to recognize shortcomings and

seek solutions. It is the right to put forth an idea, scoffed at by the experts, and watch it catch fire among the people. It is the right to dream—to follow your dream, or stick to your conscience, even if you're the only one in a sea of doubters.

Freedom is the recognition that no single person, no single authority of government has a monopoly on the truth, but that every individual life is infinitely precious.

Ronald Reagan often said that "the very heart and soul of conservatism is libertarianism." I heard him say that at Vanderbilt University in 1975, when I had the honor to dine with him before his speech and get his signature on my "Reagan for President" newsletter. These days I put it somewhat differently: the best aspect of American conservatism is its commitment to protecting the individual liberties proclaimed in the Declaration of Independence and guaranteed in the Constitution. Ronald Reagan spoke for that brand of conservatism. That's the conservatism we sorely miss in today's Washington and today's Republican party.

National Post's Financial Post, June 11, 2004

Pat Robertson's Crackpopulism

Asked about Pat Robertson as a candidate for the presidency, a longtime conservative was quoted in the *Washington Post* recently as saying: "On the three big issues—the family, right to life and a strong economy—Robertson's the clear choice." He and other conservatives who view Mr. Robertson as a committed advocate of the free market should read the former reverend's books.

Indeed, little attention has been paid to the rather odd economic ideas in those books. One of the oddest of Mr. Robertson's economic ideas is his remedy for the nation's fiscal crises, as set down in his 1984 book, *Answers to 200 of Life's Most Probing Questions*: "The Bible contains a solution to the problem of excess accumulation of wealth and power. Every 50 years during the year of Jubilee the people had to . . . cancel debts. Every debt outstanding, by every debtor, was canceled. . . . All agricultural land, what we would term today the means of production, was to be returned to the families who had originally owned it. . . . The biblical year of Jubilee is something that our society ought to learn."

On his TV show, "The 700 Club," Mr. Robertson maintained that the year of Jubilee "is the only way to solve the recession and national debt." But when Marvin Kalb recently challenged him to defend that idea, he responded: "No, a president obviously can't cancel debts. We have to honor the debts that we have." He went on to say that "as a nation we have to do something about paying them off"—apparently something that would fly in the face of his repeated endorsement of public and private debt repudiation. Was Mr. Robertson seeking to renounce a biblical precept for political gain?

The year of Jubilee is not the strangest of Mr. Robertson's economic notions. That title must surely go to his suggestion that the microchips in credit cards are the mark of the Beast, or Antichrist. Mr. Robertson has suggested that electronic-funds transfers and "the drive toward a checkless, cashless society . . . could easily fulfill what [the New Testament book of] Revelation says: that people could not buy or sell without the mark of the Beast."

Throughout Mr. Robertson's books there is an undercurrent of hostility toward credit as well as toward bankers and the rich. Take his economic history lesson in *America's Dates With Destiny* (1986): "Three times federal banking systems and regulatory agencies were tried in the United States. Each time political pressure by private banking interests overturned the national banking system, and private banking interests regained control. . . . The people wanted to control their financial institutions. They did not want to be victims of powerful, unregulated bankers."

In *America's Dates With Destiny*, Mr. Robertson blamed the Great Depression on "greed and easy credit." He wrote: "The banks were greedy when they fueled the period of frantic speculation. . . . The rich owners and bosses were greedy when they didn't share the profits with the people. And the people were greedy when they overspeculated, using credit in their attempts to get rich quick." In other books, he has railed against "unbridled capitalism" and "free-booting robber barons." That is not exactly the sophisticated analysis of the market process that might be expected from a candidate who presents himself as a defender of the free market.

There is a name for Mr. Robertson's economic notions: crackpot. Crackpot ideas have a long history in America, from the "free coinage of silver" advocated by William Jennings Bryan and the Populist Party to such Depression-era cure-alls as Huey Long's "Every man a king," Father Coughlin's deliberate inflationism, and Dr. Francis E. Townsend's plan to grant pensions to the elderly on the condition that they spend the money promptly. (Granted, crackpot ideas have a habit of becoming law; the Townsend Plan was a forerunner of Social Security, and even the Populists never advocated the free coinage of paper.)

Mr. Robertson can best be understood not as a new figure in the conservative movement but as the heir of the Populists and Father Coughlin. As the Populists did, he appeals to less-educated, lower-middle-class people who find economic and social change frightening. Populist meetings had a revivalist flavor, with banners urging people to vote as they prayed.

Populist movements never concede that their followers' problems might be of their own making or a result of spontaneous social processes; demon figures and scapegoats are required. For the Populist Party, they were immigrants, the railroads and Wall Street. For Father Coughlin, they were the banks, the Jews, and—of course—Wall Street. For Mr. Robertson, they are gays, secular humanists, and—at least in his evangelical incarnation— Wall Street.

Because populists always seem to present crackpot economic schemes— usually involving inflationism or debt repudiation—as miraculous cures for the nation's problems, it seems appropriate to note that relationship by dubbing such movements "crackpopulist." Mr. Robertson is not the only modern exponent of crackpopulism; Democrats Jesse Jackson and Richard Gephardt have made serious bids for the crackpopulist vote as well.

Mr. Robertson's attempt to erase his past is understandable. (His latest campaign brochure contains several lines of biographical information but doesn't mention his career as an evangelist. That's as if a biography of George Bush failed to mention that he has held public office.)

Perhaps he believes that just as he washed away the sins of his youth when he was born again as a Christian, he can wash away the taint of evangelism when he was born yet again as a politician. But voters need to judge all Mr. Robertson's ideas, not just the ones he mentions in tele- vised debates.

Wall Street Journal, February 10, 1988

Rick Santorum: Left, Right, and Wrong

The *New York Times* reports that Sen. Rick Santorum . . .

> . . . distributed a brochure this week as he worked a sweltering round of town hall meetings and Fourth of July parades: "Fifty Things You May Not Know About Rick Santorum." It is filled with what he called meat and potatoes, like his work to expand colon cancer screenings for Medicare beneficiaries (No. 3), or to secure money for "America's first ever coal to ultra-clean fuel plant" (No. 2). . . .
> He said he wanted Pennsylvanians to think of him as a political heir to Alfonse M. D'Amato of New York, who was known as Senator Pothole for being acutely attuned to constituent needs.

So . . . the third-ranking Republican leader in the Senate wants to be known as a porker, an earmarker, and Senator Pothole.

Santorum had already dismissed limited government in theory. He told NPR last year:

> One of the criticisms I make is to what I refer to as more of a libertarianish right. You know, the left has gone so far left and the right in some respects has gone so far right that they touch each other. They come around in the circle. This whole idea of personal autonomy, well I don't think most conservatives hold that point of view. Some do. They have this idea that people should be left alone, be able to do whatever they want to do, government should keep our taxes down and keep our regulations low, that we shouldn't get involved in the bedroom, we shouldn't get involved in cultural issues. You know, people should do whatever they want. Well, that is not how traditional conservatives view the world and I think most conservatives understand that individuals can't go it alone. That there is no such society that I am aware of, where we've had radical individualism and that it succeeds as a culture.

He declared himself against individualism, against libertarianism, against "this whole idea of personal autonomy, ... this idea that people should be left alone." Now he's also against the conservative idea that taxpayers matter, that the federal government has a limited role.

No wonder Jonathan Rauch wrote last year that, "America's Anti-Reagan Isn't Hillary Clinton. It's Rick Santorum." Rauch noted:

> In his book he comments, seemingly with a shrug, "Some will reject what I have to say as a kind of 'Big Government' conservatism."

They sure will. A list of the government interventions that Santorum endorses includes national service, promotion of prison ministries, "individual development accounts," publicly financed trust funds for children, community-investment incentives, strengthened obscenity enforcement, covenant marriage, assorted tax breaks, economic literacy programs in "*every* school in America" (his italics), and more. Lots more.

Rauch concluded,

> With *It Takes a Family*, Rick Santorum has served notice. The bold new challenge to the Goldwater-Reagan tradition in American politics comes not from the Left, but from the Right.

At least Santorum is right about one thing: sometimes the left and the right meet in the center. In this case the big-spending, intrusive, mommy-AND-daddy-state center. But he's wrong that we've never had a firmly individualist society where people are "left alone, able to do whatever they want to do."

It's called America.

Cato@Liberty, July 10, 2006

Stalin's Songbird

The *New Yorker* has another of its affectionate profiles of old Stalinists, this time the folk singer Pete Seeger. A regular old American, they say, a guy who would stand by the side of the road at 85 holding up a sign reading simply "Peace." A "conservative" really, who "believes ardently in the Constitution and the Bill of Rights." And over the years he sang for peace, and for civil rights, and for the workers. And he built his own house on a hilltop. What's not to like?

Oh, sure, they mention in parentheses that he "knew students at Harvard who were Communists and, with the idea in mind of a more equitable world, he eventually became one himself." Outside parentheses, writer Alec Wilkinson reassures us that Seeger did eventually quit the Party.

Somehow, though, they didn't quite find room to detail Seeger's long habit of following the Stalinist line. Take the best example, his twists and turns during the FDR administration. Seeger tells Wilkinson that when he was at Harvard during the late 1930s he was trying to "stop Hitler" and he became disgusted with a professor who counselled appeasement. Maybe so. But after the Hitler-Stalin pact, he and his group the Almanac Singers put out an album titled *Songs of John Doe* that called Franklin D. Roosevelt a warmongering lackey of J. P. Morgan.

> Franklin D, listen to me,
> You ain't a-gonna send me 'cross the sea.
> You may say it's for defense
> That kinda talk ain't got no sense.

Then within months Hitler invaded the Soviet Union. The album was pulled from the market and reportedly destroyed. The Almanac Singers quickly produced a new album, *Dear Mr. President*, that took a different view of FDR and the war:

> Now, Mr. President
> You're commander-in-chief of our armed forces
> The ships and the planes and the tanks and the horses
> I guess you know best just where I can fight ...
> So what I want is you to give me a gun
> So we can hurry up and get the job done!

As the ex-communist scholar Ronald Radosh puts it, "Seeger was anti-war during the period of the Nazi-Soviet Pact; pro-war after the Soviet

Union was the ally of the United States; and anti-war during the years of the Cold War and Vietnam."

Seeger is not the only aging Stalinist to get the misty-eyed treatment from elite journalists. It's a staple of the *New York Times* and other eastern establishment journals: features on communist summer camps or communist old folks' homes or communist schools in Greenwich Village ("the Little Red School House for little Reds"); profiles of aging but still feisty communist journalists; glowing obituaries of lifelong communists who "championed civil liberties."

And it's an appalling double standard. Imagine a morally neutral, affectionate profile of a nostalgic 80-year-old Nazi. It doesn't happen, it wouldn't happen. We're still making movies about the crimes of Nazism, a totalitarian regime that lasted 12 years, while you can count on the fingers of one hand the Hollywood movies about the bloody 70-year rule of the Communist Party. Alan Charles Kors, the editor of the *Oxford Encyclopedia of the Enlightenment*, wrote recently: "We rehearse the crimes of Nazism almost daily, we teach them to our children as ultimate historical and moral lessons, and we bear witness to every victim. We are, with so few exceptions, almost silent on the crimes of Communism."

To everything there is a season. We can only hope that soon it will be the season for holding accountable those who worked for Stalinist tyranny, as we have held accountable those who worked for National Socialist tyranny.

Comment Is Free, April 14, 2006

The Man Who Told the Truth

Robert Heilbroner, the bestselling writer of economics, died early this month at the age of 85. He and John Kenneth Galbraith may well have sold more economics books than all other economists combined. Alas, their talents lay more in the writing than the economics. Heilbroner was an outspoken socialist; if only a libertarian could write an introductory book on economics that could—like Heilbroner's *The Worldly Philosophers*—sell 4 million copies.

Reading some of Heilbroner's essays over the years, I admired his honesty about the meaning of socialism. Consider this excerpt from a 1978 essay in *Dissent*:

> Socialism . . . must depend for its economic direction on some
> form of planning, and for its culture on some form of commitment
> to the idea of a morally conscious collectivity. . . .

> If tradition cannot, and the market system should not, underpin
> the socialist order, we are left with some form of command as
> the necessary means for securing its continuance and adaptation.
> Indeed, that is what planning means...
>
> The factories and stores and farms and shops of a socialist socio-
> economic formation must be coordinated ... and this coordination
> must entail obedience to a central plan...
>
> The rights of individuals to their Millian liberties [are] directly
> opposed to the basic social commitment to a deliberately embraced
> collective moral goal... Under socialism, every dissenting voice
> raises a threat similar to that raised under a democracy by those
> who preach antidemocracy.

Few socialists outside the Communist Party are willing to acknowledge
that real socialism means trading our "Millian liberties" for the purported
good of economic planning and "a morally conscious collectivity."

He was not entirely impervious to new evidence, however. In 1989, he
famously wrote in *The New Yorker*:

> Less than 75 years after it officially began, the contest between
> capitalism and socialism is over: capitalism has won. ... Capitalism
> organizes the material affairs of humankind more satisfactorily
> than socialism.

In *The New Yorker* again the next year, he reminisced about hearing of
Ludwig von Mises at Harvard in the 1930s. But of course his professors
and fellow students scoffed at Mises's claim that socialism could not work.
It seemed at the time, he wrote, that it was capitalism that was failing.
Then, a mere 50 years later, he acknowledged: "It turns out, of course,
that Mises was right" about the impossibility of socialism. I particularly
like the "of course." Fifty years it took him to grasp the truth of what
Mises wrote in 1920, and he blithely tossed off his newfound wisdom as
"of course."

Alas, in that same article he went on to say that while socialism might
not in fact produce the goods, we would still need to reject capitalism on
the grounds of ... let's see ... I've got it—environmental degradation.
Yeah, that's the ticket. While he had managed to wriggle free of the ideas
he learned in the 1930s, he was still stuck in the 1970s when, like Paul
Ehrlich, he issued dire predictions about the imminent exhaustion of
natural resources. In his 1974 book *An Inquiry into the Human Prospect*,
Heilbroner wrote, "Ultimately, there is an absolute limit to the ability of
the Earth to support or tolerate the process of industrial activity, and
there is reason to believe that we now are moving toward that limit
very rapidly."

On the big issue of capitalism vs. socialism, though, he did continue his rueful acknowledgment of error. In 1992, he explained the facts of life to *Dissent* readers:

> Capitalism has been as unmistakable a success as socialism has been a failure. Here is the part that's hard to swallow. It has been the Friedmans, Hayeks, and von Miseses who have maintained that capitalism would flourish and that socialism would develop incurable ailments. All three have regarded capitalism as the 'natural' system of free men; all have maintained that left to its own devices capitalism would achieve material growth more successfully than any other system. From [my samplings] I draw the following discomforting generalization: The farther to the right one looks, the more prescient has been the historical foresight; the farther to the left, the less so.

He also noted then that "democratic liberties have not yet appeared, except fleetingly, in any nation that has declared itself to be fundamentally anticapitalist."

May the socialists in Cambridge and Cambridge, and the people struggling to create decent societies around the world, especially in Africa, the Arab world, and the ex-Communist countries, take the frank (albeit delayed) honesty of Robert Heilbroner to heart.

Reason.com, January 21, 2005

The Charismatic Collectivists of the '30s

Review of *Three New Deals: Reflections on Roosevelt's America, Mussolini's Italy, and Hitler's Germany, 1933–1939,* by Wolfgang Schivelbusch. New York: Metropolitan Books, 2006

On May 7, 1933, just two months after the inauguration of Franklin Delano Roosevelt, the *New York Times* reporter Anne O'Hare McCormick wrote that the atmosphere in Washington was "strangely reminiscent of Rome in the first weeks after the march of the Blackshirts, of Moscow at the beginning of the Five-Year Plan. . . . America today literally asks for orders." The Roosevelt administration, she added, "envisages a federation of industry, labor and government after the fashion of the corporative State as it exists in Italy."

That article isn't quoted in *Three New Deals*, a fascinating study by the German cultural historian Wolfgang Schivelbusch. But it underscores his central argument: that there are surprising similarities between the programs of Roosevelt, Mussolini, and Hitler.

With our knowledge of the horrors of the Holocaust and World War II, we find it almost impossible to consider such claims dispassionately. But in the 1930s, when everyone agreed that capitalism had failed, it wasn't hard to find common themes and mutual admiration in Washington, Berlin, and Rome, not to mention Moscow. (*Three New Deals* does not focus as much on the latter.) Nor is that a mere historical curiosity, of no great importance in the era following democracy's triumph over fascism, National Socialism, and communism. Schivelbusch concludes his essay with the liberal journalist John T. Flynn's warning, in 1944, that state power feeds on crises and enemies. Since then we have been warned about many crises and many enemies, and we have come to accept a more powerful and more intrusive state than existed before the '30s.

Schivelbusch finds parallels in the ideas, style, and programs of the disparate regimes—even their architecture. "Neoclassical monumentalism," he writes, is "the architectural style in which the state visually manifests power and authority." In Berlin, Moscow, and Rome, "the enemy that was to be eradicated was the laissez-faire architectural legacy of nineteenth-century liberalism, an unplanned jumble of styles and structures." Washington erected plenty of neoclassical monuments in the '30s, though with less destruction than in the European capitals. Think of the "Man Controlling Trade" sculptures in front of the Federal Trade Commission, with a muscular man restraining an enormous horse. It would have been right at home in Il Duce's Italy.

"To compare," Schivelbusch stresses, "is not the same as to equate. America during Roosevelt's New Deal did not become a one-party state; it had no secret police; the Constitution remained in force, and there were no concentration camps; the New Deal preserved the institutions of the liberal-democratic system that National Socialism abolished." But throughout the '30s, intellectuals and journalists noted "areas of convergence among the New Deal, Fascism, and National Socialism." All three were seen as transcending "classic Anglo-French liberalism"—individualism, free markets, decentralized power.

Since 1776, liberalism had transformed the Western world. As *The Nation* editorialized in 1900, before it too abandoned the old liberalism, "Freed from the vexatious meddling of governments, men devoted themselves to their natural task, the bettering of their condition, with the wonderful results which surround us"—industry, transportation, telephones and telegraphs, sanitation, abundant food, electricity. But the editor worried that "its material comfort has blinded the eyes of the present generation to the cause which made it possible." Old liberals died, and younger liberals began to wonder if government couldn't be a positive force, something to be used rather than constrained.

Others, meanwhile, began to reject liberalism itself. In his great novel *The Man Without Qualities*, Robert Musil wrote, "Misfortune had decreed that . . . the mood of the times would shift away from the old guidelines of liberalism that had favored Leo Fischel—the great guiding ideals of tolerance, the dignity of man, and free trade—and reason and progress in the Western world would be displaced by racial theories and street slogans."

The dream of a planned society infected both right and left. Ernst Junger, an influential right-wing militarist in Germany, reported his reaction to the Soviet Union: "I told myself: granted, they have no constitution, but they do have a plan. This may be an excellent thing." As early as 1912, FDR himself praised the Prussian-German model: "They passed beyond the liberty of the individual to do as he pleased with his own property and found it necessary to check this liberty for the benefit of the freedom of the whole people," he said in an address to the People's Forum of Troy, New York, on March 3, 1912.

American Progressives studied at German universities, Schivelbusch writes, and "came to appreciate the Hegelian theory of a strong state and Prussian militarism as the most efficient way of organizing modern societies that could no longer be ruled by anarchic liberal principles." The pragmatist philosopher William James's influential 1910 essay "The Moral Equivalent of War" stressed the importance of order, discipline, and planning.

Intellectuals worried about inequality, the poverty of the working class, and the commercial culture created by mass production. (They didn't seem to notice the tension between the last complaint and the first two.) Liberalism seemed inadequate to deal with such problems. When economic crisis hit—in Italy and Germany after World War I, in the United States with the Great Depression—the anti-liberals seized the opportunity, arguing that the market had failed and that the time for bold experimentation had arrived.

In the *North American Review* in 1934, the progressive writer Roger Shaw described the New Deal as "Fascist means to gain liberal ends." He wasn't hallucinating. FDR's adviser Rexford Tugwell wrote in his diary that Mussolini had done "many of the things which seem to me necessary." Lorena Hickok, a close confidante of Eleanor Roosevelt who lived in the White House for a spell, wrote approvingly of a local official who had said, "If [President] Roosevelt were actually a dictator, we might get somewhere." She added that if she were younger, she'd like to lead "the Fascist Movement in the United States." At the National Recovery Administration (NRA), the cartel-creating agency at the heart of the early New Deal, one report declared forthrightly, "The Fascist Principles are very similar to those we have been evolving here in America."

Roosevelt himself called Mussolini "admirable" and professed that he was "deeply impressed by what he has accomplished." The admiration was mutual. In a laudatory review of Roosevelt's 1933 book *Looking Forward*, Mussolini wrote, "Reminiscent of Fascism is the principle that the state no longer leaves the economy to its own devices. . . . Without question, the mood accompanying this sea change resembles that of Fascism." The chief Nazi newspaper, *Volkischer Beobachter*, repeatedly praised "Roosevelt's adoption of National Socialist strains of thought in his economic and social policies" and "the development toward an authoritarian state" based on the "demand that collective good be put before individual self-interest."

In Rome, Berlin, and D.C., there was an affinity for military metaphors and military structures. Fascists, National Socialists, and New Dealers had all been young in World War I, and they looked back with longing at the experiments in wartime planning. In his first inaugural address, Roosevelt summoned the nation: "If we are to go forward, we must move as a trained and loyal army willing to sacrifice for the good of a common discipline. We are, I know, ready and willing to submit our lives and property to such discipline, because it makes possible a leadership which aims at a larger good. I assume unhesitatingly the leadership of this great army. . . . I shall ask the Congress for the one remaining instrument to meet the crisis—broad executive power to wage a war against the emergency, as great as the power that would be given to me if we were in fact invaded by a foreign foe."

That was a new tone for a president of the American republic. Schivelbusch argues that "Hitler and Roosevelt were both charismatic leaders who held the masses in their sway—and without this sort of leadership, neither National Socialism nor the New Deal would have been possible." This plebiscitary style established a direct connection between the leader and the masses. Schivelbusch argues that the dictators of the 1930s differed from "old-style despots, whose rule was based largely on the coercive force of their praetorian guards." Mass rallies, fireside radio chats, and in our own time television can bring the ruler directly to the people in a way that was never possible before.

To that end, all the new regimes of the '30s undertook unprecedented propaganda efforts. "Propaganda," Schivelbusch writes, "is the means by which charismatic leadership, circumventing intermediary social and political institutions like parliaments, parties, and interest groups, gains direct hold upon the masses." The NRA's Blue Eagle campaign, in which businesses that complied with the agency's code were allowed to display a "Blue Eagle" symbol, was a way to rally the masses and call on everyone to display a visible symbol of support. NRA head Hugh Johnson made its purpose clear: "Those who are not with us are against us."

Scholars still study that propaganda. Earlier this year a Berlin museum mounted an exhibit titled "Art and Propaganda: The Clash of Nations—1930–45." According to the critic David D'Arcy, it shows how the German, Italian, Soviet, and American governments "mandated and funded art when image-building served nation-building at its most extreme. . . . The four countries rallied their citizens with images of rebirth and regeneration." One American poster of a sledgehammer bore the slogan "Work to Keep Free," which D'Arcy found "chillingly close to 'Arbeit Macht Frei,' the sign that greeted prisoners at Auschwitz." Similarly, a reissue of a classic New Deal documentary, *The River* (1938), prompted *Washington Post* critic Philip Kennicott to write that "watching it 70 years later on a new Naxos DVD feels a little creepy. . . . There are moments, especially involving tractors (the great fetish object of 20th-century propagandists), when you are certain that this film could have been produced in one of the political film mills of the totalitarian states of Europe."

Program and propaganda merged in the public works of all three systems. The Tennessee Valley Authority, the autobahn, and the reclamation of the Pontine marshes outside Rome were all showcase projects, another aspect of the "architecture of power" that displayed the vigor and vitality of the regime.

You might ask, "Where is Stalin in this analysis? Why isn't this book called *Four New Deals*?" Schivelbusch does mention Moscow repeatedly, as did McCormick in her *New York Times* piece. But Stalin seized power within an already totalitarian system; he was the victor in a coup. Hitler, Mussolini, and Roosevelt, each in a different way, came to power as strong leaders in a political process. They thus share the "charismatic leadership" that Schivelbusch finds so important.

Schivelbusch is not the first to have noticed such similarities. B.C. Forbes, the founder of the eponymous magazine, denounced "rampant Fascism" in 1933. In 1935 former President Herbert Hoover was using phrases like "Fascist regimentation" in discussing the New Deal. A decade later, he wrote in his memoirs that "the New Deal introduced to Americans the spectacle of Fascist dictation to business, labor and agriculture," and that measures such as the Agricultural Adjustment Act, "in their consequences of control of products and markets, set up an uncanny Americanized parallel with the agricultural regime of Mussolini and Hitler." In 1944, in *The Road to Serfdom*, the economist F. A. Hayek warned that economic planning could lead to totalitarianism. He cautioned Americans and Britons not to think that there was something uniquely evil about the German soul. National Socialism, he said, drew on collectivist ideas that had permeated the Western world for a generation or more.

In 1973 one of the most distinguished American historians, John A. Garraty of Columbia University, created a stir with his article "The New

Deal, National Socialism, and the Great Depression." Garraty was an admirer of Roosevelt but couldn't help noticing, for instance, the parallels between the Civilian Conservation Corps and similar programs in Germany. Both, he wrote, "were essentially designed to keep young men out of the labor market. Roosevelt described work camps as a means for getting youth 'off the city street corners,' Hitler as a way of keeping them from 'rotting helplessly in the streets.' In both countries much was made of the beneficial social results of mixing thousands of young people from different walks of life in the camps. . . . Furthermore, both were organized on semimilitary lines with the subsidiary purposes of improving the physical fitness of potential soldiers and stimulating public commitment to national service in an emergency."

And in 1976 presidential candidate Ronald Reagan incurred the ire of Sen. Edward Kennedy (D-Mass.), pro-Roosevelt historian Arthur M. Schlesinger Jr., and the *New York Times* when he told reporters that "fascism was really the basis of the New Deal."

But Schivelbusch has explored these connections in greater detail and with more historical distance. As the living memory of National Socialism and the Holocaust recedes, scholars—perhaps especially in Germany—are gradually beginning to apply normal political science to the movements and events of the 1930s. Schivelbusch occasionally overreaches, as when he writes that Roosevelt once referred to Stalin and Mussolini as "his 'blood brothers.'" (In fact, it seems clear in Schivelbusch's source—Arthur Schlesinger's *The Age of Roosevelt*—that FDR was saying communism and fascism were blood brothers to *each other*, not to *him*.) But overall, this is a formidable piece of scholarship.

To compare is not to equate, as Schivelbusch says. It's sobering to note the real parallels among these systems. But it's even more important to remember that the U.S. did *not* succumb to dictatorship. Roosevelt may have stretched the Constitution beyond recognition, and he had a taste for planning and power previously unknown in the White House. But he was not a murderous thug. And despite a population that "literally waited for orders," as McCormick put it, American institutions did not collapse. The Supreme Court declared some New Deal measures unconstitutional. Some business leaders resisted it. Intellectuals on both the right and the left, some of whom ended up in the early libertarian movement, railed against Roosevelt. Republican politicians (those were the days!) tended to oppose both the flow of power to Washington and the shift to executive authority.

Germany had a parliament and political parties and business leaders, and they collapsed in the face of Hitler's movement. Something was different in the United States. Perhaps it was the fact that the country was formed by people who had left the despots of the Old World to find freedom in the new, and who then made a libertarian revolution. Americans tend to think of themselves as individuals, with equal rights and equal freedom. A nation whose fundamental ideology is, in the words of the sociologist Seymour Martin Lipset, "antistatism, laissez-faire, individualism, populism, and egalitarianism" will be far more resistant to illiberal ideologies.

Reason, October 2007

Galbraith's Mirror

John Kenneth Galbraith, the bestselling economist, has died at the age of 97. Many people, including his ideological adversaries Milton Friedman and William F. Buckley Jr., have testified to his personal charm and geniality. So does the much younger Pete Boettke, who writes of expecting not to like Galbraith at a dinner in the 1990s, "only to be completely charmed by the man and his stories of JFK and India, of battles with Milton Friedman and William F. Buckley, or a profession which has succumbed to too much formalism, disrespect for history, and an inability to address the institutional contingencies of our age."

As an economist, however . . . well, he was an excellent writer. His books had a great influence on non-economists in the 1960s and 1970s, many of whom were required to read them in college classes. The best known was probably *The Affluent Society*. As I wrote in *Libertarianism: A Primer*:

> Galbraith observed "private opulence and public squalor"—that is, a society in which privately owned resources were generally clean, efficient, well-maintained, and improving in quality while public spaces were dirty, overcrowded, and unsafe—and concluded, oddly enough, that we ought to move more resources into the public sector.

Galbraith's ideas played a major role in the vast expansion of government during the 1960s and 1970s. And so now we have more public enterprises that are overused, unsafe, poorly maintained, or insolvent. But Galbraith and American politicians missed the real point of his observation. The more logical answer is that if privately owned resources are better maintained, then we should seek to expand private ownership.

The *New York Times* obituary is headlined "John Kenneth Galbraith, 97, Dies; Economist Held a Mirror to Society." In a mirror, of course, everything is backward.

Galbraith was a man of wit and charm. But as a public intellectual he got more things wrong than anyone other than Paul Ehrlich and Lester Brown.

Comment Is Free, May 2, 2006

Murdoch vs. The Man

There's been a lot of hand-wringing lately about Rupert Murdoch's drive for total world domination. I'd be as disappointed as anyone if he took over the *Wall Street Journal* and wrung out of it what makes the *Journal* a great paper.

But a recent *New York Times* story on "Murdoch, Ruler of a Vast Empire" rather off-handedly made clear what real power is—and it isn't what Murdoch has. As the *Times* reported,

> Shortly before Christmas in 1987, Senator Edward M. Kennedy taught Mr. Murdoch a tough lesson in the ways of Washington.
>
> Two years earlier, Mr. Murdoch had paid $2 billion to buy seven television stations in major American markets with the intention of starting a national network. To comply with rules limiting foreign ownership, he became an American citizen. And to comply with rules banning the ownership of television stations and newspapers in the same market, he promised to sell some newspapers eventually. But almost immediately he began looking for ways around that rule.
>
> Then Mr. Kennedy, Democrat of Massachusetts, stepped in. Mr. Kennedy's liberal politics had made him a target of Murdoch-owned news media outlets, particularly the *Boston Herald*, which often referred to Mr. Kennedy as "Fat Boy." [This is an unfair claim by the *Times*; one columnist at the Herald calls Kennedy that. This is like saying "The *Times* often refers to Cheney as 'Shooter'" because Maureen Dowd does.] He engineered a legislative maneuver that forced an infuriated Mr. Murdoch to sell his beloved *New York Post*.

Murdoch could spend $2 billion on American media properties and change his citizenship—but one irritated senator could force him to sell his favorite American newspaper. The *Times* continued,

> "Teddy almost did him in," said Philip R. Verveer, a cable television lobbyist. "I presume that over time, as his media ownership in this country has grown and grown, he's realized that you can't throw spit wads at leading figures in society with impunity."

Well, actually you can in a free society. That's what makes it a free society—that you can criticize the powerful. And true, nobody tried to put Murdoch in jail. They just forced him to change his citizenship and sell his newspaper.

He ran into similar problems in Britain. His newspapers there, unsurprisingly, usually supported the Conservative Party. But in 1997 two of them endorsed Labour Party leader Tony Blair for prime minister. Blair reacted warmly to the support, but some Labour leaders still wanted to enact media ownership limits, which might have forced Murdoch to sell some of his properties.

> "Blair's attitude was quite clear," Andrew Neil, the editor of the *Sunday Times* under Mr. Murdoch in London from 1983 to 1994, said in an interview. "If the Murdoch press gave the Blair government a fair hearing, it would be left intact."

Is this what the long British struggle for freedom of the press has come to? A prime minister can threaten to dismantle newspapers if they don't give him "a fair hearing"?

Murdoch has been a realist about politics. He knows that while he may buy ink by the barrel, governments have the actual power. They can shut him down at the behest of a prime minister or a powerful senator. So he plays the game, in Britain and the United States and even China.

After the 2006 elections, for instance, News Corporation and its employees started giving more money to Democrats than Republicans.

> "We did seek more balance," said Peggy Binzel, Mr. Murdoch's former chief in-house lobbyist. "You need to be able to tell your story to both sides to be effective. And that's what political giving is about."

Rupert Murdoch's empire may become yet more vast, but he'll still be subject to the whims of powerful politicians. This is hardly surprising in China. But one would hope that in the country of John Milton and the country of John Peter Zenger, and especially in the country of the First Amendment, a publisher would be free to say whatever he chooses without fear of government assault on either his person or his property.

Cato@Liberty, July 6, 2007

Chavez: Do We Need Any More Evidence?

In his three-hour inaugural address—yet another characteristic he shares with his hero, Fidel Castro—Venezuelan strongman Hugo Chavez eliminated any remaining doubt about his plans to rule as a socialist dictator. Yet some journalists still can't bring themselves to speak truth about power.

Take the *Washington Post*, for instance. Reporter Juan Forero's story is headlined "Chavez Would Abolish Presidential Term Limit." He notes Chavez's stirring mantra, borrowed from Castro: "Socialism or death!" He reports:

> All week in Caracas, Chavez has shaken markets and angered the Bush administration by promising to nationalize utilities, seek broader constitutional powers and increase the state's control of the economy. He has also frequently referred to the new, more radical phase in what he calls his revolution—drawing comparisons with Castro's famous declaration on Dec. 2, 1961: "I am a Marxist-Leninist and will be one until the day I die."

But then in the next paragraph Forero cautions:

> If the theatrics are similar, however, the apparent goal is not. Chavez stresses that Venezuela will remain a democracy, and analysts do not believe his government will embark on a wholesale expropriation of companies, as Castro's government set out to do soon after taking power in 1959.

Remain a democracy, eh? Well, that's good news.
At the end of his article, Forero does note:

> He has installed military officers in all levels of government and packed the Supreme Court, and now says he will end the autonomy of the Central Bank.

Good thing Venezuela is going to remain a democracy, or those actions could be worrisome.

In his 1,000-word story, Forero failed to note a key point that other journalists pointed out: Chavez said he would ask the National Assembly, all 167 of whose members are his supporters, for special powers allowing him to enact a series of "revolutionary laws" by decree.

What more would it take for a journalist to conclude that Chavez's "apparent goal" is the same as Castro's and that, of course, he does not intend for Venezuela to "remain a democracy"?

Even people usually thought of as on the left have viewed Chavez's consolidation of power with alarm. Human Rights Watch yesterday issued a report saying that Chavez and his supporters "have sought to consolidate power by undermining the independence of the judiciary and the press, institutions that are essential for promoting the protection of human rights."

In a recent study for the Cato Institute, Gustavo Coronel, former Venezuelan representative to Transparency International, shows that "corruption has exploded to unprecedented levels ... and Chávez has created new state-run financial institutions, whose operations are also opaque, that spend funds at the discretion of the executive."

We know from theory and history that socialism—state ownership of the means of production and the attempt to eliminate for-profit economic activity—leads inevitably to tyranny. We saw it in Russia, China, and Cuba. We know that Cuba is one of the poorest countries in the world after almost 50 years of Castro and that its people daily risk their lives in rickety boats to escape.

Chavez has promised to bring socialism to Venezuela. If he succeeds, we know that the result will be tyranny. But meanwhile, he's not waiting for the advent of socialism. He has packed Congress and the Supreme Court with his supporters. He has installed his military officers in all levels of government. He is trying to end the autonomy of the Central Bank, nationalize major industries, abolish constitutional limits on presidential tenure, and perhaps most clearly, get his followers in Congress to give him the power to rule by decree.

"Remain a democracy" indeed.

Cato@Liberty, January 12, 2007

A Toast to Yeltsin

More than any other man, Boris Yeltsin moved the Russian people from tyranny to a rough approximation of freedom. For that he was one of the authentic heroes of the 20th century.

In a way he personalizes Mikhail Gorbachev's accidental liberation of the Russian and Soviet people. Gorbachev intended to reform and reinvigorate communism. He brought Yeltsin from the rural region of

Sverdlovsk in 1985 to shake up the stagnant party as the Moscow party boss. But Gorbachev set in motion forces that he couldn't contain. Once people were allowed to criticize the communist system and glimpse an alternative, things moved rapidly—partly because of Yeltsin's unexpectedly radical leadership.

Two years later Gorbachev and the party hierarchy pushed him out of the Politburo. But he turned around and ran for the Congress of People's Deputies, won, and then was elected to the Supreme Soviet. He created Russia's first parliamentary opposition (in the Supreme Soviet) and then won election to the new Russian parliament. Against the continuing opposition of Gorbachev, he was elected to the chairmanship of that body, thus becoming president of the Russian Soviet Federative Socialist Republic. He stunned politicos by resigning from the Communist Party.

And then in 1991, less than four years after being pushed out of politics by Gorbachev, Boris Yeltsin became the first elected leader in a thousand years of Russian history, winning a popular election for president. Six weeks later he hit his high point. When hard-line communists tried to stage a coup, Yeltsin courageously raced to parliament to rally opposition. He jumped on a tank to address the crowd, creating one of the iconic images of the collapse of communism.

At that point Yeltsin was the boss, eclipsing Gorbachev, and the Soviet Union was on its way out. Yeltsin effectively dissolved the Soviet Union, leaving 15 newly independent states in the vast expanse that was once the USSR. As John Morrison says:

> His greatest achievement was to avoid the violent "Yugoslav scenario" and allow the Soviet Union's 15 republics to go their separate ways peacefully in 1991–92 without civil war. Yeltsin defied nationalist demands for the restoration of a greater Russia and made huge concessions to the other successor states, notably Ukraine, but got little credit for it.

Not many political leaders happily let their subjects go. What other political leader ever gave up control over 14 countries? But by doing so, he avoided years of bloodshed. Yeltsin then set about freeing prices and privatizing state property, the largest privatization in the history of the world. As the *New York Times* notes, he was one communist leader capable of learning from—and feeling shame about—the success of capitalism:

> On a visit to the United States in 1989, he became convinced that Russia had been ruinously damaged by its state-run economic system, in which people stood in long lines to buy the most basic needs of life and more often than not found the shelves bare. Visiting a Houston supermarket, he was overwhelmed by the kaleidoscopic variety of meats and vegetables available to ordinary Americans.

A Russia scholar, Leon Aron, quoting a Yeltsin associate, wrote that Mr. Yeltsin was in a state of shock. "For a long time, on the plane to Miami, he sat motionless, his head in his hands," Mr. Aron wrote in his 2000 biography, *Yeltsin, A Revolutionary Life*. "'What have they done to our poor people?' he said after a long silence."

Yeltsin wasn't perfect. He was often boorish and apparently had an excessive taste for alcohol. Despite letting the other Soviet republics go, he launched the devastating war in Chechnya. He unconstitutionally dissolved parliament in 1993; when communist lawmakers defied him, he sent tanks to shell parliament.

But it should be noted that Yeltsin at that time was seeking to defend liberal democracy against a return to communism. Imagine if Nazi legislators had stayed in the German parliament into 1949, resisting Adenauer's policies and threatening to bring back National Socialism. Would it be undemocratic to call out the military to counter them? Fareed Zakaria's worry in 1997 that Yeltsin's creation of a "Russian super-presidency" might be abused by his successors looks all too prescient now. But a reversion to communism would have been worse.

And finally, after becoming the first elected leader in Russia's history, he became something even more important—the first Russian leader to voluntarily give up power. True, he turned Russia over to Vladimir Putin, making him more like Ronald Reagan, who delivered the United States to the Bushes, than George Washington, who left us in the capable hands of John Adams and Thomas Jefferson.

Still, the words that President Reagan addressed to the American soldiers who invaded Normandy could also be applied to Boris Yeltsin: "These are the champions who helped free a continent. These are the heroes who helped end a war."

Raise a glass tonight to Boris Yeltsin, the man who freed a continent and helped end the Cold War.

Comment Is Free, April 25, 2007

PART **17**

The Politics of Freedom

A Free and Prosperous New Year

The sun rises in 2005 on the freest and most prosperous world in history. According to *Economic Freedom of the World: 2004 Annual Report*, the average economic freedom rating for 123 countries rose from 5.1 in 1980 to 6.5 in 2002, on a scale from 1 to 10, with 10 representing full economic freedom. China showed a particularly strong move in the direction of economic freedom, moving from 3.8 in 1980 to 5.7 in 2002 (down slightly from 5.9 in 2000). But other countries also moved toward economic freedom, notably Australia, Chile, El Salvador, India, Ireland, Mauritius, New Zealand, and Uganda.

Hong Kong was rated the freest economy in the world, but it declined slightly from 9.1 in 1995 to 8.7 in 2002.

The authors of the report, published by the Fraser Institute in Vancouver, pointed to several ways in which economic freedom has grown:

- The use of extremely high marginal tax rates fell sharply. In 2002, not a single country imposed a 60 percent marginal tax rate on personal income; in 1980, 49 did so.
- Exchange-rate controls were liberalized substantially. In 2002, there were only four countries with black-market exchange rate premiums of 25 percent or more compared to 36 countries in 1980.
- Tariffs were reduced. In 2002, the mean tariff rate was 10.4 percent compared to 26.1 percent in 1980.
- Controls on both capital markets and interest rates were relaxed.

Over the past 25 years, several factors have contributed to the growth in economic freedom. The collapse of the Soviet Union allowed Russia and its former colonies to give their citizens more freedom. Ronald Reagan and Margaret Thatcher challenged the concept of ever-bigger government and showed that tax cuts and privatization can create prosperity. The spread of world trade—often called "globalization"—brought more countries into the world economy and gave their citizens more comfortable lives.

All those trends should continue. On Ronald Reagan's 93rd birthday last February, China's deputy finance minister Lou Jiwei told the *Wall Street Journal* that China would cut tax rates. "It's a lot like Reaganomics," Lou said. "We feel that only through simplifying things and lowering tax rates will revenue collection become more efficient."

Countries compete more than ever to attract businesses, investors, and citizens. High tax rates, capital controls, and excessive regulation drive investors away, so many countries have been trying to cut taxes and regulation. "Tax competition" helps protect taxpayers from their own governments.

But there are powerful forces that resist the call for less government. The European Union started as a free-trade area—it was first known as the Common Market—but today it is largely a giant cartel for high taxes. Its leaders try to "harmonize" tax rates by pressuring member countries with low taxes to raise them.

President Vladimir Putin has been tightening restrictions on press freedom in Russia and also moving to reverse some of the post-Soviet industrial privatization. The arrest of Yukos CEO Mikhail Khodorkovsky and the renationalization of part of Yukos serve as a powerful warning to other Russian executives and to international investors.

Africa and the Arab world still have not tasted much economic freedom. Despite the Bush administration's promise to bring democracy and free enterprise to Iraq, progress in Arab countries looks likely to be very slow.

The Bush years have been a mixed bag for economic freedom in the United States. Tax rates have been cut, but government spending has soared—a combination that can't go on forever. Since his reelection, President Bush has promised to let American workers invest their Social Security taxes in private retirement accounts. If Congress goes along, that would be the biggest boost for economic freedom in many decades.

Hong Kong is in a curious position: It is the freest economy in the world, but it is now part of a country run by the Communist Party. Although China's economy is getting more free, Beijing is exerting more control over Hong Kong. That creates great risks for both freedom and prosperity in Hong Kong.

We must not forget the real importance of economic freedom. Besides the value of freedom itself, economic freedom leads to economic growth. And growth is not just an abstract concept. It means that women have running water, rather than having to carry water from a well that may be miles away. It means enough food for children. It means medical care and dramatically lower rates of infant mortality.

The hurricanes that devastated Haiti earlier this year and the Asian tsunamis last week both reminded us of the real costs of poverty. It is the lack of wealth that forced so many people to live in homes that could be easily destroyed by hurricanes and tsunamis. Economic freedom means more wealth for the whole society, which means better-built homes and better warning systems in case of disaster.

For those of us who want the poorest people in the world to have better lives, the challenge is to continue the spread of globalization, resist tax cartels, and give more people more opportunity to own stocks, bonds, and other real assets.

Pittsburgh Tribune Review, January 7, 2005

Libertarian Orphans

Imagine a minority of 20 percent with no voice.

The Gallup Poll's latest annual survey on American government finds that 21 percent of Americans hold libertarian views, compared to 27 percent who are conservative and 24 percent who are liberal.

The liberal percentage was up sharply from earlier surveys, probably because the poll was taken just 12 days after Hurricane Katrina hit the Gulf Coast. After any such disaster, including the Sept. 11 attacks, support rises sharply for the proposition that "government should do more to solve our country's problems." But it tends to fall again within a few months.

For the past dozen years, Gallup's surveys have consistently found that around 20 percent of Americans are neither liberal nor conservative but libertarian, generally opposing the use of government either to "promote traditional values" or to "do too many things that should be left to individuals and businesses." Another 20 percent are "populist"—supporting government action in both areas—and about 10 percent can't be defined. Libertarian support is spread broadly across demographic groups but is strongest among better educated and more affluent voters, and those who call themselves moderates.

So where are the libertarians in politics and the media?

Especially since the bitter fights over impeachment of President Bill Clinton and then the Florida recount in 2000, there's been a significant polarization among the chattering classes. Both members of Congress and television pundits define themselves as red or blue, pro or anti-Bush, partisan Democrat or partisan Republican. And thus they take rigid liberal or conservative positions on a whole range of unrelated issues: the Iraq war, tax cuts, Social Security reform, gay marriage, abortion, Mel Gibson vs. Michael Moore.

But the polls tell us that Americans aren't so partisan. Some are staunchly liberal or conservative, red or blue, but others see the world differently.

With big-government conservatives spending taxpayers' money like Imelda Marcos in a shoe store, and big-government liberals supporting the Patriot Act, the pro-government populists seem well represented in Washington.

It's the libertarian voters who seem leaderless. Democrats stand like a stone wall against tax cuts and Social Security privatization. Republicans want to ban abortion, gay marriage, and saying "Happy Holidays" instead of "Merry Christmas." It's not just Congress—in Virginia's recent elections for governor and legislature, all the Democrats were tax-hikers and all the Republicans were religious rightists. What's a libertarian to do?

The worst aspect of all this is the editors, columnists, and political observers who appear on television talk shows to analyze politics and policy. You'd think they'd be thoughtful and independent, right? Yet they seem almost as partisan as the politicians. The typical cable show brings the viewers two guests, a liberal and a conservative. You can count on conservative writers to defend everything President Bush and suspended House Majority Leader Tom DeLay do. You can count on liberal editors to denounce the Republicans no matter what the issue.

Of course, it could be that most Americans are in fact liberals and conservatives. Maybe Gallup is wrong, year after year after year. It turns out that the exit polls on election day 2004 offer some confirmation.

According to the exit polls, 17 million people voted for John Kerry but do not think the government should do more to solve the country's problems. And 28 million Bush voters support either gay marriage or civil unions for gay couples. That's 45 million voters who don't seem to fit into the redstate/bluestate, pro-Bush/anti-Bush model. Instead, they seem to have broadly libertarian attitudes.

In fact, it's no secret that libertarian voters make up a big chunk of America. In a recent book, lefty professors Cass Sunstein and Stephen Holmes grumbled that libertarian ideas are "astonishingly widespread in American culture."

But you'd never know it from watching television.

Wall Street Journal, January 31, 2006

Libertarian Voters in 2004 and 2006

Did libertarians swing the 2006 election? Election and poll results suggest it's possible. While partisans still voted along party lines, Republicans lost big among independents. By our analysis in our paper "The Libertarian Vote," libertarians may be the largest bloc of such independent-minded swing voters. Particularly in states with high concentrations of libertarians such as Arizona, Nevada, Colorado, Montana, and New Hampshire, disaffected libertarians likely cost Republicans House and Senate seats. But

American Ideologies: A Four-Way Matrix

		Government Intervention in Economic Affairs	
		For	Against
Expansion of Personal Freedoms	For	Liberal	Libertarian
	Against	Populist	Conservative

SOURCE: William S. Maddox and Stuart A. Lilie, *Beyond Liberal and Conservative* (Washington: Cato Institute, 1984), p. 5.

an obsession with political polarization and the red-blue divide has prevented most pundits from seeing the impact of libertarian-leaning voters.

Ever since the impeachment of President Clinton and the Florida ballot problems in 2000, we've been told that we're a polarized nation, sharply split between "red state" Republicans and "blue state" Democrats. And the rise of blogs has intensified that sense, by allowing people to get their daily, even hourly, dose of the liberal or conservative party line.

But in fact millions of people don't fit the liberal-conservative dichotomy. They may be fiscally conservative and socially liberal (or tolerant), that is, broadly libertarian. Or they may be liberal on economic issues and conservative on issues of personal freedom, and we might call them statist or populist. Either way, they don't fit neatly into the liberal or conservative box, and they often find themselves torn between conservative Republican and liberal Democratic candidates for office.

Several recent polls suggest that 10 to 20 percent of Americans fall into the libertarian quadrant. Indeed, libertarians are a bigger share of the electorate than the much-discussed "soccer moms" or "NASCAR dads," and they are increasingly a swing vote. Over the past six years Republicans have expanded entitlements and spent taxpayers' money faster than Democrats, giving libertarians less reason to stick with their traditional voting patterns. Polls show that in both 2004 and 2006 libertarian voters shifted toward the Democrats, and they may well have cost Republicans control of Congress.

Why is this substantial and growing libertarian strength not better recognized? Political scientists have taught for more than 50 years that

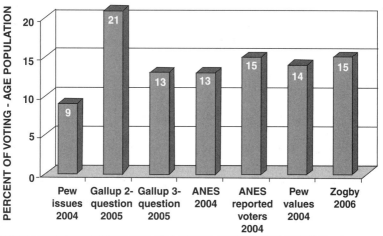

Measures of Libertarians in the Electorate

politics is arranged on a liberal-conservative continuum, so we're all used to that. And indeed, political activists and elected officials do seem to have arranged themselves into those two camps, rather than a more accurate reflection of the total electorate. Because of the constant repetition of the liberal-conservative spectrum, most libertarian-minded voters don't identify themselves as libertarians, and they aren't organized in libertarian groups. But it's time for pundits, pollsters, and politicians to pay more attention to the libertarian vote.

Libertarians Today

For more than a dozen years now, the Gallup Poll has been using two broad questions to categorize respondents by ideology about economic and social freedom. Gallup consistently finds about 20 percent of respondents to be libertarian. In 2006 they found 21 percent libertarians, along with 21 percent liberals, 20 percent populists, and 25 percent conservatives (12 percent were unclassifiable). Adding a third question from the Gallup survey to create a more robust definition, we found that 13 percent of Gallup's 2006 respondents could be classified as libertarians.

Using similar questions from the Pew Research Center, we found 14 percent libertarians. And from the generally acknowledged gold standard of public opinion data, the surveys of the American National Election Studies, which has asked the same questions for 15 years, we selected three questions about political attitudes. Using those questions, we found that in 2004 libertarians were 13 percent of the voting-age population and 15 percent of actual voters.

After publishing that study, we commissioned Zogby International to ask the same ANES questions to 1,012 actual (reported) voters in the 2006 election. Once again, we found that 15 percent of them could be defined as libertarian on our three-question screen.

Swinging Libertarians

So how do libertarians vote? That's the bottom line for candidates and consultants. We find good evidence not only that libertarians exist, and that they vote, but that their votes are currently in flux. Libertarians may be the next great swing vote. Given the dominance of fiscal and economic issues over the past generation, it is perhaps not surprising that libertarians have tended to vote Republican. Using ANES data, we find that libertarians have voted heavily Republican in recent presidential elections, but with interesting variations. In 1988, given a choice between George H. W. Bush's watered-down Reaganism and Michael Dukakis's combination of big-government orthodoxy and "card-carrying membership in the ACLU," libertarians voted 74 to 26 percent for Bush. In 2000 libertarians gave 72 percent of their votes to George W. Bush, who said every day on the campaign trail, "My opponent trusts government. I trust you," and only 20 percent to Al Gore, of whom Bush's claim seemed entirely too accurate.

But in 1992, after the senior Bush's tax increase, libertarians split their previously Republican majority almost evenly between Bush and third-party candidate Ross Perot. That suggests that the libertarian affinity for Republicans is easily broken. Libertarians also gave a high percentage of their votes to third-party candidates in 1980 (independent John B. Anderson and Libertarian Party candidate Ed Clark) and 1996 (again Perot).

But the striking fact in our data analysis is what happened in 2004. The libertarian vote for Bush dropped from 72 to 59 percent, while the libertarian vote for the Democratic nominee almost doubled. It's not hard to imagine why. Bush's record on federal spending, centralization of education, expansion of entitlements, the war in Iraq, executive authority, the federal marriage amendment, and civil liberties was certainly sufficient to dissuade many libertarian voters. Sen. John F. Kerry offered little for libertarians other than "not Bush." He voted for the war and the Patriot Act, never articulated a clear alternative position on either, and offered standard Democratic support for higher taxes and spending. Nevertheless, he narrowed the Republican majority among libertarians from 52 points to 21 points.

After two more years of war, wiretapping, and welfare-state social spending, we found similar patterns in 2006. In the Zogby survey, 59 percent of libertarians voted for Republican candidates for Congress, and

36 percent voted for Democrats. Comparing those results to the last off-year election in 2002, we find a 24 percentage point swing to the Democrats. That is, libertarians voted for Republican congressional candidates by a margin of 47 percentage points in 2002, and of only 23 points in 2006.

To put this in perspective, front-page stories since the election have reported the dramatic 7-point shift of white conservative evangelicals away from the Republicans. The libertarian vote is about the same size as the religious right vote measured in exit polls, and it is subject to swings more than three times as large.

After the 2000 election Karl Rove was convinced that 4 million Christian evangelicals had stayed home, and he was determined to get them to the polls in 2004. By our calculations, Republicans carried the libertarian vote by 5.5 million votes in the off-year election of 2002 and by only 2.9 million votes in 2006. That's a swing of 2.6 million libertarian voters. Remember, it takes two new base voters to replace one swing voter who switches from one party to the other. Rove and his colleagues should have been watching out for the libertarian vote as well.

Libertarians who said the war in Iraq was the most important issue voted 64-31 for Democratic congressional candidates. Libertarians who stuck with Republican candidates were most likely to describe terrorism or security as the most important issue. Libertarians for whom federal spending was the most important issue were most likely to vote for third-party candidates: 39 percent Democratic, 38 percent Republican, 22 percent other. It's a sad commentary on today's Republican Party when its candidates do so poorly among voters concerned about federal spending.

Republicans should be particularly troubled about their standing with young voters, including young libertarian voters. Voters in the 18–34 age groups are more likely than voters over 55 to be libertarian, and the younger libertarians voted more Democratic.

How Libertarians Voted, 2006

AGE GROUP	DEMOCRATIC	REPUBLICAN	OTHER
18–24	29%	51%	20%
25–34	40%	51%	8%
35–54	27%	67%	6%
55–69	24%	72%	5%
70 +	18%	81%	2%

SOURCE: Telephone survey of 1,012 reported voters conducted by Zogby International, Nov. 7–10, 2006. Margin of error + / − 3.1 percent.

State by State

Congressional elections are held in states and districts. How did the libertarian vote affect specific races? An interesting sidebar to our story is the impact of Libertarian Party candidates, who may have cost Sens. Jim Talent and Conrad Burns their seats, tipping the Senate to Democratic control.

In Montana, the Libertarian candidate got more than 10,000 votes, or 3 percent, while Democrat Jon Tester edged Burns by fewer than 3,000 votes. In Missouri, Claire McCaskill defeated Talent by 41,000 votes, a bit less than the 47,000 Libertarian votes. This isn't the first time Republicans have had to worry about losing votes to Libertarian Party candidates. In 1998 incoming Majority Leader Harry Reid was reelected by only 428 votes while the Libertarian candidate pulled in 8,000. In 2000 Maria Cantwell defeated Sen. Slade Gorton (R-Wash.) by 2,228 votes as the Libertarian took 65,000 votes. And in 2002, in the country's most hard-fought Senate race, John Thune lost to Sen. Tim Johnson (D-S.D.) by 524 votes, far less than the 3,000 votes for the Libertarian candidate.

But a narrow focus on minor party candidates significantly underestimates the role libertarian voters played in 2006. It's libertarian voters who swung Democratic who likely cost Republicans the House and the Senate—dealing blows to Republican candidates in Arizona, Colorado, Iowa, Nevada, New Hampshire, Ohio, and Pennsylvania.

Republicans can win the South without libertarians. But this was the year that New Hampshire and the Mountain West turned purple if not blue, and libertarians played a big role there. New Hampshire may be the most libertarian state in the country; its license plates read "Live Free or Die," and its senators are strong fiscal conservatives who both voted against the Federal Marriage Amendment. But this year both the state's Republican congressmen lost, and both houses of the state legislature went Democratic for the first time since 1874.

Meanwhile, in the Goldwateresque, "leave us alone" Mountain West, Republicans not only lost a Montana Senate seat; they also lost the governorship of Colorado, two House seats in Arizona, and one in Colorado. They had close calls in the Arizona Senate race and House races in Idaho, New Mexico, Colorado, Nevada, and Dick Cheney's Wyoming. In libertarian Nevada, the Republican candidate for governor won a plurality but not a majority against a Democrat who promised to keep the government out of guns, abortion, and gay marriage. Arizona also became the first state to vote down a state constitutional amendment to define marriage as between one man and one woman. Aspiring presidential candidates might note that in Iowa libertarians helped vote out Rep. Jim Leach (R), who championed the Internet gambling ban.

If Republicans can't win New Hampshire and the Mountain West, they can't win a national majority. And they can't win those states without libertarian votes. They'll have to stop scaring libertarian, centrist, and independent voters with big-government social conservatism and become once again the party of fiscal responsibility. In a *Newsweek* poll just before the election, 47 percent of respondents said they trusted the Democrats more on "federal spending and the deficit," compared to just 31 percent who trusted the Republicans. That's not Ronald Reagan's Republican Party.

How Libertarians See Themselves

In all of these calculations, we use a broad definition of libertarian. Certainly we are not claiming that 15 percent of American voters have the deep and well-informed commitment to liberty and limited constitutional government of Cato Sponsors or *Reason* magazine readers. Rather, we include both individuals who would self-identify as libertarian and individuals who hold generally libertarian views but may be unfamiliar with the word. It is clear that many people who hold libertarian views don't identify themselves that way. One Rasmussen poll found that only 2 percent of respondents characterized themselves as libertarians, even though 16 percent held libertarian views on a series of questions.

In our Zogby survey we found that only 9 percent of voters with libertarian views identify themselves that way. Voters we identified as libertarian identified themselves this way:

Ideological Self-Identification of Libertarian Voters
Progressive/Very liberal—4%
Liberal—6%
Moderate—31%
Conservative—41%
Very conservative—9%
Libertarian—9%

We also asked a new question. We asked half the sample, "Would you describe yourself as fiscally conservative and socially liberal?" We asked the other half of the respondents, "Would you describe yourself as fiscally conservative and socially liberal, also known as libertarian?"

The results surprised us. Fully 59 percent of the respondents said "yes" to the first question. That is, by 59 to 27 percent, poll respondents said they would describe themselves as "fiscally conservative and socially liberal."

The addition of the word "libertarian" clearly made the question more challenging. What surprised us was how low the drop-off was. A robust

44 percent of respondents answered "yes" to that question, accepting a self-description as "libertarian."

Surely that question is overinclusive. Still, it's encouraging that 59 percent of Americans think they lean in a libertarian direction on both economic and social issues and that 44 percent are willing to be described as libertarian. And that 59 percent interestingly matches a *Los Angeles Times* poll that found that Americans preferred "smaller government with fewer services" to "larger government with many services" by 59 to 26 percent.

Conclusion

The era of polarization and base mobilization is officially over. In 2006 voters broke 52-45 for Democrats for the House. This is the largest winning margin of any party since the Republican sweep in 1994.

Polarized elections are fought over turnout. Thus in 2002, 2004, and even 2006, campaign strategists fought over small marginal gains in target demographics. In contrast, the 2008 election will likely be fought more over larger blocs of independent-minded swing voters. By any reasonable estimate, libertarians are a key part of this swing group.

Since we published our initial findings in "The Libertarian Vote," libertarians are being talked about. There seems to be a dawning awareness among pundits, pollsters, and party strategists of the importance of winning libertarian votes.

Libertarian voters have been noticed by writers in *The Economist* and major newspapers. Cato's Brink Lindsey even took to the pages of the *New Republic* to test the waters for a liberal-libertarian alliance, provoking a spirited debate across the political spectrum.

In a revealing exchange, Jon Stewart recently hosted neoconservative Bill Kristol of the *Weekly Standard* on the *Daily Show*, often considered the de facto television news program for younger viewers. Kristol called Stewart an "Upper West Side liberal." To which Stewart quickly responded, "No, I'm a downtown libertarian."

Libertarian-leaning voters are a larger group than many other much-discussed voter blocs, and they tend to be younger than other voters. More important for political strategists, libertarian voters are "in play." Dissatisfied with big-government policies in both parties, they have shown a willingness to switch their votes from one to the other. The party that can best appeal to libertarian voters may dominate the political future.

With David Kirby. *Cato Policy Report*, January/February 2007

Misunderstanding Politics:
Stockman and His Revolution

David Stockman's book—which has just been published in paperback—has been discussed primarily in terms of Stockman's support for a tax increase or of his disregard for the sensitivities of his elders.

The real story of the book, however, is how Stockman forgot what he knew about the political process. Stockman sums up his argument this way: "We have had a tumultuous national referendum on everything in our half-trillion-dollar welfare state budget.... Lavish Social Security benefits, wasteful dairy subsidies, futile UDAG grants, and all the remainder of the federal subventions do not persist solely due to weak-kneed politicians or the nefarious graspings of special-interest groups."

But this is where he goes wrong. "We" did not have a national referendum on spending—Congress and the White House did. The crucial question is whether the lack of support from President Reagan, the White House staff, the Cabinet, and Congress for an assault on the welfare state—what might be termed the Stockman Revolution, in contrast to the largely mythical Reagan Revolution—does, in fact, reflect popular sentiment. Stockman assumes, without much argument, that it does.

But in a mixed-economy democracy, the actions of government reflect not the will of the majority but the pressure of interest groups. For any spending program, Congress hears from those who benefit from the program—while those who pay for it are silent.

Stockman understood this in his younger days. When he returned to Michigan in 1976 to run for Congress, he found that "the solid entrepreneurs of southern Michigan's hamlets" were willing to give up their subsidies in return for smaller government overall. But when "their" voices were heard in Washington, it was in the form of trade associations lobbying for their own pet programs.

The point, then, is that American society has not held a referendum on UDAG grants, dairy subsidies, water projects, Amtrak, the Export-Import Bank, Social Security benefit levels, and so on. Stockman's position, as he himself acknowledged, "was utterly repudiated by the combined forces of the politicians"—not by the people.

And even if Stockman does believe that we had a national referendum on government spending, consider another referendum: During the past tumultuous decade, from Proposition 13 in 1978, to the election of Ronald Reagan in 1980, to the tax cut of 1981, to the overwhelming 1984 defeat of a man who openly and honestly proclaimed his intention to raise taxes, we had a national referendum on the level of taxes. The voters made it clear that taxes were too high. Interestingly, the name "Walter Mondale" does not appear in Stockman's book, despite the light his defeat sheds on the desires of the American people.

After all the hysteria over Reagan's budget cuts, not a single Republican congressman was defeated in 1982, 1984, or 1986 because he voted for budget cuts, a pretty good sign that Republicans had not found the limits of budget cutting that the American people would accept.

In his disillusionment with the political process, Stockman has forgotten the lessons he entered the White House with. He has become what he warned Republicans against: "the tax collector for the welfare state."

David Stockman has given up too easily. His vision of society has not been rejected by the American people. It was never offered to them. If Walter Mondale had offered his program of all the government we have now and enough taxes to pay for it, and President Reagan or another candidate had offered a vision of smaller government, fewer spending programs (with the cuts identified), deregulation, and lower taxes, does Stockman believe that the American people would have preferred Mondale's program?

The Reagan Revolution—an attempt to reduce the size of government by cutting taxes and painlessly eliminating waste and fraud—was doomed to failure. But the Stockman Revolution—a frontal assault on the welfare state to liberate the "limitless possibilities" of the free market—has not yet been tried.

Cato Policy Report, January/February 1987

The Good News and the Bad News

As we enter a new century and indeed a new millennium, it seems appropriate to take stock of where we stand in the ongoing struggle for individual freedom and limited, constitutional government. We should remember that the big picture is pretty good. Given what the human race has gone through—conquest and subjugation, theocracy, slavery, feudalism, absolute monarchy, military dictatorship, communism, fascism, national socialism, apartheid—the political and economic systems of more and more of the world reflect a great deal of learning and improvement. Most readers of this column live in societies based *largely* on private property, markets, the rule of law, religious freedom, freedom of speech, and legal equality for people of different classes, races, and sexes. And because of that we have made enormous strides in the past two centuries in material prosperity, health, and life expectancy. That is a tremendous achievement.

Still, those of us with a more complete appreciation for the free society realize that we have much left on our political agenda for the 21st century. Here is a quick survey of our current political situation. First, the good news:

The Collapse of Socialism. It seemed endless at the time, but in fact the era of state socialism lasted only 75 years. With the collapse of the Soviet Union and the shift toward capitalism in China, the energy has gone out of socialism, which is no longer a significant ideological adversary to market liberalism.

Appreciation for Markets. We also see a greater appreciation for markets as an organizing principle of society. Although much of this appreciation is grudging and nonideological, it is real.

The Information Age. The shift to an information economy is undermining the power of nation-states. Global markets make it more difficult for states to impose taxes and controls on their citizens. Unprecedented access to information undermines claims of authority based on special knowledge. The shift from physical to human capital empowers individuals and makes physical control less relevant.

The New Economy. In an economy characterized by increasing labor mobility and entrepreneurship, it will be more difficult to maintain old regulatory and entitlement structures. Bureaucratic schools won't meet lifelong education needs; industrial-era labor regulations are increasingly onerous in an age of knowledge workers; a one-size-fits-all retirement system that promises to deliver 1 percent on your investment will not long remain popular; in a world where employees move around, it's absurd for employers to handle health care and retirement savings.

Now, some bad news:

The Collapse of the Constitutional Consensus. For more than a century Americans knew that the federal government had a very limited role. But after the federal government created veterans' programs, and then farm programs and retirement programs, people reacted as if a piñata had burst: the federal government has lots of money, they concluded, so let's go get it. Restoring the enumerated powers of the Constitution would solve many of our political problems, but it won't be easy.

Dismal Political Leadership. No political leader in recent years has offered an articulate defense of liberty and limited constitutional government. The traditional American individualism and skepticism toward expansive government are still there, just waiting for leadership.

Prosperity. Hard times—like the 1970s—make voters more tenacious in holding on to their money and more skeptical of government demands for higher taxes and spending. In prosperous times like these, two things happen: more tax money rolls in and people feel flush, so politicians can go on spending sprees. That's why it's essential to put limits on taxes and spending whenever the opportunity arises—because politicians will never stop pushing and prodding for opportunities to spend more.

The Urge to Centralize. Despite the collapse of socialism and the growing appreciation for markets, there is a tendency to see centralization as a way of producing quality and equality in government services. Competitive systems produce better solutions than centralized systems, but people who see only a snapshot view of the world—inevitably with inefficiencies and inequalities—don't understand the dynamic nature of competition. Ironically, the success of private enterprise may be partly responsible for this trend: companies like McDonald's, General Motors, and IBM aren't broken down into municipal or state divisions, so why should government enterprises be so fragmented? Obviously, understanding of the differences between voluntary and coercive entities is still lacking.

Media Bias. American journalists don't all think alike, and they don't get together on Monday mornings to discuss how to undermine capitalism and the Constitution. But there does seem to be a tendency among elite journalists to be more skeptical of business than of government; to think that compassion for the less fortunate entails government spending; to think that, if we know what's best, it should be federally legislated. The rise of new media will erode the power of the agenda-setting media, but this will continue to be a problem for advocates of smaller government.

In the long run, freedom works, and people figure that out. I have no doubt that at the dawn of the fourth millennium more of the human beings in the universe will live in freer societies than do today. In the shorter run the outcome is less predictable, and it will depend on our own efforts to capitalize on our strengths and learn to counter the trends that work against a free and civil society.

Cato Policy Report, January/February 2000

Are We Freer?

In the 1980s, before he was appointed to the Supreme Court, Clarence Thomas spoke at the Cato Institute. He read from Cato's standard description of itself the line, "Since [the American] revolution, civil and economic liberties have been eroded." It didn't seem that way to black Americans, he noted. Duly chastened, we changed it.

But it's still a common theme among libertarians: we're losing our freedom, year after year. We quote Thomas Jefferson: "The natural progress of things is for liberty to yield and government to gain ground." We read books with titles like *Freedom in Chains*, *Lost Rights*, *The Rise of Federal Control over the Lives of Ordinary Americans*, and *The Road to Serfdom*.

But is it true? Are we less free? Less free than when? I think libertarians often find it difficult to rouse most Americans with dire warnings about the state of freedom. Most Americans don't feel unfree. Maybe that's because they're "sheeple," or maybe it's because we really aren't losing our freedom.

One of the problems with discussing whether Americans are more or less free is some confusion over the meaning of "freedom." There are three things that at least feel like freedom: wealth, which gives us options; openness, which also gives more people more options; and political liberty.

First, let's consider the effects of widespread wealth. Air travel is so cheap today that young Cato staffers fly off to Iceland to attend a rock concert. That feels like a kind of freedom, a choice barely open to me 30 years ago and unimaginable to my parents. Wealth allows us to choose where to live. It gives us more freedom to choose careers, or to opt out of the career rat-race and still have a decent standard of living. We are less constrained by the necessity of eking out a living.

Wealth gives us cars, computers, iPods, cellphones, knowledge beyond belief organized and accessible at Google.com, and other really cool stuff. It gives us far more options for how to spend our leisure time; indeed, a downside of affluence may be that it gives us so many options that we feel overstressed, conscious of all the interesting things we don't have time to do.

Wealth is not liberty (though it is a product of political and economic liberty). But having ever more abundant resources feels a lot like freedom.

Second, we live in a more open society. Liberalism has always campaigned for a society of merit, not of status. That meant in the first place the dismantling of the privileges of nobility and aristocracy. Over the centuries it has also meant extending liberty and equality to people of other races and creeds, to women, to Jews, to gays and lesbians. Sometimes that involves dismantling actual legal barriers, and sometimes it means only a falling away of social prejudices and codes. For the most part laws didn't keep women and Jews out of colleges and careers in the 1950s; deep-seated social customs did. Sodomy laws imposed real legal penalties on gays, but the closet door was kept firmly shut more by social pressures and the fear of losing jobs, friends, and families.

Even if we're seeing mostly the decline of social restrictions, it's hard to tell blacks, women, Jews, and gays that they're less free in modern America than they were at some earlier point.

Finally, let's look at actual political and economic liberty. It's easy to point to the ways that government has grown and liberty has yielded: soaring federal and state spending; a shift to federal and presidential power; the growth of surveillance and databases; intrusive regulations on hiring and firing, on eating and drinking and smoking; expanding entitlements; and all the threats to civil liberties in the post-9/11 era (which just might, if not reined in by the courts and political reaction, make my optimism outdated). The list could go on endlessly, and that's what causes lots of libertarians to deplore "the road to serfdom" and our "lost rights."

But that list doesn't tell the whole story. In so many ways we are freer today than we were at various points in the past. Depending on just when you think was the golden age of liberty, I could counter by reminding you of oriental despotism, slavery, the Dark Ages, absolute monarchy, rigid class privilege, and so on. In the 20th century, fascism, communism, and national socialism. And even in our own country in my lifetime, we lived with military conscription, 90 percent income tax rates, wage and price controls, restricted entry to transportation and communications, indecency laws, and Jim Crow.

I think that, on balance, Americans today are more free than any people in history. And certainly when you combine liberty, wealth, and social openness, we have more choices and options than any people in history. So take a moment to reflect on our history, have a glass of wine, and celebrate what we've achieved after centuries and millennia of hard work and political struggle.

And then, refreshed and rejuvenated, return to the struggle. There never was a golden age of liberty, and there never will be. People who value freedom will always have to defend it from those who claim the right to wield power over others. Foreign and domestic, right and left, there are still plenty of people seeking to take our liberty, to force us into collectivist schemes, to promise us security or handouts in return for our freedom, or to impose their agendas on the rest of us. But slowly, over time, with high points and low points, freedom is winning.

Cato Policy Report, July/August 2007

Index

Acknowledgments

For the opportunity to write the essays in this book over the past two decades, I am grateful to the directors and Sponsors of the Cato Institute for their support; to my colleagues, who have developed so many of the ideas presented here; and especially to Edward H. Crane, the founder and president of the Institute, for his vision and determination in building the institution in which I have been fortunate to work for the past 27 years. I am also indebted to Tom G. Palmer for much of what I know about the history, economics, and politics of liberty, as well as for invaluable advice about this volume. In producing the book, I have been ably assisted by Zach Skaggs, Jason Kuznicki, Lauren Belliveau, and Kevin Scobey.

I am also grateful to the editors of the numerous newspapers, magazines, and websites where these articles originally appeared, both for giving me an opportunity to publish and for allowing me to republish the essays in this volume.

"Rights, Responsibilities, and Community," in *International Rights and Responsibilities for the Future*, ed. Kenneth W. Hunter and Timothy C. Mack, © 1996. Reproduced with permission of Greenwood Publishing Group, Inc., Westport, CT.

"How the Republicans and Democrats Maintained Their Market Share," "Chrysler, Microsoft, and Industrial Policy," "Prisoner Held for Ransom," "The Budget Two-Step," "Obesity and 'Public Health'?" and "What to Be Thankful For," © 1994, 2000, 2004, 2005 The Washington Times LLC.

"The Who and Why of Big Bucks Politics," "Junking Jobs: The War on Sidewalk Sales," "Pat Robertson's Crackpopulism," "Yellow Peril Reinfects America," and "Libertarian Orphans," reprinted from the *Wall Street Journal*, ©1983, 1984, 1988, 1989, 2006 Dow Jones & Company. All rights reserved.

"The Tentacles of Federal Funding," © June 20, 1991, Chicago Tribune Co. All rights reserved.

"George Will and the Ideological Switcheroo," © 2007. Reprinted by courtesy of Encyclopedia Britannica Inc.; used with permission.

"Don't Forget the Kids," "Domestic Justice," "Budget Cuts: Less Than Meets the Eye," "The Big Flaw in School Reform," "Privatize Social Security," and "Let's Quit the Drug War." Reprinted from the *New York Times*.

About the Author

David Boaz is the executive vice president of the Cato Institute, described by the *Wall Street Journal* as "Washington's bastion of libertarian thought." He has played a key role in the development of the libertarian movement and is the coauthor of the landmark 2006 study, "The Libertarian Vote." He is the author of *Libertarianism: A Primer*, which has been translated into nine languages, and the editor of 10 books, including *The Libertarian Reader*. He is the former editor of *New Guard* magazine and was executive director of the Council for a Competitive Economy prior to joining Cato in 1981. His articles have been published in the *Wall Street Journal*, the *New York Times*, the *Washington Post*, the *Los Angeles Times*, *National Review*, and *Slate*. He is a frequent guest on national television and radio shows and has appeared on ABC's *Politically Incorrect with Bill Maher*, CNN's *Crossfire*, NPR's *Talk of the Nation* and *All Things Considered*, John McLaughlin's *One on One*, Fox News Channel, BBC, Voice of America, Radio Free Europe, and other media.

Cato Institute

Founded in 1977, the Cato Institute is a public policy research foundation dedicated to broadening the parameters of policy debate to allow consideration of more options that are consistent with the traditional American principles of limited government, individual liberty, and peace. To that end, the Institute strives to achieve greater involvement of the intelligent, concerned lay public in questions of policy and the proper role of government.

The Institute is named for *Cato's Letters*, libertarian pamphlets that were widely read in the American Colonies in the early 18th century and played a major role in laying the philosophical foundation for the American Revolution.

Despite the achievement of the nation's Founders, today virtually no aspect of life is free from government encroachment. A pervasive intolerance for individual rights is shown by government's arbitrary intrusions into private economic transactions and its disregard for civil liberties.

To counter that trend, the Cato Institute undertakes an extensive publications program that addresses the complete spectrum of policy issues. Books, monographs, and shorter studies are commissioned to examine the federal budget, Social Security, regulation, military spending, international trade, and myriad other issues. Major policy conferences are held throughout the year, from which papers are published thrice yearly in the *Cato Journal*. The Institute also publishes the quarterly magazine *Regulation*.

In order to maintain its independence, the Cato Institute accepts no government funding. Contributions are received from foundations, corporations, and individuals, and other revenue is generated from the sale of publications. The Institute is a nonprofit, tax-exempt, educational foundation under Section 501(c)3 of the Internal Revenue Code.

CATO INSTITUTE
1000 Massachusetts Ave., N.W.
Washington, D.C. 20001
www.cato.org